CAMBRIDGE TEXTS IN THE
HISTORY OF POLITICAL THOUGHT

━━

MORE
Utopia

CAMBRIDGE TEXTS IN THE HISTORY OF POLITICAL THOUGHT

Series editors

RAYMOND GEUSS, *Reader in Philosophy, University of Cambridge*
QUENTIN SKINNER, *Regius Professor of Modern History in the University of Cambridge*

Cambridge Texts in the History of Political Thought is now firmly established as the major student textbook series in political theory. It aims to make available to students all the most important texts in the history of western political thought, from ancient Greece to the early twentieth century. All the familiar classic texts will be included, but the series seeks at the same time to enlarge the conventional canon by incorporating an extensive range of less well-known works, many of them never before available in a modern English edition. Wherever possible, texts are published in complete and unabridged form, and translations are specially commissioned for the series. Each volume contains a critical introduction together with chronologies, biographical sketches, a guide to further reading and any necessary glossaries and textual apparatus. When completed the series will aim to offer an outline of the entire evolution of western political thought.

For a list of titles published in the series, please see end of book

THOMAS MORE

Utopia

EDITED BY
GEORGE M. LOGAN
AND
ROBERT M. ADAMS
Revised Edition

CAMBRIDGE
UNIVERSITY PRESS

PUBLISHED BY THE PRESS SYNDICATE OF THE UNIVERSITY OF CAMBRIDGE
The Pitt Building, Trumpington Street, Cambridge, United Kingdom

CAMBRIDGE UNIVERSITY PRESS
The Edinburgh Building, Cambridge CB2 2RU, UK
40 West 20th Street, New York, NY 10011-4211, USA
477 Williamstown Road, Port Melbourne, VIC 3207, Australia
Ruiz de Alarcón 13, 28014 Madrid, Spain
Dock House, The Waterfront, Cape Town 8001, South Africa

http://www.cambridge.org

The translation of *Utopia* used in this edition is based on
The Norton Critical Edition of *Utopia* by Sir Thomas More,
translated and edited by Robert M. Adams.
Copyright © 1975 by W. W. Norton & Company, Inc.
By permission of W. W. Norton & Company, Inc.

© in the introduction and other new material
Cambridge University Press 1989, 2002

First published 1989 and reprinted ten times
Revised edition first published 2002
Fourth printing 2005

Printed in the United Kingdom at the University Press, Cambridge

British Library Cataloguing in Publication data
More, *Sir* Thomas, *Saint, 1478–1535*
Utopia.
I. Utopia – Early works
I. Title II. Logan, George M.
III. Adams, Robert M.
321′07

Library of Congress Cataloguing in Publication data
More, Thomas, Sir, Saint, 1478–1535.
Utopia
(Cambridge texts in the history of political thought)
Translated from the Latin.
Bibliography.
Includes index.
I. Utopias
I. Logan, George M.
II. Adams, Robert M.
III. Title
IV. Series.
HX810.5.E54   1988
335′.02′   88-25660

ISBN 0 521 34573 1 hardback 1st edition
ISBN 0 521 34797 1 paperback 1st edition

ISBN 0 521 81925 3 hardback
ISBN 0 521 52540 3 paperback

Contents

Preface   *page* vii

Textual practices   ix

Introduction   xi

Note on the translation   xxx

Chronology   xxxii

Suggestions for further reading   xxxiv

Utopia   1

   Thomas More to Peter Giles   3

   Book I   8

   Book II   41

   Ancillary materials from the early editions   108

Index   130

For Cathy

Preface

This revised edition of the Cambridge Texts *Utopia* (originally published in 1989) was undertaken primarily to incorporate the extensive changes to the Robert M. Adams translation of *Utopia* that were made for the 1995 Latin–English edition that I prepared with the late Professor Adams and, after failing health forced him to withdraw from the project, with Clarence H. Miller. Especially since the latter edition is now standard for most purposes, it seemed desirable to incorporate the reworked translation into the Cambridge Texts edition. I have also revised the introductory materials in the light of scholarship published since the first edition went to press, and have incorporated a few of the expansions to these materials, and to the commentary, that I made for the 1995 edition. All these materials were, in the 1989 edition, written by me, with the exception of the 'Note on the translation', which was (apart from its final paragraph) by Adams. Since the translation itself was also his – and still is, overwhelmingly, despite the revisions subsequently made to it – I have left the note unchanged.

The Adams translation began life in the Norton Critical Edition of *Utopia* that Adams published in 1975 (second edition 1992). I remain grateful to the late, deeply lamented John Benedict, Vice President and Editor of W. W. Norton and Company, who secured the blessing of that estimable firm on the incorporation of a revised version of the translation in the Cambridge Texts edition. For that edition, Adams also made new translations of some of the ancillary letters and poems that buttress the text of *Utopia* in the four early editions of the work.

The many revisions of 1995 were almost all made for the sake of greater accuracy.[1] Adams, who was a wonderful stylist, was sometimes inclined to sacrifice accuracy to grace; nor did he claim to be a Neo-Latin scholar. Many of the new renderings were suggested by Father Germain Marc'hadour, the paterfamilias of the international community of More students and admirers, who, with his usual generosity, at my request gave the 1989 edition a meticulous going-over; many other changes were suggested by Professor Miller, whose help and friendship, to 1995 and after, I cannot adequately acknowledge, any more than I can convey the depth of my admiration for his scholarship.

I also remain grateful, as I was in 1989, to Richard Tuck and Quentin Skinner for their valuable comments on the first version of the introductory materials; Skinner also vetted the 1995 introductory materials. His own published work is responsible for much of what I know about the context of *Utopia* in the history of political thought; and he has, on various occasions dating back twenty years, given me comments on my work that have been invaluable both professionally and personally. Elizabeth McCutcheon's review of the 1995 edition was responsible for the first of the five changes I have made to the translation this time around; and I owe this exemplary scholar and friend far more than that. In general, my greatest reward for working on More has been the profit and pleasure of his company and that of the More scholars whom I have been privileged to know.

I am also grateful to Richard Fisher, the Press's Director for Humanities and Social Sciences, with whom I have worked comfortably since the late 1980s, and whose backing made this revised edition possible. And once again I want to express my thanks to Ruth Sharman and Virginia Catmur, who served as the Press's very capable editors for, respectively, the 1989 and 1995 editions.

Finally, I want to acknowledge my associates and friends at Massey College (in the University of Toronto), the academic utopia where, during an idyllic year as Senior Resident, I completed work on this revision.

G. M. L.

---

[1] For the same reason, I have made five additional small changes for the present edition, which thus includes a translation identical to that of the 1995 edition except in the following places: p. 12: 'man-eating' to 'people-eating' (*populivoros*); p. 19: 'cattle' to 'animals' (cf. 'other kinds of livestock' two lines earlier); p. 25: 'tripped over themselves to get on his side' to 'sided with him' (*pedibus in eius ibant sententiam* – a common classical idiom); p. 104: 'completely useless to' to 'not especially necessary for' (*non . . . magnopere necessarium*), restoring More's litotes; p. 113 (middle): deleted extraneous comma after 'rule'.

Textual practices

(1) *Documentation.* The paraphernalia of documentation have been kept to a minimum. Publication data for some standard works are given in 'Suggestions for further reading': in the footnotes, these works are cited only by author and title. With the exceptions noted in 'Suggestions for further reading', all citations of classical works are to the editions of the Loeb Classical Library. Neither editors' names nor publication data are given for these editions. References to the Bible are to the King James Version – except for the Apocrypha, where references are to the Vulgate.

(2) *Abbreviations.* CW = Yale *Complete Works of St Thomas More*; CWE = Toronto *Collected Works of Erasmus*.

(3) *Names.* Names of historical figures of More's era are spelled as in *Contemporaries of Erasmus: A Biographical Register of the Renaissance and Reformation.* The sole exception is Pieter Gillis, for whom we use the familiar anglicised form Peter Giles.

(4) *Modernisation.* Whenever sixteenth-century English is quoted, spelling (and sometimes punctuation) is silently modernised.

(5) *Gendered language.* Where More uses nouns or pronouns that, in classical Latin, encompass not just males but human beings of either sex (for example, *homo, puer* and *nemo*), the translation employs similarly inclusive English equivalents. We have also avoided gendered pronouns in passages where the Latin does not positively *forbid* our doing so and where More may plausibly be thought not to have intended to restrict his reference to males. But *Utopia* – like all other Renaissance works, and despite the fact that one of its notable features is the nearly equal treatment that the

Utopian republic accords to women and men in education, work and military training and service – is the product of a culture in which intellectual and political life were generally regarded as almost exclusively male domains; and the truth is that we have probably translated into gender-neutral language some passages where More had in mind only males.

Introduction

I

The word 'utopia' entered the world with the publication of More's little book in December 1516. More coined it by fusing the Greek adverb *ou* – 'not' – with the noun *topos* – 'place' – and giving the resulting compound a Latin ending. Within the book's fiction, 'Noplace' is a newly discovered island somewhere in the New World. The meaning that 'utopia' has come to have as a common noun – a perfect society, or a literary account of one – seems authorised by the full title of the book, which is (translating from the Latin), 'On the Best State of a Commonwealth and on the New Island of Utopia'. The same Hellenist readers who recognised the etymology of 'Utopia' would also find this meaning suggested by the fact that the word puns on another Greek compound, *eutopia* – 'happy' or 'fortunate' place.

When we begin to read the book itself, though, the plausible supposition that *Utopia* is a utopia is rapidly undermined. First, the explorer whose account of the new island the book purports to record turns out to be named 'Hythloday' – another Greek compound, signifying 'nonsense peddler'. Second, the introductory, scene-setting pages are followed not by an account of Utopia but by a lengthy debate on the question of whether it is worthwhile for Hythloday to enter practical politics by joining a king's council. Within this debate is another, recounted by Hythloday, on the problem of theft in More's England. Apart from a comic postlude to the latter one, these two debates seem deadly serious, and they are powerfully written: but what are they doing in a book on the ideal commonwealth? And when, at the beginning of the second part (or 'Book') of *Utopia*, we at last reach Hythloday's account of the new island, it is still not clear that we've reached eutopia.

The commonwealth of Utopia turns out to be a highly attractive place in some ways, but a highly unattractive one in others. No one goes hungry there, no one is homeless. The commonwealth is strikingly egalitarian. On the other hand, personal freedom is restricted in ways large and small. The authorities maintain the population of households, cities and the country as a whole at optimal levels by transferring people between households, between cities and between Utopia and its colonies; and even those citizens who are not uprooted in this fashion must exchange houses by lot every ten years (though all the houses are essentially the same). There is no opportunity to pass even one's leisure hours in unsanctioned activities: there are no locks on doors; 'no wine-bars, or ale-houses, or brothels; no chances for corruption; no hiding places; no spots for secret meetings' (p. 59). A citizen must get permission from the local magistrates to travel, and from spouse and father even to go for a walk in the country. In general, if Utopia anticipates the welfare democracies of our own time in many respects, the elaborate constraints imposed on its inhabitants also frequently put us in mind of modern totalitarian regimes. More's own society was rigidly hierarchical and highly regulated, so Utopia may not have seemed as restrictive to him as it does to us. Still, it is difficult to believe that he would have regarded as ideal all the features of Utopia that we find unattractive. Moreover, every Utopian proper noun embodies the same kind of learned joke as 'Utopia' and 'Hythloday'; and a few, at least, of the Utopian exploits and customs we are told about are hard to take seriously. Finally, at the end of the book More partly dissociates himself – or at least the dramatic character who goes by his name – from Utopia, saying that many of its laws and customs struck him as absurd, though there are many others that he would 'wish rather than expect' to see in Europe.

These observations suggest three fundamental questions about *Utopia*. First, why did More invent a flawed commonwealth? It is easy to understand why a writer would want to create a fictional account of an ideal commonwealth, or a satire of a bad one. But what is the point of inventing a commonwealth that is partly good and partly bad? Second, what do the debates of Book I have to do with the account of Utopia in Book II, and with the subject of the best condition of the commonwealth? Third, how are we to understand the fact that More represents himself as disapproving of much of what Hythloday says – and that, by peppering the book with jokes, he even seems to deny its seriousness?

Utopia is endlessly enigmatic, and we as editors don't (and shouldn't) pretend to have definitive answers to these questions, or to many others that the book prompts. We are, though, convinced that answers to the key questions – and, still more, a comprehensive interpretation of the book – need to take into account certain fundamental facts about *Utopia* and its background, and that it is our role to provide the necessary starting points for interpretation, by setting the book in its contexts in More's life and times, and in the history of political thought. In this process, the 'Introduction' provides the broad outlines, and the footnotes to the translation fill in details; in turn, these materials, together with 'Suggestions for further reading', point the reader to texts on which a fuller and deeper understanding of *Utopia* depends.

II

More was born in London on 7 February 1478, or possibly 1477.[1] His father, John More, evidently hoped his eldest son would follow him into the legal profession. Thomas spent a few years at St Anthony's School, learning the fundamentals of Latin grammar and composition. At the age of about twelve, he was placed as a page in the household of Henry VII's Lord Chancellor, John Morton. (Morton was also Archbishop of Canterbury and, from 1493, a cardinal.) This placement was ideally suited to exposing More to the ways of public life, and to securing him a powerful patron. After two years at Morton's, the boy was sent to Oxford, presumably to sharpen the skills in rhetoric and logic that would be important to a legal career. He was then, at about sixteen, brought back to London to begin legal training in the Inns of Court.

During his years as a law student, however, More came increasingly under the influence of a group of literary scholars, central figures of the emerging tradition of Renaissance humanism in England. As modern studies have made clear, the term 'humanism', when applied to the Renaissance, is best used not to designate a particular philosophical position – for no single position is shared by all those Renaissance figures whom we are accustomed to regard as humanists – but to designate a particular scholarly orientation. 'Humanism' is a nineteenth-century coinage; but 'humanist' (like its cognates in other European languages) is found in the Renaissance itself, where it derived, first as Italian university-student

---

[1] See Richard Marius, *Thomas More*, p. 7; Peter Ackroyd, *The Life of Thomas More*, p. 4.

slang, from *studia humanitatis*, a Ciceronian phrase that came to designate a family of disciplines comprising grammar, rhetoric, history, poetry and moral philosophy.[2] In the Renaissance as in the Middle Ages, Latin was the normal language of learning. Beginning in the fourteenth century, humanists like Petrarch attempted to revive the classical form of that language; by the early fifteenth century, they had undertaken a parallel attempt for classical Greek. More studied Latin composition with the grammarian John Holt, and Greek with the first Englishman to teach it, William Grocyn. He also fell strongly under the influence of John Colet. Like Grocyn, Colet had studied in Italy, the centre of humanist learning. After his return to England in 1496, he gave several series of lectures at Oxford on the epistles of St Paul, lectures that constituted the earliest English application of some of the exegetical and historiographical techniques of Italian humanism; later he became Dean of St Paul's Cathedral, and founded there the first of the humanist grammar schools in England. And in 1499, More made the acquaintance of the great Dutch humanist Erasmus, who in that year first visited England.

Indeed, at this period More seems to have been as intent on the pursuit of literary scholarship as of the law. He may also seriously have considered becoming a priest. According to a biographical sketch of More that Erasmus wrote in 1519, for a time 'he applied his whole mind to the pursuit of piety, with vigils and fasts and prayer and similar exercises preparing himself for the priesthood' (*CWE*, VII, 21). In fact More seems to have tested his vocation not merely for the priesthood – a calling that, as Morton's example shows, need not have precluded a career in law (and politics) – but also for a life of religious withdrawal. The biography by his son-in-law William Roper says that at about this time More lived for four years with the Carthusians, the strictest of the monastic orders.[3]

Eventually More made his choices. By early 1505, he had closed the door to the priesthood and monasticism by marrying Joan Colt, the daughter of a wealthy landowner;[4] nor is there any sign, in the years following his marriage, that he thought of abandoning the law. Given the necessity

---

[2] See especially Paul Oskar Kristeller, *Renaissance Thought: The Classic, Scholastic, and Humanist Strains* (New York, 1961), pp. 8–23.

[3] *The Life of Sir Thomas More*, p. 198. Roper says that More 'gave himself to devotion and prayer in the Charterhouse of London, religiously living there without vow about four years'. The biography by his great-grandson Cresacre More, however, says he dwelt 'near' the Charterhouse: *The Life of Sir Thomas More*, ed. Joseph Hunter (London, 1828), p. 25.

[4] On her first name, usually given as 'Jane', see Germain Marc'hadour, 'More's first wife... Jane? or Joan?', *Moreana*, 29, no. 109 (1992), 3–22.

of supporting a growing family – Joan bore him four children before her death in 1511, at twenty-three; shortly afterward, More married a middle-aged widow, Alice Middleton – he could in any case scarcely have afforded to entertain such thoughts.

In the decade following his first marriage, More rose rapidly in his profession. Roper says that he was a member of the Parliament of 1504, and he almost certainly represented the City of London in that of 1510. In the same year, he began to act as a city judge, having been appointed an undersheriff of London. Increasingly he won assignments that drew on his literary and rhetorical as well as his legal skills. In March 1518, he entered Henry VIII's council.[5] His duties in this role spanned a broad range of activities, but his main employment, before he became Lord Chancellor in 1529, was as secretary to the king. He also served frequently as the king's orator. And when Henry decided to write against Martin Luther (in 1520), More acted as his literary adviser and editor.

In the earlier part of his professional life, More also managed to carry out a substantial amount of independent scholarship and writing. It is striking how precisely his works of this period conform to the five associated disciplines of the *studia humanitatis*.[6] As grammarian (in the Renaissance understanding of the term), he translated (into Latin) Greek poems, and four short prose works of the Greek ironist Lucian. As rhetorician, he wrote a declamation in reply to Lucian's *Tyrannicide*. (The declamation was a standard rhetorical exercise, a speech on a paradoxical or otherwise ingenious topic, often involving the impersonation of some historical or mythical figure.) Erasmus reports a lost dialogue, evidently in the spirit of a declamation, defending the community of wives advocated in Plato's *Republic*. Several of More's longer, polemical letters of these years belong to the rhetorical genre of invective. As poet, he wrote, in addition to a few English poems, a large number of Latin epigrams. As historian, he practised the humanist genre of historical biography, in Latin and English versions of his unfinished *History of King Richard III* (a splendid, sardonic work that became the main source of Shakespeare's play) and in his translation of a biography of the fifteenth-century Italian philosopher Pico della Mirandola. As moral and political philosopher, he wrote *Utopia*. The publication of *Utopia* came near the end of this phase of More's literary career. Apart from four lengthy open letters in defence of Erasmus and

5 See J. A. Guy, *Thomas More*, pp. 52–3.
6 See P. O. Kristeller, 'Thomas More as a Renaissance Humanist', *Moreana*, no. 65–6 (1980), 5–22.

humanist learning, for several years after 1516 he wrote little other than what was required of him in his profession; and when he resumed writing books in the 1520s – works opposing the Lutheran 'heresy', and a series of devotional works – they no longer fitted the humanist categories.

III

Utopia was conceived in the summer of 1515. In May of that year, More left England for Flanders, as a member of a royal trade commission. The negotiations conducted by this commission and its Flemish counterpart at Bruges were stalled and recessed by 21 July, but More did not return to England until 25 October. In the three months from late July to late October, he enjoyed a rare period of leisure; it was during this period that *Utopia* began to take shape.

At some point in the summer More visited Antwerp, where he met Peter Giles, to whom Erasmus had recommended him. Giles was a man after More's own heart. A classical scholar and an intimate of Erasmus and his circle, he was also a man of practical affairs, city clerk of Antwerp and as such deeply involved in the business of that cosmopolitan shipping and commercial centre. Book I of *Utopia* opens with a brief account of the trade mission, which leads into an account of More's acquaintance with Giles. At this point, the book glides from fact into fiction. More says he encountered Giles after Mass one day, when Giles introduced him to Raphael Hythloday, with whom they proceeded to have the conversation that is recorded in *Utopia*. This fictional conversation is presumably a transformation and expansion of actual conversations between More and Giles.[7] Be that as it may, More's visit to Antwerp served to crystallise and fuse a range of concerns most of which had (on the evidence of his earlier writings) been in his mind for years.

We have no direct information as to when More began writing. In the biographical sketch referred to above, Erasmus reported that his friend wrote the second book of *Utopia* 'earlier, when at leisure; at a later opportunity he added the first in the heat of the moment' (*CWE*, VII, 24). As J. H. Hexter argues, if More wrote Book II first, it seems probable that he initially regarded it as a complete work; presumably this version of *Utopia*

---

[7] Giles seems to hint as much in the commendatory letter he wrote for the first edition of *Utopia:* see p. 120.

was well in hand by the time he returned to England.[8] Back in London, though, he found reason to add the dialogue of Book I.

Hexter points out that the first version of *Utopia* must have included not only the account of Utopia that now occupies all of Book II except its last few pages but also an introduction something like the opening of the present Book I. Otherwise it would not be clear who is speaking in the monologue on Utopia, and under what circumstances. The second phase of composition is likely to have begun, then, not with the narrative account of the embassy to Bruges and the diversion to Antwerp but with the dialogue that now follows this introductory section. Indeed the precise point where More, as Hexter says, 'opened a seam' in the first version of *Utopia* to insert the dialogue can be identified with some confidence (see below, p. 12n.). After writing the dialogue, More must also have revised the conclusion of the work as a whole. In the final paragraph of Book II, as Hexter points out, the narrator recalls that Hythloday 'had reproached certain people who were afraid they might not appear knowing enough unless they found something to criticise in the ideas of others'. But Hythloday's censures occur in the dialogue of Book I (p. 14), so that this allusion to them must have been written after the dialogue.

The fact that *Utopia* was composed in this odd sequence surely has implications for its interpretation. As with many other facts about the book, though, this one cuts two ways. On the one hand, it may suggest that More split open a complete, unified book to insert a dialogue which, though interesting in itself, doesn't really belong with the original material – that *Utopia* is really *two* books. Or it may suggest that More had second thoughts about the account of Utopia and saw a need to insert a new section which would be in effect an introduction to it. In any event, the dialogue affects our view of Utopia. For one thing, it gives us a much sharper sense of Hythloday, who is both our only source of information about the island commonwealth and its foremost enthusiast.

IV

More's book benefited greatly both from his experience in law and politics and from his humanist learning. Though the social problems *Utopia* addresses are perennial, the particular formulations of them, and the data

[8] See *More's 'Utopia': The Biography of an Idea*, pp. 15–30; *CW*, IV (*Utopia*), xv–xxiii.

of recent and contemporary English and European life that the book deploys, reflect More's personal and professional experience. But the intellectual paradigms that he brings to bear on the understanding of these problems, and the form and style of his book, derive primarily from his literary humanism.

The most obvious relation between *Utopia* and More's humanist learning is that with the central Greek works of political philosophy. The first part of the book's title – *On the Best State of a Commonwealth* – identifies it as belonging to the oldest genre of political writing, the discourse on the ideal commonwealth initiated by Plato's *Republic* and *Laws* and continued in Aristotle's *Politics* (and subsequently in many other works). Plato's and Aristotle's discussions of the ideal commonwealth are, however, purely argumentative, whereas the Utopian part of More's book consists of Hythloday's fictional travelogue. The decision to present his imaginary society in the form of a long speech by a fictional personage is responsible both for much of the book's interest and for much of its enigmatic quality. Fictions are attractive, but in their very nature they are not apt to resolve into unambiguous meanings.[9]

For the debate of Book I, the primary formal models are the dialogues of Plato – and, perhaps even more, those of Cicero. Like *Utopia*, and unlike the Platonic exemplars, Cicero's dialogues consist mainly of long speeches punctuated by brief interruptions, and are more concerned with expounding alternative positions than with reaching definite and prescriptive conclusions. There are also precedents for the main *topic* of More's debate, in humanist as well as classical literature. Arguing about whether Hythloday should join a king's council is a way of getting at the general, and very frequently discussed, problem of 'counsel': the problem of ensuring that rulers receive – and take – appropriate advice. As Quentin Skinner observes, this problem could be approached either from the point of view of the ruler, in which case the focus is on 'the importance of choosing good councillors and learning to distinguish between true and false friends', or from the point of view of the prospective councillor, when the focus is on the question of whether a scholar should commit himself

---

[9] More's decision to present Utopia as a fiction has also been responsible for much of his book's literary influence: the genre of the utopia, which *Utopia* initiated, differs from the philosophical discourse on the ideal commonwealth precisely in that it offers a fictionalised account of the eutopia as if it already existed. In the second of the two letters on *Utopia* that More addressed to Giles, he commented obliquely on the advantage of this way of proceeding. See p. 109.

to practical politics.[10] Viewed in the second perspective, it is an aspect of the ancient question of the relative merits of the active and contemplative lives.[11] Since, as Skinner says, 'humanists tended to see themselves essentially as political advisers', counsel was the political topic that most intrigued them. More himself had special reason to be intrigued: he had been edging closer to full-time royal service. Joining Henry's council (which, as noted above, More eventually did, in 1518) would be a step toward which his career as lawyer and diplomat led naturally; and yet contemplating this step may have prompted some anxiety in a man who was also imbued with the ideals of scholarly and religious detachment.[12]

Though the topic of counsel is commonplace, More's treatment of it is distinctive. This is also the case with his treatment (in the debate-within-a-debate referred to earlier) of the problem of theft, which expands into a general analysis of the condition of England. More's handling of these matters differs from that of most other social or political writers of the period in what we may call its systemic or holistic approach. As Hexter puts it, More sees 'in depth, in perspective, and in mutual relation problems which his contemporaries saw in the flat and as a disjointed series' (*CW*, IV, ci). He understands that the problem of counsel cannot be solved by sending a few wise men to court, because, in the existing structure of society, most of the people they would encounter there – including especially the rulers – are motivated by blinkered self-interest. Similarly, the problem of theft cannot be solved by punishing thieves, because theft stems primarily from poverty, which is in turn the product of a number of social factors. The polity as a whole is a complex network of reciprocally affecting parts.

The social analysis of Book I is also distinguished by its passionate intensity, its pervasive moral outrage at the status quo. The treatment of the problem of theft constitutes a scathing indictment of a system of 'justice' in which the poor are 'driven to the awful necessity of stealing and then dying for it' (p. 16). The root cause of this situation lies in the pride, sloth

---

[10] *The Foundations of Modern Political Thought*, 1, 216–17.

[11] Influential – and durably interesting – treatments of this issue are found in Plato (*Republic* VI.496C–497B and Epistle VII) and Seneca ('On Leisure' and 'On Tranquillity of Mind', in *Moral Essays*), who make the case for non-involvement, and in one of Plutarch's *Moral Essays*, 'That a Philosopher Ought to Converse Especially with Men in Power'. Cicero sees merit in both courses (*On Moral Obligation* I.xx.69–xxi.72, xliii.153–xliv.156).

[12] The most authoritative account of More's entry into royal service is that in Guy, *Thomas More*, pp. 46–58.

and greed of the upper classes. Noblemen live idly off others' labour, and also 'drag around with them a great train of idle servants', who, when they are later dismissed, know no honest way of making a living. The practice of enclosure (fencing common land as pasturage for sheep) deprives farm labourers of their livelihood and sets them to wander and beg – or to steal and be hanged.

Though it is Hythloday who delivers this indictment, one can hardly doubt that it embodies More's own views; and in fact More represents himself as concurring in Hythloday's analysis (p. 27). In the debate on counsel, however, More portrays Hythloday and himself as taking opposite positions, with Hythloday opposing involvement and More favouring it. Both positions are powerfully argued, and they are never bridged: in the closing pages of Book I, the disputants simply drop the topic and go on to another – the desirability of abolishing private property – about which they also never reach agreement.

These facts suggest an additional aspect of the relation between *Utopia* and its author's character and experience, one that helps to explain More's apparent dissociation of himself from Utopia: that the personality and views of his two main characters project his own persistent dividedness of mind. That 'More' closely resembles the author is clear. Yet it is equally clear that this cautious, practical lawyer and family man is More without his passion and vision – a More who could not have written *Utopia*, nor ever have chosen martyrdom. The most obvious literary models for Hythloday are the stern experts on comparative politics of Plato's political dialogues. In the book's generic economy, Hythloday corresponds to the austere Stranger of the *Statesman* or the Old Athenian of the *Laws*, whose detachment from practical affairs enables them to see and speak the truth. But this is as much as to say that Hythloday is to some extent More's fantasy – partly wistful, partly critical – of what he himself might have been, had he made different choices a decade earlier; even as 'More' is his mildly deprecating representation of the practical man he had become.[13]

More's dividedness of mind is also related, via his humanist learning, to the seriocomic mode of *Utopia*. Here the key author is Lucian, four

---

[13] Hythloday also recalls Erasmus (who, though he wrote about politics, kept himself clear of practical involvement with it) and, more strikingly, the fifteenth-century Florentine philosopher Pico della Mirandola, who was to More a particularly intriguing exemplar of contemplative withdrawal from worldly business. On More and Pico, see Dominic Baker-Smith, *More's 'Utopia'*, pp. 15–21.

of whose works, as we noted above, More had translated. (These were published in 1506, together with some additional translations by Erasmus.)

A Syrian sophist of the second century AD, Lucian was one of the last writers of classical Greek. In a series of dialogues and other short prose pieces, he played a key part in the development of a tradition of making serious points under the guise of jokes, other examples of which are *The Golden Ass* of Apuleius, numerous mock orations and festive treatises (like those listed as precedents in Erasmus' preface to *The Praise of Folly*), and works of later writers such as Rabelais and Swift. This tradition is sometimes characterised by the Latin phrase *serio ludere* – 'to play seriously'.[14]

As More says in his preface to the translations of Lucian, this kind of writing satisfies the Horatian injunction that literature should combine delight with instruction (*CW*, III, Part I, 3); in his second letter to Giles, he indicates that it was such considerations that led him to choose a seriocomic mode for *Utopia* (p. 109). But More was also attracted to the tradition of *serio ludere* for a deeper reason. The divided, complex mind, capable of seeing more than one side of a question and reluctant to make a definite commitment to any single position, has a proclivity for ironic discourse; and *serio ludere* – in which the play can serve to qualify or undercut any statement – is one of the great vehicles of irony. The first major humanist work in the Lucianic tradition is *The Praise of Folly* (written in More's house in 1509). This is a declamation of bewilderingly complex irony, in which Erasmus has Folly (supposed to be a goddess) praise folly – thus setting up a verbal hall of mirrors. The situation in *Utopia* is equally complex: a 'nonsense peddler' condemns Europe and praises Noplace; and his views – many of which are clearly not nonsense – are reported by a character who bears the author's name, and who dissociates himself from most of them.

V

Turning now to the question of the relation between the two books of *Utopia*, it is evident, first, that an analysis of the evils of the existing society forms an appropriate prelude to a discussion of a possibly better one; and that the juxtaposition of Europe and Utopia throws sharply

---

[14] See, for example, Edgar Wind, *Pagan Mysteries in the Renaissance*, rev. edn (New York, 1968), esp. pp. 236–7, and Rosalie L. Colie, *Paradoxia Epidemica: The Renaissance Tradition of Paradox* (Princeton, 1966).

into relief what is distinctive about each. The resulting comparisons are the burden of the peroration of Book II, in which Hythloday eloquently sums up what we have seen about Europe and Utopia, and makes, very powerfully, the contrasts that are begging to be made. But Book I also prepares us for Book II in another way, which becomes apparent if we consider the structure of Hythloday's arguments in Book I.

The discussion of theft opens with the question of why this problem persists, despite the continual execution of thieves – 'with as many as twenty at a time being hanged on a single gallows' (p. 15). Hythloday's response begins with, and is organised by, the contention that executing thieves is neither moral nor practical: 'The penalty is too harsh in itself, yet it isn't an effective deterrent. Simple theft is not so great a crime that it ought to cost a man his head, yet no punishment however severe can restrain those from robbery who have no other way to make a living.' Correspondingly, Hythloday argues that the milder punishment he recommends is both just and expedient.

As More's contemporaries would have recognised, this strategy of argument originates in rhetorical theory. Rhetoric (like logic) provided lists of subject-matter categories, called 'topics', of proven utility in constructing arguments. Since the subject of Hythloday's remarks is the advisability or inadvisability of particular policies, his speeches belong to the 'deliberative' genre, the oratory of persuasion and dissuasion. (Deliberative is one of the three great *genera* of classical rhetoric, along with the demonstrative genre – the oratory of praise or blame – and the judicial.) The central topics of deliberative oratory are *honestas* and *utilitas* – honour and expediency.[15] The deliberative orator normally argues that a particular course of action is advisable on the ground that it is honourable, or on the ground that it is expedient – or argues that it is *in*advisable, as being either dishonourable or inexpedient. Naturally, the strongest case is made when it can be shown that considerations of honour and expediency point in the same direction.

This turns out to be the nature of Hythloday's argument not only on the problem of theft but on all the questions he addresses. To 'More' and Giles he argues that joining a king's council would be neither honourable nor useful, since kings employ councillors only to tell them how best to accomplish dishonourable and destructive ends. In the two narratives of imaginary privy council meetings that he uses as examples (pp. 28–34),

---

[15] See, for example, Cicero, *On Invention* II.li.156–8; Quintilian, *The Education of the Orator* III.viii.1–3, 22–5.

he portrays himself as arguing that the supposedly expedient courses recommended by the other councillors are both immoral and self-defeating. When 'More', at the climax of the debate on counsel (pp. 34–7), argues for an 'indirect', temporising approach, in which the councillor, knowing that he cannot turn all to good, will at least try to make things as little bad as possible, Hythloday responds that such a strategy is neither practical nor consistent with Christian morality. Indeed, we get the strong impression that he would say that the moral and the expedient *never* truly conflict, that correct analysis will always show that a dishonourable course is also impractical. This position links him with the Stoics, for whom the identity of the moral and the expedient is a key doctrine.[16]

Evidently the question of the relation of the moral and the expedient interested More deeply, as it did other humanists. The claim that the two are identical was a standard theme of early humanist political thought, which is permeated by Stoicism; but in the fifteenth century some Italian humanists began to assert that *honestas* is *not* always the same as *utilitas*. In 1513, Machiavelli produced, in *The Prince*, the most famous of all statements of this position. More could not have known Machiavelli's book (it wasn't published until 1532), but he certainly knew the tradition of thought that it crystallised.

It is also evident that the question of the relation of *honestas* and *utilitas* is linked with the subject of the best condition of the commonwealth. If the moral and the expedient – the practical – are ultimately identical, then it is theoretically possible to design a viable commonwealth that would always act morally. But if the moral and the expedient cannot be fully reconciled, then this ideal could never be achieved, even in theory.

That More recognised the importance of this issue to the theory of the ideal commonwealth seems clear from what follows the exchange about the indirect approach to counsel. The question of the validity of this approach is never resolved – surely because More was of two minds about it. In his *fiction*, though, the question is left unresolved because it is sidetracked by Hythloday's sudden confession that he thinks the abolition of private property offers the only route to social justice. 'More' disputes this claim, not on the ground that communism is unjust, but on the basis

---

[16] Doubtless the most widely read account of this Stoic doctrine was that in Book III of Cicero's *On Moral Obligation*. Cicero – who is, along with Seneca, the only Roman in whom the graecophile Hythloday finds any philosophic merit (see p. 10) – gained a place in the history of philosophy not by original thought but, as in this instance, by popularising the ideas of various schools.

of arguments (derived from Aristotle's critique of the *Republic*) that it is impractical. The commonwealth cannot be stable, prosperous and happy without private property and the inequality that goes with it. Hythloday counters that More would think differently if he had seen Utopia: for that commonwealth embodies the equality that More thinks impractical, and yet it is uniquely happy and well-governed, with institutions that are both 'wise and sacred' (p. 37).

This, then, is the context that More provided for the account of Utopia: a dispute about the degree of compatibility of the moral and the expedient in political life, and, in particular, on the question of whether the ideal of equality is compatible with stability and prosperity. This context suggests that the account of Utopia may be – whatever *else* it may be – an attempt to answer this fundamental question about the best condition of the commonwealth: is it possible, even theoretically, for a commonwealth to be both moral and expedient?[17]

VI

If Book I of *Utopia* is affiliated with deliberative oratory, Book II has an equally clear connection with the demonstrative or epideictic genre, the oratory of praise or blame. Whatever More's readers (or More himself) might think of Utopia, for Hythloday it is 'that commonwealth which I consider not only the best but indeed the only one that can rightfully claim that name' (p. 103). Praise of a city or state was a recognised subgenre of demonstrative oratory, and a perusal of the discussions of this subgenre in classical textbooks of rhetoric suggests that these discussions may have contributed something to both the substance and the organization of Hythloday's long speech.[18]

---

[17] We may note in passing that these considerations suggest a solution to the much-discussed problem of why More made Utopia non-Christian. More and all his contemporaries – including Machiavelli – believed that moral, and Christian, behaviour is advisable on religious grounds. One of the liveliest questions in early sixteenth-century political thought, though, is that raised in Book I of *Utopia*: how far, in political life, is this kind of behaviour advisable on purely prudential grounds? More realised that this question could be answered by seeing what a society pursuing perfect expediency through purely rational calculations would be like.

[18] See Quintilian III.vii.26–7. There is another important treatment of the subgenre in the treatise on epideictic oratory by the Greek rhetorician Menander. His treatise (without translation) can be found in *Rhetores Graeci*, ed. Christianus Walz, 9 vols. (Osnabrück, 1968; originally published 1832–6), IX, 127–330; for a summary, see Theodore C. Burgess, 'Epideictic literature', *University of Chicago Studies in Classical Philology*, 3 (1902), 109–12.

If the selection and order of topics in the account of Utopia to some extent reflect the dicta of rhetorical theory, though, the structure of the commonwealth itself certainly derives from *political* theory. First, More took many of the institutional arrangements of Utopia from the discussions of the ideal commonwealth by Plato and Aristotle, and from idealised accounts of historical polities and their lawgivers by such authors as Tacitus and, especially, Plutarch. These appropriations range from small (but often striking) items such as the Utopians' custom of having wives stand 'shoulder to shoulder' (p. 90) with their husbands in battle, which seems to have been inspired or authorised by a passage in Plato's *Republic*, to fundamental features of Utopian life such as the restrictions on property and privacy, the institution of the common tables, and the heavy use, in the inculcation of desirable behaviour, of what we should call positive and negative reinforcement.

Second, the structure into which the borrowed institutions were fitted appears to have been constructed by applying the method for designing an ideal commonwealth devised by Plato and Aristotle. In this method, creating such a commonwealth is not simply a matter of piling together all the desirable features one can think of. On the contrary, the design premise is the principle of *autarkeia*, self-sufficiency: the best commonwealth will be one that includes everything that is necessary to the happiness of its citizens, and nothing else. Starting from this economical premise, Plato developed, and Aristotle refined, a four-step procedure for constructing an ideal commonwealth.[19] First, one must determine what constitutes the happiest life for the individual. This is the central question of ethical theory, and, as Aristotle explains at the beginning of Book VII of the *Politics*, its answer constitutes the starting point of political theory. Second, from these conclusions about the most desirable life, the theorist derives the communal goals whose attainment will result in the happiness of the citizens. Third, it is necessary to form a sort of checklist of the physical and institutional components that the commonwealth must include: a certain size of population will be required, and a certain kind and extent of territory; certain occupational functions will have to be performed; and so on. Finally, the theorist determines the particular form that each of these components should be given in order to assure that, collectively, they will constitute the best commonwealth. For More, most of these forms are (as we have noted) appropriated from Plato's and Aristotle's

[19] See Plato, *Republic* II.369B–372E; Aristotle, *Politics* VII.i–viii.

discussions of the ideal commonwealth and from idealised accounts of actual commonwealths.

Though there are many other useful things to say about Book II of *Utopia*, it seems beyond dispute, and fundamental, that the book presents the results of a best-commonwealth exercise conducted according to the Greek rules. This fact is obscured by More's decision to present his results in the form of a speech in praise of a supposedly existing commonwealth – the decision, as it were, to invent the genre of the utopia instead of writing a work of political theory in one of the standard forms. This decision entailed suppressing or disguising the various components of the dialectical substructure of his model. But once we recognise that Book II of *Utopia* constitutes a best-commonwealth exercise, some mystifying aspects of the work begin to make sense. In particular, this recognition tells us how to take the lengthy account of Utopian moral philosophy (pp. 64–74); and it can suggest an answer to one of the key questions we posed in starting out: why did More labour to invent a *flawed* commonwealth?

The passage on moral philosophy is in fact the cornerstone of the Utopian edifice: it constitutes the first step of the best-commonwealth exercise, the determination of the happiest life for the individual. The Utopians (who take it for granted that self-interest is the basic fact about human nature) maintain that pleasure is the goal of life, but they find that the most pleasurable life is the life of virtue. This is also the conclusion of Plato and Aristotle, but for them the virtuous life is that of contemplative leisure, made possible by the labour of slaves and artisans whose happiness is not a goal of the commonwealth. By contrast, the Utopians conclude that individual felicity is incompatible with special privilege, and think that the foremost pleasure 'arises from practice of the virtues and consciousness of a good life' (p. 73). Thus, though the Utopians are not Christians and their arguments consider only self-interest, they conclude that the best life for the individual is one lived in accordance with the moral norms of Christianity. Moreover, parallels between their arguments and passages in others of More's works confirm that he thought these arguments valid – though many readers have found them convoluted and strained.

But even if we grant that, for each individual, morality is always expedient, is this also true for the commonwealth as a whole? For the most part, Utopia supports this view. If, as the Utopians conclude, one's happiness is incompatible with spoiling the happiness of others, then it follows that the institutions of the commonwealth, whose goal is to maximise the happiness of its citizens, must be structured so as to implement the

Golden Rule. Indeed, the institutions and policies of Utopia (many deriving as they do from previous treatments of the ideal commonwealth) are on the whole much preferable to those of European nations and are in many respects completely consistent with Christian standards, as those are interpreted in the writings of More and his associates.

Yet some Utopian practices appear to be incompatible with these standards, and to be justifiable only in terms of expediency. To take the most disturbing examples, there is, first, the severe restriction of personal freedom. In Book I, Hythloday criticises repressive policies on the ground that 'it's an incompetent monarch who knows no other way to reform his people than by depriving them of all life's benefits' (p. 33), and this attitude harmonises with many passages in the writings of More's humanist circle. The Utopians themselves believe that 'no kind of pleasure is forbidden, provided harm does not come of it' (p. 58). To be sure, More was not a man to countenance laxity in himself or in others, and he regarded some activities as harmful that, to most of us nowadays, seem quite innocuous. But the numerous proscriptions and rigid controls hedged round life in Utopia include some that do not appear capable of being explained in this fashion. Is taking an unsanctioned walk in the country (pp. 58–9) really such a pernicious act?

Then there are the troubling aspects of Utopian foreign policy. For the most part, the Utopians are generous toward their neighbours. They distribute their surplus commodities among them 'at moderate prices', and they are always happy to provide them with skilful and honest administrators (pp. 59, 83). They detest war, and, whenever it cannot be avoided, go to great lengths to minimise its destructiveness. Yet it turns out that they will go to war for a good many reasons – including to obtain territory for colonisation, whenever the Utopian population exceeds the optimum number. Furthermore, some of their military tactics are of very dubious morality. They offer rewards for the assassination of enemy leaders. They employ mercenaries to do as much of their fighting as possible – and the mercenaries they prefer are the savage Zapoletes (pp. 88–9), whose use is hard to reconcile with the aim of minimising war's destructiveness. Moreover, despite their compassion for the common citizens of enemy nations, the Utopians enslave the prisoners taken in wars in which they have employed their own forces.[20]

---

[20] Robert P. Adams shows that many of the 'antichivalric' Utopian military practices are consonant with Stoic and Erasmian humanist ideas (*The Better Part of Valor*, pp. 152–4). But this argument cannot account for the particular practices mentioned here.

The explanation of these discrepancies between Utopian practices and More's own ideals would seem to lie in his recognition of the fact that even in the best commonwealth there will always be conflicts between valid goals – a problem that occurs but rarely to theorists of the ideal commonwealth or writers of utopias. More's awareness of the conflict of goals is first apparent in the section on moral philosophy. Utopian ethics is a strange fusion of Stoicism and Epicureanism. One feature of Epicureanism that struck More is the so-called 'hedonic calculus', Epicurus' rule that, in choosing among pleasures, one should always choose a greater pleasure over a lesser, and should reject any pleasure that will eventually result in pain: this rule occurs three times, in one formulation or another, in the passage on moral philosophy. It seems clear that More thought similar principles should be applied to resolving conflicts between goals at the collective, political level; and it is possible to understand most of the unattractive features of Utopia in terms of such principles.

More was evidently impressed by the Aristotelian objections to egalitarianism that he has 'More' voice at the end of Book I. If Utopia does not manifest the chaos that 'More' had claimed would be inevitable in a communist society, this is presumably because of the elaborate system of restraints that More has built into it. Apparently he believed that too much freedom would threaten the stability and security of the commonwealth – which, in the nature of things, has to be the political goal of highest priority.

The same line of explanation can be applied to the disturbing Utopian practices in foreign policy. It is impossible to believe that More approved of all these practices; yet apparently he thought them necessary. The internal arrangements of Utopia or any other commonwealth will not really matter unless the commonwealth can be made externally secure; and as long as other commonwealths are not utopian, it is hard to see how to secure it without indulging in some practices that are expedient but certainly not moral.

Despite its abundant wit, *Utopia* is in fact a rather melancholy book. More evidently shared with St Augustine (whose *City of God* he had expounded in a series of lectures about 1501) the conviction that no human society could be wholly attractive; and he knew, too, that even the attractive arrangements that are theoretically possible are in practice difficult to achieve. Is there any reason not to take at face value the final judgement of 'More' that Utopia includes 'very many features that in our own societies I would wish rather than expect to see'? Yet 'More' also insists, in the debate on the 'indirect approach' to counsel, that things can be made at least a little less bad, by working tactfully on rulers and their councillors. Here as in other ways history has generally borne him out. In the centuries since he wrote, many of the reforms proposed in *Utopia* have been effected in various countries – though not always by peaceful means (any more than was the case in Utopia, where they were imposed by a foreign conqueror (p. 42)), and not always resulting in clear net improvements.

Note on the translation

A translation of *Utopia* has to be based on one of the first four editions – the only ones in which More or his direct agents had a hand. (There is no manuscript of the work.) These editions were published at Louvain (1516), Paris (1517) and Basel (March and November 1518). Like other recent editors, we have concluded that the Basel editions most nearly and fully represent More's intent, both for his text itself and for its appendages (contributions by other humanists) and format. The second of these Basel editions is a close resetting of the first, with nothing, in our judgement, to suggest that its changes from the earlier version have authorial sanction. We have therefore based the translation on the edition of March 1518, occasionally corrected by better readings in the other three early editions, and here and there emended by editorial judgement – our own or that of our predecessors.

Utopia is not cast in artificial or ornate literary language, as More's age understood it. Though More occasionally uses rare words, on the whole his Latin is simple, conversational, everyday prose such as a lawyer, a diplomat or a humanist scholar might employ about the normal occasions and business of daily existence. It is far from Ciceronian; it is seldom deliberately mannered. But it is quite unlike modern English in several important ways. The sentences are longer and less tightly knit in patterns of subordination. The main idea of a sentence may be hidden in an ablative absolute, or hung out at a considerable distance in space and syntax. Because it is a highly inflected language, Latin can scatter the ingredients of a sentence about more loosely than English does, in the assurance that a reader will be able to assemble them within his or her own mind. An English sentence is expected to do more of the reader's work. At the same time, Latin, or at least More's lawyerly Latin, has a mass of delicate innuendoes and qualifications at its disposal – double negatives, ironic appositives, pseudo-antitheses and formal (but only formal) correlatives. To represent the structure of More's Latin syntax in English would create the impression of a whirling chaos; reproducing his stylistic nuances would give rise to a mincing and artificial English. And in either case, the real flavour of More's book, which is casual and colloquial, would be lost.

The almost inevitable solution is to translate into natural, unmannered, everyday prose, and let the flowers of rhetoric wither by the wayside. With some texts this procedure might produce a flat or neutral version; but *Utopia* is not only free and various in itself, it is so crowded with thought that shoehorning More's overflowing amplitude of meaning into pronounceable English sentences provides work enough for a translator. The complexities of interpreting *Utopia* don't, on the whole, derive from intricacies of language; they are matters of attitude and levels of ironic reversal – both controlled by the sort of moral feeling one brings to the book.

Finally, a word about the appendages to the text. More entrusted the publication of *Utopia* to Giles and Erasmus. One or both of them composed a series of marginal glosses on the text (see p. 121 and note), and, in accordance with More's wish, Erasmus secured a series of commendatory letters, poems and other materials to buttress the work (see p. 110n.). These commendations appeared in different combinations in all four early editions, some preceding the text of *Utopia* itself, and others following it. Since the commendations – and, we assume, the glosses – were appended to the text with More's approval, and since all these materials are useful in indicating how *Utopia* struck the readers for whom it was originally intended, we have included them in this edition. We have, though, relegated all the commendations to the end of the text.

Chronology

1478 (1477?) 7 February: More born, in London.

c. 1482–90 Attends St Anthony's School.

1485 Defeat and death of Richard III at Bosworth Field; accession of Henry VII.

c. 1490–2 More serves as page in Cardinal Morton's household.

c. 1492–4 More at Oxford.

c. 1494 More enters the Inns of Court to study law.

1499 More meets Erasmus.

1504 More in Parliament?

1504 or 1505 More marries Joan Colt.

1505–7 Publication of accounts of the New World voyages of Amerigo Vespucci.

1509 Death of Henry VII; accession of Henry VIII. Erasmus writes *The Praise of Folly* (published 1511).

1510 More appointed an undersheriff of London; in Parliament.

1511 Death of Joan Colt; More marries a widow, Alice Middleton.

1512–13 Henry VIII at war with France.

1513 Machiavelli writes *The Prince* (published 1532).

c. 1513–19 More writes *The History of King Richard III*.

1515 May–October: More on embassy to Flanders; meets Peter Giles; begins *Utopia*.

1516 December: *Utopia* published at Louvain.

1517 Second edition of *Utopia* published at Paris. Martin Luther's ninety-five theses on indulgences signal the beginning of the Reformation.

1518 More joins Henry VIII's council. March and November: third and fourth editions of *Utopia* published at Basel, together with *Epigrams*.

(These are the last editions of *Utopia* in which More could have had a hand.)

1521 More becomes Under-Treasurer of the Exchequer; knighted. His daughter Margaret marries William Roper.

1523 More made Speaker of the House of Commons. Writes a defence of Henry VIII against Luther.

1525 More appointed Chancellor of the Duchy of Lancaster.

1529 More publishes *A Dialogue Concerning Heresies*, against William Tyndale and Luther. 25 October: appointed Lord Chancellor of England (first layman to occupy that office).

1532 16 May: More resigns the chancellorship over the 'Submission of the Clergy', which ceded veto power over ecclesiastical legislation to Henry VIII.

1533 Henry VIII marries Anne Boleyn and is excommunicated.

1534 13 April: More refuses to swear support for the Act of Succession (acknowledging Henry's male heirs by Anne Boleyn as heirs to the throne). 17 April: More imprisoned in the Tower of London, where he writes *A Dialogue of Comfort against Tribulation* and other devotional works.

1535 1 July: More tried and convicted of treason. 6 July: beheaded.

1551 *Utopia* first translated into English, by Ralph Robinson.

1557 Collected edition of More's English works.

1565–6 Collected edition of More's Latin works.

1935 More canonised.

Suggestions for further reading

The earliest biography of More is the brief, engaging *Life of Sir Thomas More* by his son-in-law William Roper. It is published with the other famous English biography of the early sixteenth century, George Cavendish's *The Life and Death of Cardinal Wolsey*, in *Two Early Tudor Lives*, ed. Richard S. Sylvester and Davis P. Harding (New Haven and London, 1962). The most influential modern biography (though now dated) has been R. W. Chambers's highly readable, laudatory *Thomas More* (London, 1935). The two most recent full biographies are Richard Marius, *Thomas More* (New York, 1984), a revisionist work that develops a generally unflattering portrait of More as a deeply conflicted man, and Peter Ackroyd, *The Life of Thomas More* (London, 1998), which presents him as a healthy defender of a dying medieval Catholic culture. John Guy's *Thomas More* (London and New York, 2000) is both a compact biography and a salutary examination of the ways in which the problematic nature of the sources makes it impossible to give definitive answers to many key questions about More. Guy had previously traced More's professional life, in *The Public Career of Sir Thomas More* (Brighton and New Haven, 1980). There is an engrossing psychobiographical study in Stephen Greenblatt's *Renaissance Self-fashioning from More to Shakespeare* (Chicago and London, 1980), pp. 11–73. In *Thomas More: History and Providence* (New Haven and London, 1983), Alistair Fox interprets all of More's works in the context of an exploration of his complex psychology; his book has affinities with Marius's revisionism. A rich and convenient source of biographical information about More's contemporaries is *Contemporaries of Erasmus: A Biographical Register of the Renaissance and Reformation,* ed. Peter G. Bietenholz and Thomas B. Deutscher, 3 vols. (Toronto/Buffalo/London, 1985–7).

Authoritative editions of More's works are found in the monumental Yale *Complete Works of St Thomas More*, 15 vols. (New Haven and London, 1963–97). A Modernized Series supplement to the Yale edition provides translations of forty-four of More's Latin letters and texts of twenty-two English ones: *Selected Letters*, ed. Elizabeth F. Rogers (rev. edn, 1967). *Utopia* (Latin and English), ed. Edward Surtz, SJ, and J. H. Hexter (1965), is Volume IV of the Yale edition. Hexter's section of the introduction to that volume constitutes an especially challenging and interesting interpretation of *Utopia*; Surtz's section, and his 300-page commentary, supply a wealth of information on the literary and historical contexts of the book. For detailed information on any passage of *Utopia*, Surtz's commentary is the first place to look. More recent and more compact is *Utopia: Latin Text and English Translation*, ed. George M. Logan, Robert M. Adams and Clarence H. Miller (Cambridge, 1995), which includes, in addition to the revised version of the Adams translation reproduced in the present volume, a modern-spelling edition of the Latin text and a somewhat fuller commentary than the one found here. J. H. Lupton's 1895 edition of *Utopia* (Oxford) reprints the earliest English translation of the book, by Ralph Robinson (1551), together with the Latin text and a full and interesting commentary. A commentary nearly on the scale of Surtz's is found in the Latin-French edition by André Prévost (Paris, 1978).

Utopia participates in a sort of dialogue with earlier (and later) works of political thought. The Greek and Roman works in this dialogue, as well as the other classical works to which More alludes, are found in many libraries in the bilingual editions of the Loeb Classical Library. These are the editions quoted in the notes to this volume, except in the case of Aristotle's *Politics*, where we quote from the masterly edition by Ernest Barker (Oxford, 1948), and Plato's *Republic* and *Laws*, where we cite the engaging and handy Penguin translations: *The Republic*, trans. H. D. P. Lee, 2nd edn (1974); *The Laws*, trans. Trevor J. Saunders (1970). Passages in the works of More's fellow humanist Erasmus often provide the best gloss on passages of *Utopia*. Most of the major works are now available in the *Collected Works of Erasmus*, issuing from the University of Toronto Press (1974–).

For the context of *Utopia* in Renaissance political thought, see Quentin Skinner, *The Foundations of Modern Political Thought*, 2 vols. (Cambridge,

1978), and Skinner's chapter on political philosophy in *The Cambridge History of Renaissance Philosophy*, ed. Charles B. Schmitt *et al.* (Cambridge, 1988), pp. 387–452; for the context in moral philosophy, see Jill Kraye's chapter in the same work, pp. 301–86. The history of utopian literature is massively treated by Frank E. and Fritzie P. Manuel, *Utopian Thought in the Western World* (Cambridge, Mass., 1979). On the history of More's time, see G. R. Elton, *Reform and Reformation: England, 1509–1558*, The New History of England, II (London and Cambridge, Mass., 1977), or John Guy, *Tudor England* (Oxford and New York, 1988). On the social problems addressed in *Utopia*, see Joyce Youings, *Sixteenth-Century England*, The Pelican Social History of Britain (Harmondsworth, Middlesex, 1984).

The most influential books on *Utopia* have been Hexter's brilliant little *More's 'Utopia': The Biography of an Idea* (1952; rpt with an epilogue, New York, 1965), and two 1957 books by Surtz: *The Praise of Pleasure: Philosophy, Education, and Communism in More's Utopia* (Cambridge, Mass.) and *The Praise of Wisdom: A Commentary on the Religious and Moral Problems and Backgrounds of St Thomas More's 'Utopia'* (Chicago). Both contain a wealth of illuminating contextual information – much of which is, however (like much of the substance of Hexter's book), incorporated into the Yale *Utopia* (see above). Dominic Baker-Smith, *More's 'Utopia'* (London and New York, 1991), adroitly synthesises recent scholarship and criticism. Alistair Fox, *'Utopia': An Elusive Vision* (New York, 1993), includes a survey of the critical tradition and an excellent annotated bibliography. Fox's own reading purports to trace in *Utopia* More's progressive disillusionment with Utopia. Robert P. Adams, *The Better Part of Valor: More, Erasmus, Colet, and Vives, on Humanism, War, and Peace, 1496–1535* (Seattle, 1962), links *Utopia* to Erasmian pacifism. George M. Logan, *The Meaning of More's 'Utopia'* (Princeton, 1983), is primarily concerned with the relation between *Utopia* and classical and Renaissance political philosophy. This is also the focus of Quentin Skinner, 'Sir Thomas More's *Utopia* and the language of Renaissance humanism', in *The Languages of Political Theory in Early-Modern Europe*, ed. Anthony Pagden (Cambridge, 1987), pp. 123–57. Richard Halpern, *The Poetics of Primitive Accumulation: English Renaissance Culture and the Genealogy of Capital* (Ithaca and London, 1991), includes, on pp. 136–75, a sophisticated Marxist reading of *Utopia*. Elizabeth McCutcheon shows how much More's book yields to close stylistic analysis: see *My Dear Peter: The 'Arts Poetica' and Hermeneutics for More's 'Utopia'* (Angers, 1983).

She is particularly acute on More's use of the paradoxical tradition of *serio ludere*. Clarence H. Miller, 'Style and meaning in *Utopia*: Hythloday's sentences and diction', in *Acta Conventus Neo-Latini Hafniensis*, ed. Rhoda Schnur *et al.* (Binghamton, N.Y., 1994), pp. 675–83, analyses the style of Hythloday's speeches and the import of its striking variations. *Essential Articles for the Study of Thomas More*, ed. R. S. Sylvester and G. P. Marc'hadour (Hamden, Conn., 1977), reprints a number of the best articles on *Utopia*, on other works by More, and on facets of More's biography. There are two recent bibliographies of More: Michael D. Wentworth, *The Essential Sir Thomas More: An Annotated Bibliography of Major Modern Studies* (New York, 1995), and Albert J. Geritz, *Thomas More: An Annotated Bibliography of Criticism, 1935–1997* (Westport, Conn., and London, 1998). There is also an online bibliography, devoted to *Utopia* alone and covering the period *c.* 1890–1995, by Romauld Lakowski: http://www.shu.ac.uk/emls/01-2/lakomore.html. The journal *Moreana* publishes articles on More, reviews scholarship on him, and reports the many and varied activities of the global circle of More scholars and admirers.

ON THE BEST
STATE OF A COMMONWEALTH
AND ON THE NEW ISLAND
OF UTOPIA

A Truly Golden Handbook,
No Less Beneficial than Entertaining,
by the Most Distinguished and Eloquent Author
THOMAS MORE
Citizen and Undersheriff of the Famous City
of London

THOMAS MORE TO PETER GILES, GREETINGS[1]

My dear Peter Giles, I am almost ashamed to be sending you after nearly a year this little book about the Utopian commonwealth, which I'm sure you expected in less than six weeks.[2] For, as you were well aware, I faced no problem in finding my materials, and had no reason to ponder the arrangement of them.[3] All I had to do was repeat what you and I together heard Raphael[4] relate. Hence there was no occasion for me to labour over the style, since what he said, being extempore and informal, couldn't be couched in fancy terms.[5] And besides, as you know, he is a man not so well versed in Latin as in Greek;[6] so that my language would be nearer the truth, the closer it approached to his casual simplicity. Truth in fact is the only thing at which I should aim and do aim in writing this book.

I confess, my dear Peter, that having all these materials ready to hand left hardly anything at all for me to do. Otherwise, thinking through this topic from the beginning and disposing it in proper order might have demanded no little time and work, even if one were not entirely deficient in talent and learning. And then if the matter had to be set forth with eloquence,

---

[1] In the first edition of *Utopia* (1516), this letter was called the 'preface' of the work; this is also its running title in the 1518 editions. On Giles (*c.* 1486–1533), see p. 9 and, on his role in the genesis of *Utopia*, pp. 120–1 and the Introduction, p. xvi.

[2] On the chronology, see Introduction, pp. xvi–xvii. On the meaning of 'Utopia', p. xi.

[3] Finding materials, disposing them in the proper order and couching them in the appropriate style are the three steps of literary composition (*inventio, dispositio, elocutio*), as that subject is treated in the classical textbooks of rhetoric and their medieval and Renaissance successors.

[4] I.e., Raphael Hythloday. His given name links him with the archangel Raphael, traditionally a guide and healer. (On his surname, see p. 5n.)

[5] Rhetorical theory identified three levels of style: the grand, the middle and the plain. This sentence hints that *Utopia* is written in the plain style – according to theory, the appropriate one for philosophical dialogue. In point of fact, while the account of the Utopian commonwealth in Book II of the work is written in a generally simple and straightforward style, some passages of Book I, as well as the peroration of Book II, diverge very considerably from the plain style. See Clarence H. Miller, 'Style and meaning in *Utopia*: Hythloday's sentences and diction'.

[6] Knowledge of Greek was still uncommon among humanists in the early sixteenth century and thus carried considerable prestige in their circles. Greek studies had been More's own preoccupation as a scholar in the decade leading up to *Utopia*.

not just factually, there is no way I could have done that, however hard I worked, for however long a time. But now when I was relieved of all these concerns, over which I could have sweated forever, there was nothing for me to do but simply write down what I had heard. Well, little as it was, that task was rendered almost impossible by my many other obligations. Most of my day is given to the law – pleading some cases, hearing others, arbitrating others, and deciding still others. I pay a courtesy call to one man and visit another on business; and so almost all day I'm out dealing with other people, and the rest of the day I give over to my family and household; and then for myself – that is, my studies – there's nothing left.

For when I get home, I have to talk with my wife, chatter with my children, and consult with the servants. All these matters I consider part of my business, since they have to be done unless a man wants to be a stranger in his own house. Besides, you are bound to bear yourself as agreeably as you can towards those whom nature or chance or your own choice has made the companions of your life. But of course you mustn't spoil them with your familiarity, or by overindulgence turn the servants into your masters. And so, amid the concerns I have mentioned, the day, the month, the year slips away.

When do I write, then? Especially since I still have said nothing about sleeping or even eating, to which many people devote as much time as to sleep itself, which consumes almost half of our lives. My own time is only what I steal from sleeping and eating.[7] It isn't very much (hence the slow pace), but it's something, and so I've finally finished *Utopia*, and I'm sending it to you now. I hope, my dear Peter, that you'll read it over and let me know if you find anything that I've overlooked. Though on this point I do not lack all confidence in myself – I wish my judgement and learning were up to my memory, which isn't too bad – still, I don't feel so confident that I would swear I've missed nothing.

For my servant John Clement[8] has raised a great doubt in my mind. As you know, he was there with us, for I always want him to be present at conversations where there's profit to be gained. (And one of these days I

---

[7] His sixteenth-century biographer Thomas Stapleton says that More slept four or five hours a night, rising at 2 a.m. See *The Life and Illustrious Martyrdom of Sir Thomas More*, trans. Philip E. Hallett, ed. E. E. Reynolds (London, 1966), p. 28. Claiming that a book was composed in odd hours or inopportune circumstances was conventional, but in More's case there is no reason to doubt that the convention corresponded to fact.

[8] John Clement (d. 1572) was one of the first students of St Paul's School, the humanist grammar school founded by John Colet about 1509. By 1514 he had entered More's household as servant and pupil; in later life he became a respected physician.

expect we'll get a fine crop of learning from this young sprout, who has already made excellent progress in Greek as well as Latin.) Anyhow, as I recall matters, Hythloday[9] said the bridge over the Anyder at Amaurot was five hundred yards long; but my John says that is two hundred yards too much – that in fact the river is not more than three hundred yards wide there. So I beg you, consult your memory. If your recollection agrees with his, I'll yield and confess myself mistaken. But if you don't recall the point, I'll follow my own memory and keep my present figure. For, as I've taken particular pains to avoid having anything false in the book, so, if anything is in doubt, I'd rather say something untrue than tell a lie. In short, I'd rather be honest than clever.

Note the theological distinction between a deliberate lie and an untruth[10]

But the difficulty can easily be cleared up if you'll ask Raphael about it – either face-to-face or else by letter. And you must do this anyway, because of another problem that has cropped up – whether through my fault, or yours, or Raphael's, I'm not sure. For it didn't occur to us to ask, nor to him to say, in what part of the New World Utopia is to be found. I would give a sizeable sum of money to remedy this oversight, for I'm rather ashamed not to know the ocean where this island lies about which I've written so much. Besides, there are various people here, and one in particular, a devout man and a professor of theology, who very much wants to go to Utopia.[11] His motive is not by any means idle curiosity, a hankering after new sights, but rather a desire to foster and further the growth of our religion, which has made such a happy start there. To do this properly, he has decided to arrange to be sent there by the pope, and even to be named bishop to the Utopians. He feels no particular scruples about applying for this post, for he considers it a holy ambition, arising not from motives of glory or gain, but from religious zeal.

Office-seeking in a good cause

Therefore I beg you, my dear Peter, to get in touch with Hythloday – in person if you can, or by letters if he's gone – and make sure that my work contains nothing false and omits nothing true. Perhaps it would be

[9] From Greek *hythlos* ('idle talk', 'nonsense') plus *daiein* ('to distribute') or perhaps *daios* (in the rare sense of 'knowing', 'cunning'): hence 'nonsense peddler' or 'expert in nonsense'. Similarly, 'Anyder' and 'Amaurot' are from *anydros*, 'waterless', and *amauroton*, 'made dark or dim'. For the bridge, see p. 45 below.

[10] This distinction has not been located in the theological literature. More's formulation of it echoes a passage in a late classical work well known to humanists, Aulus Gellius' *Attic Nights* (XI.xi). The marginal glosses are apparently by Giles, though Erasmus may also have had a hand in them (see p. 121 and note).

[11] A note in a 1624 translation of *Utopia* identifies this learned divine as Rowland Phillips, Warden of Merton College, Oxford. But there is nothing to support the identification, and the passage may simply be one of the book's jokes at the expense of theologians.

better to show him the book itself. If I've made a mistake, there's nobody better qualified to correct me; but even he cannot do it, unless he reads over my book. Besides, you will be able to discover in this way whether he's pleased or annoyed that I have written the book. If he has decided to write out his own story himself, he may not want me to do so; and I should be sorry, too, if in publicising the commonwealth of Utopia I had robbed him and his story of the flower of novelty.

The ungrateful judgements of men

But, to tell the truth, I'm still of two minds as to whether I should publish the book at all.[12] For men's tastes are so various, the tempers of some are so severe, their minds so ungrateful, their judgements so foolish, that there seems no point in publishing a book that others will receive only with contempt and ingratitude. Better simply to follow one's own natural inclinations, lead a merry life, and avoid the harrowing task of publishing something either useful or pleasant. Most people know nothing of learning; many despise it. The clod rejects as too difficult whatever isn't cloddish. The pedant dismisses as mere trifling anything that isn't stuffed with obsolete words. Some readers approve only of ancient authors; many men like only their own writing. Here's a man so solemn he won't allow a shadow of levity, and there's one so insipid of taste that he can't endure the salt of a little wit. Some are so flat-nosed[13] that they dread satire as a man bitten by a rabid dog dreads water; some are so changeable that they like one thing when they're seated and another when they're standing.[14]

Men who can't stand satire, he calls 'flat-nosed'

These people lounge around the taverns, and over their cups they pass judgement on the intelligence of writers. With complete assurance they condemn every author by his writings, just as the whim takes them, plucking each one, as it were, by the beard. But they themselves remain safe – 'out of range', so to speak. No use trying to lay hold of them; these good men are shaved so close, there's not so much as a hair of their heads to catch them by.

A saying

---

[12] Although More's letters express considerable anxiety about the reception of *Utopia*, the claim that he is ambivalent about publishing it would seem to be largely conventional. In a letter of *c.* 20 September 1516 he told Erasmus (who saw the book through the press), 'I am most anxious to have it published soon', and on 15 December he confided that 'from day to day I look forward to my *Utopia* with the feelings of a mother waiting for her son to return from abroad' (*Selected Letters*, pp. 76, 87).

[13] The nose, traditionally the organ expressive of anger and derision, is the seat of satire. So those who don't relish satire are flat-nosed.

[14] The last phrase echoes the *Invective against Cicero* (IV.7) of the first-century BC Roman historian Sallust; the paragraph as a whole resembles Erasmus' complaints, in his letter to Maarten van Dorp, about ill-natured readers of *The Praise of Folly* (*CWE*, III, 129).

Moreover, some people are so ungrateful that even though they're delighted with a work, they don't like the author any better because of it. They are no different from rude guests who, after they have been lavishly *A neat comparison* entertained at a splendid banquet, finally go home stuffed, without a word of thanks to the host who invited them. A fine task, providing at your own expense a banquet for men of such finicky palates and such various tastes, who will remember and reward you with such thanks!

Nevertheless, my dear Peter, raise with Hythloday the points I mentioned. Afterwards I will be free to consider the matter once more. But in fact, if he himself gives his consent – since it is late to be wise now that I have finished all the work – in all other considerations about publishing I will follow the advice of my friends, and especially yours. Farewell, my very dear Peter Giles; my regards to your excellent wife. Love me as you always have; I am more fond of you than I have ever been.

THE BEST STATE OF A COMMONWEALTH,
A DISCOURSE BY THE EXTRAORDINARY
RAPHAEL HYTHLODAY, AS RECORDED BY
THE NOTED THOMAS MORE, CITIZEN AND
UNDERSHERIFF[1] OF THE FAMOUS CITY OF
BRITAIN, LONDON
BOOK I

The most invincible King of England, Henry, the eighth of that name, a prince adorned with the royal accomplishments beyond any other,[2] had recently some differences of no slight import with Charles, the most serene Prince of Castile,[3] and sent me into Flanders as his spokesman to discuss and settle them. I was companion and associate to that incomparable man Cuthbert Tunstall, whom the king has recently created Master of the Rolls, to everyone's enormous satisfaction.[4] I will say nothing in praise of this man, not because I fear the judgement of a friend might be questioned, but because his integrity and learning are greater than I can describe and too well known everywhere to need my commendation – unless I would, according to the proverb, 'show the sun with a lantern'.

Those appointed by the prince to deal with us, all excellent men, met us at Bruges by pre-arrangement. Their head man and leader was the Mayor of Bruges, a most distinguished person. But their main speaker

Cuthbert Tunstall

Adage

[1] More had been an undersheriff of London since 1510. His principal duty was to act as a judge in the Sheriff's Court (a city court that heard a wide variety of cases).

[2] When he succeeded to the throne in 1509, at the age of seventeen, Henry appeared to be something very close to the humanist ideal of a cultivated, just and peace-loving monarch, and More had enthusiastically heralded his accession in several Latin poems (*CW*, III, Part II, 101–17). By 1516, however, this view had been considerably undermined, especially by the king's fondness for martial (not yet marital) adventure.

[3] The disputes between the two nations were commercial ones, especially over tariffs. Charles was grandson of the Emperor Maximilian I, and was Duke of Burgundy after his father's death in 1506. He became, nominally though not formally, Prince of Castile after the death of Ferdinand II (23 January 1516), and Holy Roman Emperor in 1519.

[4] A royal commission of 7 May 1515 appointed five commissioners, including More, with Tunstall as their chief. Tunstall (1474–1559) was created Master of the Rolls (principal clerk of the Chancery Court) and Vice-Chancellor of the realm on 12 May 1516.

8

and guiding spirit was Georges de Themsecke, the Provost of Cassel, a man eloquent by nature as well as by training, also very learned in the law, and most skilful in diplomatic affairs through his ability and long practice. After we had met several times, certain points remained on which we could not come to agreement; so they adjourned the meeting[5] and went to Brussels for some days to learn their prince's pleasure.

Meanwhile, since my business required it, I went to Antwerp. Of those who visited me while I was there, no one was more welcome to me than Peter Giles. He was a native of Antwerp, a man of high reputation, already *Peter Giles* appointed to a good position and worthy of the very best: I hardly know whether the young man is distinguished more in learning or in character. Apart from being cultured, virtuous and courteous to all, with his intimates he is so open-hearted, affectionate, loyal and sincere that you would be hard-pressed to find another man anywhere whom you would think comparable to him in all the points of friendship. No one is more modest or more frank; no one better combines simplicity with wisdom. Besides, his conversation is so pleasant, and so witty without malice, that the ardent desire I felt to see again my native country, my home, my wife and my children (from whom I had been separated more than four months) was much eased by his most agreeable company and delightful talk.

One day after I had heard Mass at Notre Dame, the most beautiful and most popular church in Antwerp, I was about to return to my quarters when I happened to see him talking with a stranger, a man of quite advanced years, with a sunburned face, a long beard, and a cloak hanging loosely from his shoulders; from his face and dress, I took him to be a ship's captain. When Peter saw me, he came up and greeted me. As I was about to reply, he drew me aside and, indicating the man with whom I had seen him talking, said, 'Do you see that fellow? I was just on the point of bringing him straight to you.'

'He would have been very welcome on your behalf', I answered.

'And on his own too, if you knew him', said Peter, 'for there is no mortal alive today can tell you so much about unknown peoples and unexplored lands; and I know that you're always greedy for such information.'

'In that case', said I, 'my guess wasn't a bad one, for at first glance I supposed he was a ship's captain.'

---

[5] On or before 21 July 1515. See Introduction, p. xvi.

'Then you're far off the mark', he replied, 'for his sailing has not been like that of Palinurus, but more that of Ulysses, or rather of Plato.[6] This man, who is named Raphael – his family name is Hythloday – knows a good deal of Latin and is particularly learned in Greek. He studied Greek more than Latin because his main interest is philosophy, and in that field he recognised that the Romans have left us nothing very valuable except certain works of Seneca and Cicero.[7] Being eager to see the world, he left to his brothers the patrimony to which he was entitled at home (he is a Portuguese),[8] and joined Amerigo Vespucci. He was Vespucci's constant companion on the last three of his four voyages, accounts of which are now common reading everywhere,[9] but on the last voyage, he did not return home with him. After much persuasion and expostulation he got Amerigo's permission to be one of the twenty-four men who were left in a garrison at the farthest point of the last voyage. Being left in this way was altogether agreeable to him, as he was more concerned about his travels than his tomb. He would often say, "The man who has no grave is covered by the sky", and "Wherever you start from, the road to heaven is the same length."[10] Yet this attitude would have cost him dear, if God had not been gracious to him. After Vespucci's departure he travelled through many countries with five companions from the garrison. At last, by strange good fortune, he got via Ceylon to

Aphorism

---

[6] Palinurus was Aeneas' pilot: he dozed at the helm and fell overboard (*Aeneid* V.833–61, VI.337–83). Ulysses' reputation as a man who saw many cities and knew men's minds is based on the opening lines of the *Odyssey*. (But Ulysses could also be regarded – as in the opening of the 'True Story' of Lucian (Introduction, pp. xx–xxi) – as a notable liar.) According to the Life of Plato by Diogenes Laertius (fl. third century AD), Plato travelled widely in the Mediterranean world (*Lives of Eminent Philosophers* III.6, 18–19).

[7] This opinion is echoed in More's 1518 Letter to Oxford (*CW*, XV, 143). Seneca was a Stoic; and though Cicero styled himself an adherent of the sceptical philosophy associated with the later phase of the Platonic Academy, his sympathies in ethical and political theory lay mainly with the Stoics, whose views he often rehearsed at length. Hythloday's own views are permeated by Stoic ideas.

[8] Hythloday's nationality links him with several of the great explorers of the period, who were either Portuguese or sponsored by the King of Portugal. His renunciation of his patrimony recalls the Italian philosopher Pico della Mirandola (1463–94), whose biography More had translated, and whom he greatly admired. See Introduction, p. xxn.

[9] Two Latin accounts (now of disputed authenticity) of the voyages of the Florentine explorer Amerigo Vespucci (1451–1512), who sailed for the King of Portugal, were published in the years 1505–7: *New World* and *The Four Voyages of Amerigo Vespucci*. *Utopia* exhibits parallels with both. *Four Voyages* tells that Vespucci left twenty-four men at the farthest point of his last voyage.

[10] The first of these sayings is quoted from the epic poem by Seneca's nephew Lucan, *Pharsalia* (VII.819); the second is adapted from Cicero (*Tusculan Disputations* I.xliii.104).

Calicut,[11] where he opportunely found some Portuguese ships; and so, beyond all hope, he finally returned to his own country."[12]

When Peter had told me this, I thanked him for his great kindness in introducing me to a man whose conversation he hoped I would enjoy, and then I turned towards Raphael. After we had greeted each other and exchanged the usual civilities of strangers upon their first meeting, we all went off to my house. There in the garden we sat down on a bench covered with grassy turf[13] to talk together.

He told us how, after Vespucci sailed away, he and his companions who had stayed behind in the garrison met with the people of that land, and by ingratiating speeches gradually made up to them. Before long they came to dwell with them not only safely but even on friendly terms. The prince also gave them his favour (I have forgotten his name and that of his country). He told how this prince generously furnished him and his five companions not only with ample provisions but with means for travelling – rafts when they went by water, wagons when they went by land. In addition, he sent with them a most trusty guide, who was to conduct them to other princes they wanted to visit, and supplied them with strong letters of recommendation. After many days' journey, he said, they found towns and cities, and commonwealths that were both very populous and not badly governed.

To be sure, under the equator and as far on both sides of the line as the sun moves, there lie vast empty deserts, scorched with the perpetual heat. The whole region is desolate and squalid, grim and uncultivated, inhabited by wild beasts and serpents, and by men no less wild and dangerous than the beasts themselves. But as you go on, everything gradually grows milder. The sun is less fierce, the earth greener, the creatures less savage. At last you reach people, cities and towns which not only trade among themselves and with their neighbours but even carry on commerce by sea and land with remote countries. After that, he said, they were able to visit different lands in every direction, for there was no ship readied for a journey on which he and his companions were not welcome as passengers.

---

[11] Calicut is a seaport on the west coast of India. Portuguese ships landed there several times in the early sixteenth century.

[12] Hythloday was thus the first European to circumnavigate the globe. (Magellan's men completed the trip in 1522.)

[13] The small woodcut of the scene in the 1518 editions shows the bench as a long wooden box filled with earth and covered on top with growing grass.

The vessels they saw in the first regions were flat-bottomed, he said, with sails made of stitched papyrus-reeds or wicker, elsewhere of leather. Farther on they found ships with pointed keels and canvas sails, in every respect like our own. The seamen were not unskilled in managing wind and water; but they were most grateful to him, Raphael said, for showing them the use of the compass, of which they had been entirely ignorant. For that reason they had formerly sailed with great timidity, and only in summer. Now they have such trust in that loadstone that they no longer fear winter at all, and tend to be careless rather than safe. There is some danger that through their imprudence this device, which they thought would be so advantageous to them, may become the cause of much mischief.

It would take too long to repeat all that Raphael told us he had observed in each place, nor would it serve our present purpose. Perhaps on another occasion we shall tell more about these things, especially those that it would be useful not to be ignorant of – above all, the wise and prudent provisions that he observed among the civilised nations. We asked him many eager questions about such things, and he answered us willingly enough. We made no inquiries, however, about monsters, for nothing is less new or strange than they are. There is no place where you will not find Scyllas, ravenous Celaenos, people-eating Laestrygonians[14] and that sort of monstrosity, but well and wisely trained citizens you will hardly find anywhere. While he told us of many ill-considered usages in these new-found nations, he also described quite a few other customs from which our own cities, nations, races and kingdoms might take lessons in order to correct their errors. These I shall discuss in another place, as I said. Now I intend to relate only what he told us about the customs and institutions of the Utopians,[15] but first recounting the conversation that drew him into speaking of that commonwealth. Raphael had been discoursing very thoughtfully on the faulty arrangements both in that hemisphere and in this (and there are many in both places), and had also spoken of the wiser provisions among us or among them, talking as shrewdly about the

---

[14] Scylla, a six-headed sea monster, appears in both the *Odyssey* (XII.73–100, 234–59) and the *Aeneid* (III.420–32). Celaeno, one of the Harpies (birds with women's faces), appears in the *Aeneid* (III.209–58). The Laestrygonians were gigantic cannibals in the *Odyssey* (X.76–132).

[15] At this point the dialogue suddenly goes off on a different tack. The account of Utopia is postponed; and the ensuing conversation includes, among other things, precisely those matters that More has just said he won't relate: Hythloday's descriptions of the practices of other new-found nations. As J. H. Hexter argues (*More's 'Utopia': The Biography of an Idea*, pp. 18–21; *CW*, IV, xviii–xx), it was almost certainly here that More opened a seam in the first version of *Utopia* to insert the additions that constitute the remainder of Book I. See Introduction, p. xvii.

customs and institutions of each place he had visited as if he had lived there all his life. Peter was amazed. 'My dear Raphael', he said, 'I'm surprised that you don't enter some king's service; for I don't know of a single prince who wouldn't be very glad to have you. Your learning and your knowledge of various countries and peoples would entertain him while your advice and supply of examples would be helpful at the counsel board. Thus you might admirably advance your own interests and be of great use at the same time to all your relatives and friends.'

'About my relatives and friends', he replied, 'I'm not much concerned, because I consider I've already done my duty by them tolerably well. While still young and healthy, I distributed among my relatives and friends the possessions that most men do not part with till they're old and sick (and then only reluctantly, when they can no longer keep them). I think they should be content with this gift of mine, and not insist, or even expect, that for their sake I should enslave myself to any king whatever.'

'Well said', Peter replied; 'but I do not mean that you should be in servitude to any king, only in his service.'

'The difference is only a matter of one syllable', said Raphael.

'All right', said Peter, 'but whatever you call it, I do not see any other way in which you can be so useful to your friends or to the general public, in addition to making yourself happier.'

'Happier indeed!' said Raphael. 'Would a way of life so absolutely repellent to my spirit make my life happier? As it is now, I live as I please,[16] and I fancy very few courtiers, however splendid, can say that. As a matter of fact, there are so many men soliciting favours from the powerful that you need not think it will be a great loss if they have to do without me and a couple of others like me.'

Then I said, 'It is clear, my dear Raphael, that you seek neither wealth nor power, and indeed I prize and revere a man of your disposition no less than I do the mightiest persons in the world. Yet I think if you could bring yourself to devote your intelligence and energy to public affairs, you would be doing something worthy of your noble and truly philosophical nature, even if you did not much like it. You could best perform such a service by joining the council of some great prince and inciting him to just and noble actions (as I'm sure you would): for a people's welfare or misery flows in a stream from their prince as from a never-failing spring. Your learning is so full, even if it weren't combined with experience, and

---

[16] Hythloday paraphrases Cicero's definition of liberty, which occurs in a context similar to the present one (*On Moral Obligation* I.xx.69–70).

your experience is so great, even apart from your learning, that you would be an extraordinary counsellor to any king in the world.'

'You are twice mistaken, my dear More', he said, 'first in me and then in the situation itself. I don't have the capacity you ascribe to me, and if I had it in the highest degree, the public would still not be any better off if I exchanged my contemplative leisure for active endeavour. In the first place, most princes apply themselves to the arts of war, in which I have neither ability nor interest, instead of to the good arts of peace. They are generally more set on acquiring new kingdoms by hook or crook than on governing well those they already have. Moreover, the counsellors of kings are so wise already that they don't need to accept or approve advice from anyone else – or at least they have that opinion of themselves. At the same time they endorse and flatter the most absurd statements of the prince's special favourites, through whose influence they hope to stand well with the prince. It's only natural, of course, that each man should think his own inventions best: the crow loves his fledgling and the ape his cub.

'Now in a court composed of people who envy everyone else and admire only themselves, if a man should suggest something he has read of in other ages or seen in practice elsewhere, those who hear it act as if their whole reputation for wisdom would be endangered, and as if henceforth they would look like simpletons, unless they can find fault with the proposals of others. If all else fails, they take refuge in some remark like this: "The way we're doing it was good enough for our ancestors, and I only wish we were as wise as they were." And with this deep thought they take their seats, as though they have said the last word on the subject – implying, of course, that it would be a very dangerous matter if anyone were found to be wiser on any point than his ancestors. As a matter of fact, we have no misgivings about neglecting the best examples they have left us; but if on some point their deliberations could have been more prudent, we immediately and eagerly seize the excuse of reverence for times past and cling to it desperately. Such proud, obstinate, ridiculous judgements I have encountered many times, and once even in England.'

'What!' I said, 'Were you ever in my country?'

'Yes', he said, 'I spent several months there. It was not long after the revolt of the west-countrymen against the King had been put down with the lamentable slaughter of the rebels.[17] During my stay I was deeply

---

[17] Angered by Henry VII's rapacious taxation, an army of Cornishmen marched on London in 1497. They were defeated at the Battle of Blackheath; estimates of the number killed vary from 200 to ten times that many.

beholden to the reverend father John Morton, Archbishop of Canterbury and Cardinal, and also at that time Lord Chancellor of England.[18] He was a man, my dear Peter (for More already knows what I'm going to say), as much respected for his wisdom and virtue as for his authority. He was of medium height, not bent over despite his age; his looks inspired respect, not fear. In conversation, he was not forbidding, though serious and grave. When petitioners came to him, he liked to test their spirit and presence of mind by speaking to them sharply, though not maliciously. He liked to uncover these qualities, which were those of his own nature, as long as they were not carried to the point of effrontery; and he thought such men were best qualified to carry on business. His speech was polished and pointed, his knowledge of the law was great, he had an incomparable understanding and a prodigious memory, for he had improved excellent natural abilities by study and practice. At the time when I was in England, the King depended greatly on his advice, and he seemed the mainspring of all public affairs. He had been taken straight from school to court when scarcely more than a boy, had devoted all his life to important business, and had been whirled about by violent changes of fortune so that in the midst of great dangers he had learned practical wisdom, which is not soon lost when so purchased.

'It happened one day when I was dining with him there was present a layman, learned in the laws of your country, who for some reason took occasion to praise the rigid execution of justice then being practised on *Of unjust laws* thieves. They were being executed everywhere, he said, with as many as twenty at a time being hanged on a single gallows.[19] And then he declared he was amazed that so many thieves sprang up everywhere when so few of them escaped hanging. I ventured to speak freely before the Cardinal, and said, "There is no need to wonder: this way of punishing thieves goes beyond the call of justice, and is not in any case for the public good. The penalty is too harsh in itself, yet it isn't an effective deterrent. Simple theft is not so great a crime that it ought to cost a man his head, yet no punishment however severe can restrain those from robbery who have no other way to make a living. In this matter not only you in England but a good part of the world seem to imitate bad schoolmasters, who would

---

[18] More had greatly admired Morton (1420–1500) since serving as a page in his household (Introduction, p. xiii). There is a similar portrait of him in *The History of King Richard III* (*CW*, II, 90–1).

[19] Raphael Holinshed reports that, in the reign of Henry VIII alone, 72,000 thieves were hanged (*Holinshed's Chronicles [of] England, Scotland, and Ireland*, 6 vols. (1807; rpt New York, 1965), I, 314).

15

[handwritten note: If it is by theft that some make a living, for else they would die anyways, execution does not help.]

[handwritten marginal note: are too harsh for some of it, perhaps crimes. Eg should wonder of punishment]

How to reduce
the number of
thieves
rather whip their pupils than teach them. Severe and terrible punishments are enacted for theft, when it would be much better to enable every man to earn his own living, instead of being driven to the awful necessity of stealing and then dying for it."

' "Oh, we've taken care of that", said the fellow. "There are the trades and there is farming by which men may make a living, unless they choose deliberately to do evil."

' "No", I said, "you won't get out of it that way. We may overlook the cripples who come home from foreign and civil wars, as lately from the Cornish battle and not long before that from your wars with France.[20] These men, who have lost limbs in the service of the common good or the king, are too shattered to follow their old trades and too old to learn new ones. But since wars occur only from time to time, let us, I say, overlook these men and consider what happens every day. There are a great many noblemen who live idly like drones off the labour of others,[21] their tenants whom they bleed white by constantly raising their rents. (This is the only instance of their tightfistedness, because they are prodigal in everything else, ready to spend their way to the poorhouse.) What's more, they drag around with them a great train of idle servants, who have never learned any trade by which they could make a living.[22] As soon as their master dies, or they themselves fall ill, they are promptly turned out of doors, for lords would rather support idlers than invalids, and the heir is often unable to maintain as big a household as his father had, at least at first. Those who are turned out soon set about starving, unless they set about stealing. What else can they do? Then when a wandering life has taken the edge off their health and the gloss off their clothes, when their faces

---

[20] Since the dramatic date of the conversation is 1497 or shortly thereafter, Hythloday may be referring to the relatively small number of casualties suffered by the English during the sporadic hostilities in France in 1489–92. But More is probably thinking of the heavier casualties of Henry VIII's French excursions of 1512–13.

[21] In the *Republic*, Socrates uses the same metaphor to describe the kind of monied individual who contributes nothing to society: 'Though he may have appeared to belong to the ruling class, surely in fact he was neither ruling, nor serving society in any other way; he was merely a consumer of goods...Don't you think we can fairly call him a drone?' (VIII.552B–C). In general, Plato's characterisation of oligarchy (whence the quoted passage) seems to have provided More with a framework for his observations on the condition of England. An oligarchy is 'a society where it is wealth that counts...and in which political power is in the hands of the rich and the poor have no share of it' (VIII.550C). The 'worst defect' of such a society is that it generates functionless people (552A).

[22] Some of these retainers were household servants; others constituted the remnants of the private armies which, in a feudal society, followed every lord. In the reign of Henry VII the latter kind of retaining was sharply curtailed.

look worn and their garments are tattered, men of rank will not care to engage them. And country folk dare not do so, for they don't have to be told that one who has been raised softly to idle pleasures, who has been used to swaggering about like a bully with sword and buckler, is likely to look down on the whole neighbourhood and despise everybody else as beneath him. Such a man can't be put to work with spade and mattock; he will not serve a poor man faithfully for scant wages and sparse diet."

' "But we ought to encourage these men in particular", said the lawyer. "In case of war the strength and power of our army depend on them, because they have a bolder and nobler spirit than workmen and farmers have."

' "You may as well say that thieves should be encouraged for the sake of wars", I answered, "since you will never lack for thieves as long as you have men like these. Just as thieves are not bad soldiers, soldiers turn out to be enterprising robbers, so nearly are these two ways of life related.[23] But this problem, though frequent here, is not yours alone; it is common to almost all nations. France suffers from an even more pestiferous plague. Even in peacetime, if you can call it peace, the whole country is crowded and overrun with foreign mercenaries, imported on the same principle that you've given for your noblemen keeping idle servants.[24] Wise fools[25] think that the public safety depends on having ready a strong army, preferably of veteran soldiers. They think inexperienced men are not reliable, and they sometimes hunt out pretexts for war, just so they may have trained soldiers; hence men's throats are cut for no reason – lest, as Sallust neatly puts it, 'hand and spirit grow dull through lack of practice.'[26] But France has learned to her cost how pernicious it is to feed such beasts. The examples of the Romans, the Carthaginians, the Syrians and many other peoples show the same thing; for not only their governments but their fields and even their cities were ruined more than once by their own standing armies.[27] Besides, this preparedness is unnecessary: not even the French soldiers, practised in arms from their cradles, can boast of having

The mischief of standing armies

---

[23] The close kinship between the professions of soldier and robber is a frequent theme of Erasmus and other humanists. See, for example, Erasmus' *Complaint of Peace*, *CWE*, XXVII, 316–17.

[24] In the early sixteenth century, French infantry forces were mainly Swiss and German mercenaries.

[25] *Morosophi* (transliterated from Greek). The modern word 'sophomore' is the same combination reversed.

[26] Paraphrased from *Catiline* XVI.3.

[27] Roman history is full of such episodes, dating from the emergence of standing armies in the first century BC. At the end of the First Punic War (241 BC), the Carthaginians' mercenaries

often got the best of your raw recruits.[28] I shall say no more on this point, lest I seem to flatter present company. At any rate, neither your town workmen nor your rough farm labourers – except for those whose physique isn't suited for strength or boldness, or whose spirit has been broken by the lack of means to support their families – seem to be much afraid of those flocks of idle retainers. So you need not fear that retainers, once strong and vigorous (for that's the only sort the gentry deign to corrupt), but now soft and flabby because of their idle, effeminate life, would be weakened if they were taught practical crafts to earn their living and trained to manly labour. However that may be, though, I certainly cannot think it's in the public interest to maintain for the emergency of war such a vast multitude of people who trouble and disturb the peace: you never have war unless you choose it, and peace is always more to be considered than war. Yet this is not the only force driving men to thievery. There is another that, as I see it, applies more specially to you Englishmen."

' "What is that?" said the Cardinal.

' "Your sheep", I said, "that commonly are so meek and eat so little; now, as I hear, they have become so greedy and fierce that they devour human beings themselves.[29] They devastate and depopulate fields, houses and towns. For in whatever parts of the land sheep yield the finest and. thus the most expensive wool, there the nobility and gentry, yes, and even a good many abbots – holy men – are not content with the old rents that the land yielded to their predecessors. Living in idleness and luxury without doing society any good no longer satisfies them; they have to do positive harm. For they leave no land free for the plough: they enclose every acre for pasture; they destroy houses and abolish towns, keeping the churches – but only for sheep-barns. And as if enough of your land were not already wasted on game-preserves and forests for hunting wild animals, these worthy men turn all human habitations and cultivated fields

turned on their masters. The victimisers of the Syrians that Hythloday has in mind are probably the Mamelukes, a military caste of foreign extraction that ruled, from the thirteenth century to the early sixteenth, a state that included much of the Middle East.

[28] Past English victories over the French included Crécy (1346), Poitiers (1356) and Henry V's triumph at Agincourt (1415).

[29] This vivid image introduces Hythloday's treatment of the social dislocation brought about by 'enclosure' – the gradual amalgamation and fencing, over a period extending from the twelfth to the nineteenth century, of the open fields of the feudal system: one incentive to enclosure was the increasing profitability of the wool trade. There were (and are) apologists for enclosure, but Hythloday's view was widely shared, and there is no doubt that the increase in sheep farming, which required large grazing lands and little manpower, greatly worsened the lot of many labourers and resulted in the destruction of many villages.

back to wilderness. Thus, so that one greedy, insatiable glutton, a frightful plague to his native country, may enclose thousands of acres within a single fence, the tenants are ejected; and some are stripped of their belongings by trickery or brute force, or, wearied by constant harassment, are driven to sell them. One way or another, these wretched people – men, women, husbands, wives, orphans, widows, parents with little children and entire families (poor but numerous, since farming requires many hands) – are forced to move out. They leave the only homes familiar to them, and can find no place to go. Since they must leave at once without waiting for a proper buyer, they sell for a pittance all their household goods, which would not bring much in any case. When that little money is gone (and it's soon spent in wandering from place to place), what finally remains for them but to steal, and so be hanged – justly, no doubt – or to wander and beg? And yet if they go tramping, they are jailed as idle vagrants. They would be glad to work, but they can find no one who will hire them. There is no need for farm labour, in which they have been trained, when there is no land left to be planted. One herdsman or shepherd can look after a flock of beasts large enough to stock an area that used to require many hands to make it grow crops.

' "This enclosing has led to sharply rising food prices in many districts. Also, the price of raw wool has risen so much that poor people among you who used to make cloth can no longer afford it, and so great numbers are forced from work to idleness. One reason is that after so much new pasture-land was enclosed, rot killed a countless number of the sheep – as though God were punishing greed by sending on the beasts a murrain that rightly should have fallen on the owners! But even if the number of sheep should increase greatly, the price will not fall a penny, because the wool trade, though it can't be called a monopoly because it isn't in the hands of a single person, is concentrated in so few hands (an oligopoly, you might say), and these so rich, that the owners are never pressed to sell until they have a mind to, and that is only when they can get their price.

' "For the same reason other kinds of livestock are also priced exorbitantly, the more so because, with farmhouses being torn down and farming in decay, nobody is left to breed the animals. These rich men will not breed calves as they do lambs, but buy them lean and cheap, fatten them in their pastures, and then sell them dear. I don't think the full impact of this bad system has yet been felt. We know these dealers hurt consumers where the fattened cattle are sold. But when, over a period of time, they keep buying beasts from other localities faster than they can be bred, a

[Handwritten marginalia:] Is Raphael here trying to say that perhaps theory is not a result of evil men, but rather of a dysfunctional system which eventually creates poverty, idleness, and eventually crime.

gradually diminishing supply where they are bought will inevitably lead to severe shortages. So your island, which seemed specially fortunate in this matter, will be ruined by the crass avarice of a few. For the high cost of living causes everyone to dismiss as many retainers as he can from his household; and what, I ask, can these men do but rob or beg? And a man of courage is more easily persuaded to steal than to beg.

' "To make this miserable poverty and scarcity worse, they exist side by side with wanton luxury.[30] The servants of noblemen, tradespeople, even some farmers – people of every social rank – are given to ostentatious dress and gourmandising. Look at the cook-shops, the brothels, the bawdy houses and those other places just as bad, the wine-bars and ale-houses. Look at all the crooked games of chance like dice, cards, backgammon, tennis, bowling and quoits, in which money slips away so fast. Don't all these pastimes lead their devotees straight to robbery? Banish these blights, make those who have ruined farmhouses and villages restore them or hand them over to someone who will restore and rebuild. Restrict the right of the rich to buy up anything and everything, and then to exercise a kind of monopoly.[31] Let fewer people be brought up in idleness. Let agriculture be restored, and the wool-manufacture revived as an honest trade, so there will be useful work for the idle throng, whether those whom poverty has already made thieves or those who are only vagabonds or idle servants now, but are bound to become thieves in the future.

' "Certainly, unless you cure these evils it is futile to boast of your justice in punishing theft. Your policy may look superficially like justice, but in reality it is neither just nor expedient. If you allow young folk to be abominably brought up and their characters corrupted, little by little, from childhood; and if then you punish them as grown-ups for committing the crimes to which their training has consistently inclined them, what else is this, I ask, but first making them thieves and then punishing them for it?"

'As I was speaking thus, the lawyer had prepared his answer, choosing the solemn style of disputants who are better at summing up than at replying, and who like to show off their memory. So he said to me, "You

---

[30] Extravagant display was not in fact characteristic of the reign of the parsimonious Henry VII (the period in which Hythloday is supposed to be addressing Cardinal Morton). More seems to be projecting onto the earlier period the taste for display associated with the reign of Henry VIII.

[31] A number of laws to control gambling and ale-houses, restrict monopolies and provide for the rebuilding of towns and the restoration of pastures to tillage were in fact passed, with small result, in the reigns of both Henry VII and Henry VIII.

[Handwritten margin note: I don't think capital punishment is ever true justifiable only in very rare cases.]

have talked very well for a stranger, but you have heard more than you've been able to understand correctly, as I will make clear to you in a few words. First, I will summarise what you said; then I will show how you have been misled by ignorance of our ways; finally, I will refute all your arguments and demolish them. And so to begin with the first thing I promised, on four points you seemed to me –"

' "Hold your tongue", said the Cardinal, "for you won't be finished in a few words if this is the way you start. We will spare you the trouble of answering now and put off the whole task until your next meeting, which will be tomorrow if your affairs and Raphael's permit it. Meanwhile, my dear Raphael, I'd be glad to hear why you think theft should not be punished with the extreme penalty, or what other punishment you think would be more conducive to the common good. For surely even you don't think it should go entirely unpunished. Even as it is, fear of death does not restrain the malefactors; once they were sure of their lives, as you propose, what force or fear could withhold them? They would look on a mitigation of the punishment as an invitation to commit crimes, almost a reward." *Illustrates the Cardinal's informal way of interrupting a babbler*

' "It seems to me, most kind and reverend father", I said, "that it's altogether unjust to take someone's life for taking money. In fact, I think that nothing in the world that fortune can bestow can be put on a par with a human life. If they say the thief suffers, not for the money, but for violation of justice and transgression of laws, then this extreme justice should properly be called extreme injury.[32] We ought not to approve of edicts so Manlian that they unsheathe the sword for the smallest violations.[33] Nor should we accept the Stoic decree that all crimes are equal,[34] as if there were no difference between killing a man and taking a coin from him. If equity means anything, there is no proportion or relation at all between these two crimes. God has forbidden us to kill anyone; shall we kill so readily for the theft of a bit of small change? Perhaps it will be argued that God's commandment against killing does not apply where human law allows it. But what then prevents men from making other laws in the same way, determining to what extent rape, adultery and perjury ought *Manlian edicts from Livy*

[32] The phrase echoes the adage *summum ius, summa iniuria* (quoted by Cicero, *On Moral Obligation* I.x.33), which has a long history in discussions of equity.
[33] According to Livy, the Roman consul Manlius (fourth century BC) had his own son executed for accepting a challenge to single combat (he won) after the consuls had forbidden any engagement with the enemy (*From the Founding of the City* VIII.vii.1–22). 'Manlian edicts' was therefore proverbial for inexorable decrees.
[34] Cicero ridicules this Stoic paradox (*On the Supreme Good and Evil* IV.ix.21–3, xxvii.75–xxviii.77); it is also criticised by Horace (*Satires* I.iii.96–124).

to be permitted? God has forbidden each of us not only to take the life of another but also to take his own life. If mutual consent to certain laws about killing one another has such force that it entitles men to exempt their agents from this command and allows them to kill those condemned by human decrees where God has given us no precedent, what is this but giving that command of God only as much force as human laws allow? The result will be that in every situation men will decide for themselves how far it suits them to observe the laws of God. Finally, the law of Moses was harsh and severe, as for an enslaved and stubborn people, but it punished theft with a fine, not death.[35] Let us not think that in his new law of mercy, where he rules us as a father rules his children, God has given us greater licence to be cruel to one another.

' "These are the reasons why I think this punishment is wrong. And surely there is no one who doesn't know how absurd and even dangerous for society it is to punish theft and murder alike. If the thief realises that theft by itself carries the same peril as murder, that thought alone will encourage him to kill the victim whom otherwise he would only have robbed. Apart from the fact that he is in no greater danger if he is caught, murder is safer, since he conceals both crimes by killing the witness. Thus while we strive to terrify thieves with extreme cruelty, we really urge them to kill the innocent.

' "As for the usual question of what more suitable punishment can be found, in my judgement it would be far easier to find a better one than a worse. Why should we question the value of the punishments which we know were long used by the ancient Romans, who were most expert in the arts of government? They condemned those convicted of heinous crimes to work in shackles for the rest of their lives in stone quarries and mines. But on this point, of all the alternatives I prefer the method which I observed in my Persian travels practised among the people commonly called the Polylerites.[36] They are a nation of no small size, not badly governed, free and subject only to their own laws, except that they pay annual tribute to the Persian king. Living far from the sea, they are nearly surrounded by mountains; and since they are content with the products of their own land (it is by no means unfruitful), they do not

The Polylerite society near the Persians

---

[35] The Mosaic law on theft is spelled out in the first verses of Exodus 22. It provides various penalties for theft, but nowhere death. This law is contrasted with the 'new law' of Christ, under which England is supposed to be operating. Note, though, that the Mosaic law prescribes death as the penalty for certain other crimes, and that Hythloday does not always condemn capital punishment.

[36] More's coinage from *polus* ('much') plus *leros* ('nonsense'): 'the People of Much Nonsense'.

visit other nations and are not much visited. By ancient tradition, they make no effort to enlarge their boundaries, and they are easily protected by their mountains and by the tribute paid to their overlord. Thus they fight no wars, and live in a comfortable rather than a glorious manner, more contented than renowned or glorious. Indeed, I think they are hardly known by name to anyone but their immediate neighbours.

' "In their land, whoever is found guilty of theft must make restitution to the owner, not (as elsewhere) to the prince;[37] they think the prince has precisely as much right to the stolen goods as the thief himself. If the stolen property has disappeared, its value is made up from the thief's belongings and is paid back. All the rest is handed over to his wife and children, while the thief himself is sentenced to hard labour.

To be noted by us, who do otherwise

' "Unless their crimes were compounded with atrocities, thieves are neither imprisoned nor shackled, but go free and unconstrained about their work on public projects. If they shirk and do their jobs slackly, they are not chained, but they are whipped. If they work hard, they undergo no humiliation, except that at night after roll call they are locked in their cells. Apart from constant labour, their life is not uncomfortable. As workers for the public good, they are decently fed out of the public stores, though in different ways in different places. In some districts they are supported by alms. Unreliable as this support may seem, the Polylerites are so compassionate that no way is found more rewarding. In other places, public revenues are set aside for their support or a special tax is levied on every individual for their use; and in some localities they do not do public work, but anyone in need of workmen can go to the market and hire a convict by the day at a set rate, a little less than that for free men. If they are lazy, it is lawful to whip them. Thus the convicts never lack work, and each brings a little profit every day into the public treasury beyond the cost of his keep.

' "All of them, and only they, are dressed in clothes of the same distinctive colour. Their hair is not shaved off, but trimmed a little above the ears, and the tip of one ear is cut off. Their friends are allowed to give them food, drink or clothing, as long as it is of the proper colour; but to give them money is death, to both the giver and the taker. It is just as dangerous a crime for any free man to take money from them, for whatever reason;

Yet nowadays the servants of noblemen think such a haircut quite handsome

---

[37] Erasmus also condemns this common European practice, in *The Education of a Christian Prince* (*CWE*, XXVII, 270). In general, the principles underlying Polylerite criminal justice are similar to those expounded in Plato's *Laws*, where the legitimate aims of punishment are said to be to deter crime, reform the criminal, and redress the injury to the victim (IX.862C–D).

and it is also a capital crime for any of these slaves (as the condemned are called) to touch weapons. In each district of the country they wear a special badge. It is a capital crime to discard the badge, to be seen beyond the bounds of one's own district, or to talk with a slave of another district. Plotting escape is no more secure than escape itself: indeed, for any slave to be privy to an escape-plot is death, and for a free man, slavery. On the other hand, there are rewards for informers – money for a free man, freedom for a slave, and for both of them pardon and amnesty for knowing about the plot. Thus it can never be safer to persist in an illicit scheme than to repent of it.

' "These then are their laws and policy in this matter. It is clear how mild and practical they are, for the aim of the punishment is to destroy vices and save men. The men are treated so that they necessarily become good, and they have the rest of their lives to make up for the damage they have done. There is so little danger of recidivism that even travellers going from one part of the country to another think slaves the most reliable guides, changing them at the boundary of each district. Nowhere do the slaves have any chance of committing robbery, since they are unarmed, and any money in their possession is evidence of a crime. If caught, they would be punished, and there is utterly no hope of escaping anywhere. Since every bit of a slave's clothing is unlike the usual clothing of the country, how could one escape, unless he fled naked? And even then his cropped ear would give him away. But isn't there at least the danger of the slaves forming a conspiracy against the government? As if slaves of a single district could hope to succeed unless they involved in their plot slave-gangs from many other districts! And they are so far from being able to form a conspiracy that they are not even allowed to meet or talk together, or to greet one another. How can we believe that anyone would dare to trust his comrades with such a plot when they know it is so dangerous to remain silent and so advantageous to reveal it? Besides, no one is quite without hope of gaining his freedom eventually if he accepts his punishment in a spirit of patient obedience and gives promise of future good conduct. Indeed, never a year goes by in which some are not pardoned as a reward for submissive behaviour."

'When I had finished this account, I added that I saw no reason why this policy could not be adopted even in England, and with much greater advantage than the "justice" which my legal antagonist had praised so highly. But the lawyer said, "Such a system could never be established in England without putting the commonwealth in serious peril." And so

24

saying, he shook his head, made a wry face, and fell silent. And all who were present sided with him.

'Then the Cardinal said, "It is not easy to guess whether this scheme would work well or not, since it has never been tried. But perhaps when the death sentence has been passed on a thief, the king might reprieve him for a time without right of sanctuary,[38] and thus see how the plan worked. If it turned out well, the practice might be made law; if not, he could then carry out the punishment of the man already condemned. This would be no more perilous to the public or unjust to the criminal than if the condemned person had been put to death at once, and in the meantime the experiment would involve no risk. In fact, I think it would not be a bad idea to treat vagabonds this way too, for though we have passed many laws against them, they have had no real effect as yet."

'When the Cardinal had said this, they all vied with one another in praising enthusiastically ideas which they had received with contempt when I suggested them; and they particularly liked the idea about vagabonds because it was the Cardinal's addition.

'I don't know whether it might not be better to keep quiet about what followed, because it was silly, but I'll tell it anyhow, for there's no harm in it, and it has some bearing on our subject. There was a parasite standing around, who liked to play the fool, and did it in such a way that you could hardly tell him from the real thing. He was constantly making jokes, but so awkwardly that we laughed more at him than at them; yet sometimes a rather clever thing came out, confirming the old proverb that one who throws the dice often will sooner or later make a lucky cast. One of the company happened to say that in my speech I had taken care of the thieves, and the Cardinal of the vagabonds, so now all that was left to do was to take care of the poor, whom sickness or old age had reduced to poverty and kept from earning a living.

The friar and the fool: a merry dialogue

' "Leave that to me", said the fool, "and I'll see to it that it's taken care of properly. These are people I'm desperately eager to get out of my sight, having been so often vexed with them when they wail and whine and demand money – though they never cry out finely enough to extract a single penny from me. For they can't win with me: either I don't want to give them anything, or I haven't anything to give them. Now they're getting wise; they don't waste their breath, but let me pass without a

---

[38] In earlier days almost any criminal could take sanctuary in any church and be safe from the law. Beginning in the reign of Henry VII, the privilege was gradually abridged. The issue was much disputed in More's time, and is debated in his *Richard III* (*CW*, II, 27–33).

An old saying
bandied about
among beggars

An Horatian
allusion: 'Doused
with Italian
vinegar'⁴⁰

How his people
speak in character!

Out of ignorance the
friar uses 'zelus' as if
it were a neuter
noun, like 'scelus'⁴⁶

word or a hope – no more, by heaven, than if I were a priest. But I would make a law dividing up and parcelling out all these beggars among the Benedictine monasteries, where the men could become lay brothers, as they're called,³⁹ and the women I would make nuns."

'The Cardinal smiled and passed it off as a joke; the rest took it seriously. But a certain friar, a theologian, found such pleasure in this jest at the expense of priests and monks that he too began to make merry, though generally he was grave to the point of sourness. "Even so you will not get rid of the beggars", he began, "unless you provide for us friars too."

' "But you have been taken care of already", said the parasite. "The Cardinal provided for you splendidly when he said vagabonds should be arrested and put to work, for you friars are the greatest vagabonds of all."

'When the company, watching the Cardinal closely, saw that he did not disdain this joke any more than the other, they all took it up with a will – except for the friar. Not surprisingly, he was stung by the vinegar and flew into such a violent rage that he could not keep from abusing the fool. He called him a knave, a slanderer, a sneak and a "son of perdition",⁴¹ quoting the meanwhile terrible denunciations from Holy Scripture. Now the jester began to jest in earnest, for he was clearly on his own ground.

' "Don't get angry, good friar", he said, "for it is written, *In your patience you will possess your souls.*"⁴²

'In reply, the friar said, and I quote his very words: "I am not angry, you gallows-bird, or at least I do not sin, for the Psalmist says, *Be angry, and sin not.*"⁴³

'At this point the Cardinal gently cautioned the friar to calm down, but he answered, "No, my lord, I speak only from righteous zeal, as I ought to. For holy men have had righteous zeal. That is why it is said, *The zeal of your house has eaten me up,*⁴⁴ and we sing in church, *Those who mocked Elisha as he went up to the house of God felt the zeal of the baldhead.*⁴⁵ Just so this mocker, this joker, this guttersnipe may well feel it."

---

³⁹ 'Lay brothers' lived and worked in monasteries (performing mostly menial tasks) but were not admitted to clerical orders.

⁴⁰ *Satires* I.vii.32.   ⁴¹ John 17:12, II Thessalonians 2:3.   ⁴² Luke 21:19.

⁴³ Psalms 4:4. (The Vulgate translates as *Irascimini* ('Be angry') the Hebrew word that is rendered 'Stand in awe' in the Authorised Version.)

⁴⁴ Psalms 69:9.

⁴⁵ Some children mocked the prophet Elisha for his baldness. But his curse brought two bears out of the woods, who tore to pieces forty-two of the mockers: II Kings 2:23–4. The friar quotes a medieval hymn, ascribed to Adam of St Victor, that is based on this cautionary tale.

⁴⁶ In the Latin, the friar incorrectly says *zelus* instead of *zelum*.

' "Perhaps you mean well", said the Cardinal, "but I think you would act if not in a holier at least in a wiser way, if you didn't set your wit against a fool's wit and try to spar with a buffoon."

' "No, my lord", he said, "I would not act more wisely. For Solomon himself, wisest of men, said, *Answer a fool according to his folly*,[47] and that's what I'm doing now. I am showing him the pit into which he will fall[48] if he does not take care. For if the many mockers of Elisha, who was only one bald man, felt the zeal of a baldhead, how much more of an effect shall be felt by a single mocker of many friars, among whom are a great many baldheads! And besides, we have a papal bull, by which all who mock at us are excommunicated."

'When the Cardinal saw there was no end to the matter, he nodded to the fool to leave and tactfully turned the conversation to another subject. Soon after, he rose from table and, going to hear petitioners, dismissed us.

'Look, my dear More, what a long story I have inflicted on you. I would be quite ashamed if you had not yourself eagerly insisted on it, and seemed to listen as if you did not want any part to be left out. Though I ought to have related this conversation more concisely, I did feel bound to recount it, so you might see how those who had rejected what I said approved of it immediately afterwards, when they saw the Cardinal did not disapprove. In fact they went so far in their flattery that they indulged and almost took seriously ideas that their master tolerated only as the clowning of a parasite. From this episode you can see how little courtiers would value me or my advice.'

'Certainly, my dear Raphael', I said, 'you have given me great pleasure, for everything you've said has been both wise and witty. Furthermore, as you spoke, I seemed somehow to be a child and in my own native land once more, through the pleasant recollection of that Cardinal in whose court I was brought up as a lad. Dear as you are to me on other accounts, you cannot imagine, my friend Raphael, how much dearer you are because you honour his memory so highly. Still, I by no means give up my former opinion: indeed, I am fully persuaded that if you could overcome your aversion to court life, your advice to a prince would be of the greatest advantage to the public welfare. No part of a good man's duty – and that means

---

[47] Proverbs 26:5. The preceding verse, however, says 'Answer not a fool according to his folly, lest thou also be like unto him.'
[48] Alluding to Psalms 7:15.

yours – is more important than this.[49] Your friend Plato thinks that commonwealths will be happy only when philosophers become kings or kings become philosophers.[50] No wonder we are so far from happiness when philosophers do not condescend even to assist kings with their counsels.'

'They are not so ungracious', said Raphael, 'but that they would gladly do it; in fact, many have already done it in published books, if the rulers were only willing to take their good advice. But doubtless Plato was right in foreseeing that unless kings became philosophical themselves the advice of philosophers would never influence them deeply immersed as they are and infected with false values from boyhood on. Plato himself had this experience with Dionysius.[51] If I proposed wise laws to some king, and tried to root out of his soul the seeds of evil and corruption, don't you suppose I would be either kicked out forthwith, or made into a laughing stock?

'Imagine, if you will, that I am at the court of the King of France.[52] Suppose me to be sitting in his royal council, meeting in secret session with the King himself presiding and surrounded by all his most judicious councillors hard at work devising a set of crafty machinations by which the King might keep hold of Milan and recover Naples, which has proved so slippery;[53] then overthrow the Venetians and subdue all Italy; next add to his realm Flanders, Brabant and the whole of Burgundy, besides some other nations he has long had in mind to invade.[54] One man urges him to make an alliance with the Venetians for just as long as it suits their own convenience – to develop a common strategy with them, and even allow

Indirectly he discourages the French from seizing Italy

---

[49] The best-known locus for this position is Cicero's *On Moral Obligation* I.xliii. See Quentin Skinner, 'Sir Thomas More's *Utopia* and the language of Renaissance humanism', pp. 129–35.

[50] *Republic* V.473C–D; cf. Epistle VII.326A–B.

[51] Plato is reported to have made three visits to Syracuse, where he conspicuously failed to reform either the tyrant Dionysius the Elder or his son Dionysius the Younger. See Plato, Epistle VII; Plutarch, 'Dion' IV.i–v.3, IX.i–xx.2.

[52] At the time of writing, Francis I was King of France. At the time of Hythloday's supposed visit to England, the French King was either Charles VIII (d. 1498) or Louis XII (d. 1515). All three were would-be imperialists with hereditary claims to Milan and Naples, and all three bogged down in the intricacies of Italian political intrigue. In general, the advice of the councillors in this passage conforms closely to actual French policies in the period. Scathing denunciation of such policies is characteristic of Erasmian humanism. (See R. P. Adams, *The Better Part of Valor*.) Rabelais probably had More's passage in mind in *Gargantua and Pantagruel* I.xxxiii, where he sketched King Picrochole's insanely tottery schemes of world conquest.

[53] France gained Milan in 1499, lost it in 1512, and regained it at the Battle of Marignano in September 1515. Naples was won in 1495, lost in 1496, won again in 1501, and lost again in 1504.

[54] The rest of Hythloday's account – through 'would be received?' (p. 31) – is syntactically one very long (464 words), very intricate sentence. But the early editions break it up with numerous periods, as we also have done, to make it manageable; more boldly, we have paragraphed it.

them a share of the loot, which can be recovered later when things work out according to plan. While one recommends hiring German mercenaries,[55] his neighbour proposes paying the Swiss to stay neutral. A fourth suggests soothing the offended divinity of his imperial majesty with a votive offering, as it were, of gold.[56] Still another thinks a settlement should be made with the King of Aragon, and that, as a reward for peace, he should be given Navarre, which belongs to somebody else.[57] Meanwhile, someone suggests snaring the Prince of Castile by the prospect of a marriage alliance, and by drawing some nobles of his court onto their side by granting them pensions.[58]

Swiss mercenaries

'The knottiest problem of all is what to do, in the meantime, about England. They agree that peace should be made, and that the alliance, which is weak at best, should be strengthened as much as possible. Let the English be proclaimed as friends, yet suspected as enemies. And let the Scots be kept like sentinels in constant readiness, poised to attack the English on the spot in case they stir ever so little.[59] Also a banished nobleman with pretensions to the English throne must be secretly encouraged (treaties forbid doing it openly), and in this way they will have a bridle to restrain a king whom they do not trust.[60]

'Now in a meeting like this one, where so much is at stake, where so many distinguished men are competing to think up schemes of warfare, what if an insignificant fellow like me were to get up and advise going on another tack entirely?[61] Suppose I said the King should leave Italy alone and stay at home, because the kingdom of France by itself is almost too much for one man to govern well, and the King should not dream of adding others

---

[55] Among the mercenaries of Europe, the German foot-soldiers were surpassed only by the Swiss.

[56] Maximilian of Habsburg, the Holy Roman Emperor, was notoriously impecunious.

[57] Ferdinand II of Aragon took the southern part of Navarre in 1512, and annexed it to Castile (of which he was regent) in 1515. He died on 23 January 1516 – so More must have written this part of Book I before he heard the news (presumably within a few weeks of the event).

[58] Charles, Prince of Castile, was the future Holy Roman Emperor. The question of a French marriage for him, which would unite the two great European powers, was continually in the air. (He was engaged ten different times – always for financial or dynastic reasons – before he was twenty.) On the use of international bribery as an everyday tactic of European statecraft, see James W. Thompson and Saul K. Padover, *Secret Diplomacy*, 2nd edn (New York, 1963), pp. 56–60.

[59] The Scots, as traditional enemies of England, were traditional allies of France.

[60] The French had in fact supported various pretenders to the English throne – most recently, Richard de la Pole, the inheritor of the Yorkist claim.

[61] The advice that Hythloday imagines himself as giving is precisely the kind that Erasmian humanists offered in numerous political writings. Edward Surtz documents many parallels (*CW*, IV, 358–61).

A notable example

to it?[62] Then imagine I told about the decrees of the Achorians,[63] who live off to the south-southeast of the island of Utopia. Long ago these people went to war to gain another realm for their king, who claimed that he had rightfully inherited it by virtue of an ancient marriage tie. When they had conquered it, they saw that keeping it was going to be no less trouble than getting it had been. The seeds of fighting were always springing up: their new subjects were continually rebelling or being attacked by foreign invaders; the Achorians had to be constantly at war for them or against them, and they saw no hope of ever being able to disband their army. In the meantime, they were being heavily taxed, money flowed out of their kingdom, their blood was being shed for someone else's petty pride, and peace was no closer than it had ever been. At home the war corrupted their citizens by encouraging lust for robbery and murder; and the laws fell into contempt because their king, distracted with the cares of two kingdoms, could give neither his proper attention.

'When they saw that the list of these evils was endless, they took counsel together, and very courteously offered their king his choice of keeping whichever of the two kingdoms he preferred, because he couldn't rule them both. They were too numerous a people, they said, to be ruled by half a king; adding that a man would not willingly share even a muledriver with someone else. The worthy prince was thus obliged to be content with his own realm and give his new one to a friend, who before long was driven out.

'Moreover, suppose I showed that all this war-mongering, by which so many different nations were kept in turmoil for his sake, would exhaust his treasury and demoralise his people, yet in the end come to nothing through one mishap or another.[64] And therefore he should look after his ancestral kingdom, improve it as much as possible, and make it as flourishing as it could conceivably be made.[65] He should love his people and be loved by them; he should live among them, govern them kindly, and let other kingdoms alone, since the one that had fallen to his lot was big enough,

---

[62] Cf. More's epigram 'On the Lust for Power': 'Among many kings there will be scarcely one, if there is really one, who is satisfied to have one kingdom. And yet among many kings there will be scarcely one, if there is really one, who rules a single kingdom well' (*CW*, III, Part II, 257).

[63] From *a*- ('without') plus *choros* ('place', 'country'): 'the People without a Country'.

[64] Francis lost Milan in 1520 and, in a catastrophic effort to regain it in 1525, was defeated and taken prisoner by Charles V.

[65] Hythloday is thinking of the adage 'Spartam nactus es, hanc orna' ('Sparta is your portion; do your best for her'), which Erasmus discusses at length in *Adages* II.v.1 (*CWE*, XXXIII, 237–43).

[Handwritten marginal note: The proper management of the state must also take into account the size of population.]

if not too big, for him. How do you think, my dear More, this speech of mine would be received?'

'Not very enthusiastically, I'm sure', said I.

'Well,[66] let's go on', he said. 'Suppose that a king and his councillors are deliberating about various schemes for filling his treasury. One man recommends increasing the value of money when the king pays his debts and devaluing it when he collects his revenues. Thus he can discharge a huge debt with a small payment, and collect a large sum when only a small one is due him.[67] Another suggests a make-believe war, so that money can be raised under that pretext; then when the money is in, he can make peace with holy ceremonies – which the deluded common people will attribute to the prince's piety and compassion for the lives of his subjects.[68] Another councillor calls to mind some old moth-eaten laws, antiquated by long disuse, which no one remembers being made and therefore everyone has transgressed, and suggests that the king levy fines for breaking them. There's no richer source of income, nor any that looks more creditable, since it can be made to wear the mask of justice.[69] Another recommendation is that he forbid under particularly heavy fines many practices, especially such as are contrary to the public interest; afterwards, for money he can grant the special interests dispensations from his own rules. Thus he gains the favour of the people and makes a double profit, from fines imposed on those who've fallen into his trap and from selling dispensations. The higher the price, the better the prince, since he is very reluctant to grant a private person the right to obstruct the public welfare, and therefore does it only for a great price.

'Another councillor proposes that he work on the judges so they will decide every case in the royal interest. Moreover, they should be frequently summoned to the palace and asked to debate his affairs in the royal presence. However unjust his claims, one or another of the judges, whether from love of contradiction, or desire to seem original, or simply to serve

---

[66] Like the account of the French privy council, Hythloday's second *exemplum* consists, syntactically, of a single gargantuan sentence – comprising 926 words and continuing through 'deaf ears to me?' (p. 34).

[67] Dodges of this kind were practised by Edward IV, Henry VII and (after *Utopia* was written) Henry VIII. In general, the policies satirised in this continuation find more parallels in English practice than elsewhere, though European parallels also abound.

[68] Something like this happened in 1492, when Henry VII not only pretended war with France on behalf of Brittany and levied taxes for the war (which was hardly fought) but collected a bribe from Charles VIII for not fighting it.

[69] Henry VII's ministers Empson and Dudley were notorious masters in this practice – and Cardinal Morton was also involved in it.

his own interest, will be able to find some loophole to introduce chicanery. If the judges give differing opinions, the clearest matter in the world can be made cloudy and truth itself brought into question. The king is given a convenient handle to interpret the law in his favour, and everyone else will acquiesce from shame or fear. Thus the judgement can be boldly handed down in court; nor can there be any lack of pretexts for someone ruling in the prince's favour. Either equity is on the king's side, or the letter of the law makes for him, or a twisted interpretation of a document, or the factor which in the end outweighs all laws for scrupulous judges, the indisputable prerogative of the prince.[70]

Saying of Crassus
the Rich

'Then all the councillors agree with the famous maxim of Crassus: a king can never have enough gold, because he must maintain an army.[71] Further, that a king, even if he wants to, can do no wrong, for all property belongs to the king, and so do his subjects themselves; a man owns nothing but what the king, in his goodness, sees fit not to take from him. It is important for the king to leave his subjects as little as possible, because his own safety depends on keeping them from getting too frisky with wealth and freedom. For riches and liberty make people less patient to endure harsh and unjust commands, whereas poverty and want blunt their spirits, make them docile, and grind out of the oppressed the lofty spirit of rebellion.[72]

'Now at this point, suppose I were to get up again and declare that all these counsels are both dishonourable and ruinous to the king? Suppose I said his honour and his safety alike rest on the people's resources rather than his own? Suppose I said that people choose a king for their own sake,

[70] The limits of royal prerogative, and the duties of judges (who served by royal appointment) in respect to it, was in the course of becoming an issue of the utmost importance. For an overview, see John W. Allen, *A History of Political Thought in the Sixteenth Century* (1928; rpt London, 1957), pp. 121–68.

[71] Hythloday adapts his source, which is Cicero's *On Moral Obligation*: 'Crassus... not long since declared that no amount of wealth was enough for the man who aspired to be the foremost citizen of the state, unless with the income from it he could maintain an army' (I.viii.25). Crassus joined with Pompey and Caesar to form the First Triumvirate (60 BC).

[72] The underlying schema of the fiscal policy developed in the foregoing paragraphs was provided by Aristotle's discussion in the *Politics* of the two ways in which tyrannies can be preserved. The first embraces the traditional acts of the tyrant: he will prohibit 'everything likely to produce... mutual confidence and a high spirit' in the citizens (v.xi.5); his 'first end and aim is to break the spirit of... [his] subjects', because 'a poor-spirited man will never plot against anybody' (xi.15). Impoverishing the citizens is a principal means to this end. Alternatively, 'the tyrant should act, or at any rate appear to act, in the role of a good player of the part of King' (xi.19). He should, for example, 'levy taxes, and require other contributions, in such a way that they can be seen to be intended for the proper management of public services, or to be meant for use... on military emergencies' (xi.21).

not his, so that by his efforts and troubles they may live in comfort and safety? This is why, I would say, it is the king's duty to take more care of his people's welfare than of his own, just as it is the duty of a shepherd who cares about his job to feed the sheep rather than himself.[73]

'They are absolutely wrong in thinking that the people's poverty guarantees public peace: experience shows the contrary. Where will you find more squabbling than among beggars? Who is more eager to change things than the man who is most discontented with his present position? Who is more reckless about creating disorder than the man who knows he has nothing to lose and thinks he may have something to gain? If a king is so hated or despised by his subjects that he can keep them in hand only by maltreatment, plundering, confiscation and reducing them to beggary, he'd do much better to abdicate his throne than to retain it by such methods, through which he keeps the name of authority but loses all the majesty of a king. A king has no dignity when he exercises authority over beggars, only when he rules over prosperous and happy subjects. This was certainly what that noble and lofty spirit Fabricius meant, when he replied that he would rather be a ruler of rich men than be rich himself.[74] Indeed a lone individual who enjoys a life of pleasure and self-indulgence while all about him are grieving and groaning is acting like a jailer, not a king. Finally, just as an incompetent doctor can cure his patient of one disease only by throwing him into another, so it's an incompetent monarch who knows no other way to reform his people than by depriving them of all life's benefits. Such a king openly confesses his incapacity to rule free men.

'He should correct his own sloth or arrogance, because these are the vices that cause people to despise or hate him. Let him live on his own income without wronging others, and limit his spending to his income. Let him curb crime, and by training his subjects wisely keep them from misbehaviour, instead of letting trouble breed and then punishing it. Let him not rashly revive antiquated laws, especially if they have been long forgotten and never missed. And let him never take money as a fine for some crime when a judge would regard an ordinary subject as wicked and deceitful for claiming it.

---

[73] Again Hythloday's advice is the same as that offered by More speaking in his own person (e.g., *Epigrams*, *CW*, III, Part II, 163–5, 169), as well as by other humanists and their classical sources. See *CW*, IV, 366–71.

[74] Gaius Fabricius Luscinus took part in the wars against Pyrrhus, King of Epirus (280–275 BC). The saying that is attributed to him here was actually coined by his colleague Manius Curius Dentatus (Plutarch, *Moral Essays* 194F), but it is quite in his spirit.

'Suppose I should then describe for them the law of the Macarians,[75] a people who also live not far from the Utopians. On the day that their king first assumes office, he must take an oath confirmed by solemn ceremonies never to have in his treasury at any one time more than a thousand pounds of gold, or its equivalent in silver.[76] They say this law was made by an excellent king, who cared more for his country's welfare than for his own wealth, and wanted to prevent any king from heaping up so much money as to impoverish his people. He thought this sum would enable a king to put down rebellions or repel hostile invasions, but would not be large enough to tempt him into aggressive adventures. Though this was the primary reason for the law, he also wanted to ensure an ample supply of money for the daily business of the citizens. Finally, he thought that a king who has to distribute all the excess money in the treasury to the people will not look for ways to gain it wrongfully. Such a king will be feared by evil-doers, and just as much beloved by the good. – Now, don't you suppose if I set these ideas and others like them before men strongly inclined to the contrary, they would turn deaf ears to me?'

'Stone deaf, indeed, there's no doubt about it', I said, 'and by heaven it's no wonder! To tell you the truth, I don't think you should thrust forward ideas of this sort, or offer advice that you know for certain will not be listened to. What good can it do? When your listeners are already prepossessed against you and firmly convinced of opposite opinions, how can you win over their minds with such out-of-the-way speeches? This academic philosophy is pleasant enough in the private conversation of close friends, but in the councils of kings, where great matters are debated with great authority, there is no room for it.'[77]

'That is just what I was saying', Raphael replied. 'There is no place for philosophy in the councils of kings.'

'Yes, it is true', I said, 'that there is no place for this school philosophy which supposes every topic suitable for every occasion.[78] But there is another philosophy, better suited for the role of a citizen, that takes its cue,

Wonderful law of the Macarians

Proverb

Philosophy of the schools

---

[75] From *makarios*: 'blessed', 'happy'.

[76] Again More seems to glance at Henry VII, who died with a huge sum in his treasury.

[77] This position is informed by the rhetorical and ethical doctrine of *decorum*, propriety of words or actions. (On *decorum*, see Cicero, *Orator* XXI.69–XXII.74, *On Moral Obligation* I.xxvii–xlii, *On the Orator* III.lv.210–12.) The ensuing argument reflects the ancient conflict between rhetoric and philosophy, which centres in the tension between persuasion and truth.

[78] Complaints that philosophers fail to consider context – whether in the interpretation of literary works or in their mistaken notions about style and rhetorical strategy – constitute a main theme of humanist attacks on scholasticism. See, for example, More's 'Letter to Dorp', *CW*, XV, 49–55.

adapts itself to the drama in hand and acts its part neatly and appropriately. This is the philosophy for you to use.[79] Otherwise, when a comedy of Plautus is being played, and the household slaves are cracking trivial jokes together, you come onstage in the garb of a philosopher and repeat Seneca's speech to Nero from the *Octavia*.[80] Wouldn't it be better to take a silent role than to say something inappropriate and thus turn the play into a tragicomedy? You pervert a play and ruin it when you add irrelevant speeches, even if they are better than the play itself. So go through with the drama in hand as best you can, and don't spoil it all just because you happen to think of a play by someone else that might be more elegant.

A striking comparison

A mute part

'That's how things go in the commonwealth, and in the councils of princes. If you cannot pluck up bad ideas by the root, or cure long-standing evils to your heart's content, you must not therefore abandon the commonwealth. Don't give up the ship in a storm because you cannot hold back the winds. You must not deliver strange and out-of-the-way speeches to people with whom they will carry no weight because they are firmly persuaded the other way. Instead, by an indirect approach, you must strive and struggle as best you can to handle everything tactfully – and thus what you cannot turn to good, you may at least make as little bad as possible.[81] For it is impossible to make everything good unless all men are good, and that I don't expect to see for quite a few years yet.'

'The only result of this', he said, 'will be that while I try to cure the madness of others, I'll be raving along with them myself. For if I wish to speak the truth, I will have to talk in the way I've described. Whether it's the business of a philosopher to tell lies, I don't know, but it certainly isn't mine. Perhaps my advice may be repugnant and irksome to them, but I don't see why it should be considered outlandish to the point of folly. What if I told them the kind of thing that Plato imagines in his republic,

[79] Cf. Cicero, *Orator* XXXV.123: 'This ... is the form of wisdom that the orator must especially employ – to adapt himself to occasions and persons ... one must not speak in the same style at all times, nor before all people'; *On Moral Obligation* I.xxxi.114: 'if at some time stress of circumstances shall thrust us aside into some uncongenial part, we must devote to it all possible thought, practice, and pains, that we may be able to perform it, if not with propriety, at least with as little impropriety as possible'.

[80] Most of the plays of the Roman comic dramatist Plautus (*c.* 250–184 BC) involve low intrigue: needy young men, expensive prostitutes, senile moneybags and clever slaves, in predictable combinations. The tragedy *Octavia*, involving Seneca as a character (and long supposed to have been written by him), is full of high seriousness. In the passage to which More alludes (ll. 440–592), Seneca lectures Nero on the abuses of power.

[81] This is consistent with the advice of rhetoricians (e.g., Quintilian, *The Education of the Orator* II.xvii.26–9, III.viii.38–9) and some humanists (e.g., Erasmus, *Correspondence*, CWE, II, 79, 81–2).

Utopian institutions or that the Utopians actually practise in theirs? However superior those institutions might be (and they certainly are), yet here they would seem alien, because private property is the rule here, and there all things are held in common.

'People who have made up their minds to rush headlong down the opposite road are never pleased with the man who calls them back and points out the dangers of their course. But, apart from that, what did I say that could not and should not be said everywhere? Indeed, if we dismiss as outlandish and absurd everything that the perverse customs of men have made to seem alien to us, we shall have to set aside, even in a community of Christians, most of the teachings of Christ. Yet he forbade us to dissemble them, and even ordered that what he had whispered in the ears of his disciples should be preached openly from the housetops.[82] Most of his teachings are far more alien from the common customs of mankind than my discourse was. But preachers, like the crafty fellows they are, have found that people would rather not change their lives to fit Christ's rule, and so, following your advice, I suppose, they have adjusted his teaching to the way people live, as if it were a leaden yardstick.[83] At least in that way they can get the two things to correspond in some way or other. The only real thing they accomplish that I can see is to make people feel more secure about doing evil.

'And indeed this is all that I myself would accomplish in the councils of princes. For either I would have different ideas from the others, and that would be like having no ideas at all, or I would agree with them, and that, as Mitio says in Terence, would merely confirm them in their madness.[84] As for that "indirect approach" of yours, I simply don't know what you mean. You think I should try hard to urge my case tactfully, so that what cannot be made good can at least be made as little bad as possible. In a council, there is no way to dissemble or look the other way. You must openly approve the worst proposals and endorse the most vicious policies. A man who praised wicked counsels only half-heartedly would be suspected as a spy, perhaps a traitor. And there is no way for you to do any good when you are thrown among colleagues who would more readily corrupt the best of men than be reformed themselves. Either they will seduce you by

---

[82] Matthew 10:27; Luke 12:3.

[83] A flexible measuring rod of lead was particularly useful in the sort of ancient building known as the 'Lesbian' style, because of the great number of curved mouldings. Aristotle uses the leaden rule as a metaphor for adaptable moral standards (*Nicomachean Ethics* V.x.7).

[84] The allusion is to a comedy – *The Brothers* (I.145–7) – by the Roman playwright Terence (*c.* 190–159 BC).

their evil ways, or, if you remain honest and innocent, you will be made a screen for the knavery and folly of others. You wouldn't stand a chance of changing anything for the better by that "indirect approach".

'This is why Plato in a very fine comparison[85] declares that wise men are right in keeping away from public business. They see the people swarming through the streets and getting soaked with rain; they cannot persuade them to go indoors and get out of the wet. If they go out themselves, they know they will do no good, but only get drenched with the others. So they stay indoors and are content to keep at least themselves dry, since they cannot remedy the folly of others.

'But as a matter of fact, my dear More, to tell you what I really think, wherever you have private property, and money is the measure of all things, it is hardly ever possible for a commonwealth to be just or prosperous – unless you think justice can exist where all the best things are held by the worst citizens, or suppose happiness can be found where the good things of life are divided among very few, where even those few are always uneasy, and where the rest are utterly wretched.

'So I reflect on the wonderfully wise and sacred institutions of the Utopians, who are so well governed with so few laws.[86] Among them virtue has its reward, yet everything is shared equally, and everyone lives in plenty. I contrast with them the many other nations, none of which, though all are constantly passing new ordinances, can ever order its affairs satisfactorily. In such nations, whatever a man can get he calls his own private property; but all the mass of laws enacted day after day don't enable him to secure his own or to defend it, or even to distinguish it from someone else's property – as is shown by innumerable and interminable lawsuits, fresh ones every day. When I consider all these things, I become more sympathetic to Plato, and wonder the less that he refused to make any laws for people who rejected laws requiring all goods to be shared equally by all. Wisest of men, he saw easily that the one and only path to the public welfare lies through equal allocation of goods.[87] I doubt whether

---

[85] *Republic* VI.496D–E.

[86] On the small number of Utopian laws (though they are supplemented by an oppressive number of codes, customs and conventions), see p. 82.

[87] Diogenes Laertius reports that 'the Arcadians and Thebans, when they were founding Megalopolis, invited Plato to be their legislator; but . . . when he discovered that they were opposed to equality of possessions, he refused to go' (*Lives of Eminent Philosophers* III.23). In the *Republic* Plato recommends communism only for the ruling class (the Guardians), but in the *Laws* (V.739B–C) he says that the best commonwealth would be one in which communism was applied across the board. Given its approval by Plato, Plutarch and, traditionally,

such equality can ever be achieved where property belongs to individuals. However abundant goods may be, when everyone, by whatever pretexts, tries to scrape together for himself as much as he can, a handful of men end up sharing the whole pile, and the rest are left in poverty. The result generally is two sorts of people whose fortunes ought to be interchanged: the rich are rapacious, wicked and useless, while the poor are unassuming, modest men, whose daily labour benefits the public more than themselves.

'Thus I am wholly convinced that unless private property is entirely abolished, there can be no fair or just distribution of goods, nor can the business of mortals be conducted happily. As long as private property remains, by far the largest and best part of the human race will be oppressed by a distressing and inescapable burden of poverty and anxieties. This load, I admit, may be lightened to some extent, but I maintain it cannot be entirely removed. Laws might be made that no one should own more than a certain amount of land or receive more than a certain income. Or laws might be passed to prevent the prince from becoming too powerful and the populace too insolent. It might be made illegal for public offices to be solicited or put up for sale or made burdensome for the office-holder by great expense. Otherwise, officials are tempted to get their money back by fraud or extortion, and only rich men can accept appointment to positions which ought to go to the wise. Laws of this sort, I agree, may have as much effect as poultices continually applied to sick bodies that are past cure. The social evils I mentioned may be alleviated and their effects mitigated for a while, but so long as private property remains, there is no hope at all of effecting a cure and restoring society to good health. While you try to cure one part, you aggravate the wound in other parts. Suppressing the disease in one place causes it to break out in another, since you cannot give something to one person without taking it away from someone else.'[88]

'But I don't see it that way', I said. 'It seems to me that people cannot possibly live well where all things are in common. How can there be

---

Pythagoras, as well as the stress in the New Testament on the communal life of the earliest Christians, communism had long been respectable as a theoretical position. The first proverb discussed in Erasmus' *Adages* is *Amicorum communia omnia* ('Between friends all is common'), and Erasmus remarks that 'it is extraordinary how Christians dislike this common ownership of Plato's . . . although nothing was ever said by a pagan philosopher which comes closer to the mind of Christ' (*CWE*, XXXI, 30).

[88] Plato repeatedly uses the metaphor of disease, and of the statesman as physician, in much the same way. Cf. *Republic* IV.425E–426A; *Statesman* 297E–298E; Epistle VII 330C–331A – and Plutarch, 'Lycurgus' V.2.

plenty of commodities where every man stops working? The hope of gain does not spur him on, and by relying on others he will become lazy. If men are impelled by need, and yet no man can legally protect what he has obtained, what can follow but continual bloodshed and turmoil, especially when respect for magistrates and their authority has been lost? I for one cannot even conceive of authority existing among men who are not distinguished from one another in any respect.[89]

'I'm not surprised that you think of it this way', he said, 'since you have no image, or only a false one, of such a commonwealth. But you should have been with me in Utopia and seen with your own eyes their manners and customs, as I did – for I lived there more than five years, and would never have left, if it had not been to make that new world known to others. If you had seen them, you would frankly confess that you had never seen a well-governed people anywhere but there.'

'Come now', said Peter Giles, 'you will have a hard time persuading me that one can find in that new world a better-governed people than in the world we know. Our minds are not inferior to theirs, and our governments, I believe, are older. Long experience has helped us develop many conveniences of life, to say nothing of chance discoveries that human ingenuity could never have hit upon.'

'As for the relative ages of the governments', Raphael said, 'you might judge more accurately if you had read the histories of that part of the world. If we are to believe these records, they had cities there before there were even people here. What ingenuity has discovered or chance hit upon could have turned up just as well there as here. For the rest, I really think that even if we surpass them in natural intelligence, they leave us far behind in their diligence and zeal to learn.

'According to their chronicles, they had heard nothing of Ultra-equatorials (that's their name for us) until we arrived, except that once, some twelve hundred years ago, a ship which a storm had blown towards Utopia was wrecked on their island. Some Romans and Egyptians were cast ashore, and never departed.

'Now note how the Utopians profited, through their diligence, from this one chance event. They learned every single useful art of the Roman empire either directly from their guests or by using the seeds of ideas to discover these arts for themselves. What benefits from the mere fact that

---

[89] These objections to communism derive from the critique of the *Republic* in Aristotle's *Politics* (II.i–v).

on a single occasion some people from this part of the world landed there! If in the past a similar accident has brought anyone here from their land, the incident has been completely forgotten, as our future generations will perhaps forget that I was ever there. From one such accident they made themselves masters of all our useful inventions, but I suspect it will be a long time before we adopt any institutions of theirs which are better than ours. This readiness to learn is, I think, the really important reason for their being better governed and living more happily than we do, though we are not inferior to them in brains or resources.'

'Then let me implore you, my dear Raphael', said I, 'describe that island to us. Don't try to be brief, but explain in order their fields, rivers, towns, people, manners, institutions, laws – everything, in short, that you think we would like to know. And you can assume we want to know everything we don't know yet.'

'There's nothing I'd rather do', he said, 'for these things are fresh in my mind. But it will take quite some time.'

'In that case', I said, 'let's first go to luncheon. Afterwards, we shall have all the time we want.'

'Agreed', he said. So we went in and had lunch. Then we came back to the same spot, and sat down on the same bench. I ordered my servants to make sure that no one interrupted us. Peter Giles and I urged Raphael to fulfil his promise. When he saw that we were attentive and eager to hear him, he sat silent and thoughtful a moment, and then began as follows.

THE END OF BOOK I.
BOOK II FOLLOWS.

THE DISCOURSE OF
RAPHAEL HYTHLODAY
ON THE BEST STATE OF A COMMONWEALTH,
BOOK II:
AS RECOUNTED BY THOMAS MORE,
CITIZEN AND UNDERSHERIFF OF LONDON

The island of the Utopians is two hundred miles across in the middle *Site and shape*
part, where it is widest, and nowhere much narrower than this except to- *of Utopia the*
new island
wards the two ends, where it gradually tapers. These ends, curved round
as if completing a circle five hundred miles in circumference, make the
island crescent-shaped, like a new moon.[1] Between the horns of the cres-
cent, which are about eleven miles apart, the sea enters and spreads into
a broad bay. Being sheltered from the wind by the surrounding land, the
bay is not rough, but placid and smooth instead, like a big lake. Thus
nearly the whole inner coast is one great harbour, across which ships pass
in every direction, to the great advantage of the people. What with shal-
lows on one side and rocks on the other, the mouth of the bay is perilous.[2] *Being*
naturally
Near mid-channel, there is one reef that rises above the water, and so *safe, the*
presents no danger in itself; a tower has been built on top of it, and a *entry is*
defended by
garrison is kept there. Since the other rocks lie under the water, they *a single fort*

---

[1] Utopia is similar to England in size, though not at all in shape. For a detailed account of its
geography, and the inconsistencies thereof, see Brian R. Goodey, 'Mapping "Utopia": A com-
ment on the geography of Sir Thomas More', *The Geographical Review*, 60 (1970), 15–30.

The main topics and the order of Hythloday's account may owe something to Aristotle's
treatment of the ideal commonwealth in *Politics* VII–VIII. Aristotle's discussion of the optimal
'human material' and territory for a polis is followed by a checklist of the six 'services'
that must be provided for: food; arts and crafts; arms; 'a certain supply of property, alike
for domestic use and for military purposes'; public worship; and a deliberative and judicial
system (VII.iv–viii).

[2] A number of the geographical features of Utopia recall the dicta of ideal-commonwealth
literature. Aristotle, for example, says that the best territory for a polis is one that is 'difficult
of access to enemies, and easy of egress for its inhabitants' (*Politics* VII.v. 3). There are, though,
some features in which the Utopians' territory is *not* ideal: on the shortage of iron, see p. 59;
on the poor climate and soil, p. 74.

are very dangerous. The channels are known only to the Utopians, so hardly any strangers enter the bay without one of their pilots; and even they themselves could not enter safely if they did not direct their course *The trick of shifting* by some landmarks on the coast. Should these landmarks be shifted about, *landmarks* the Utopians could easily lure to destruction an enemy fleet, however big it was.

On the outer side of the island, harbours are found not infrequently; but everywhere the coast is rugged by nature, and so well fortified that a few defenders could beat off the attack of a strong force. They say (and the appearance of the place confirms this) that their land was not always *Utopia named* surrounded by the sea. But Utopus, who conquered the country and gave *after Utopus the* it his name (for it had previously been called Abraxa),[3] and who brought its *commander* rude, uncouth inhabitants to such a high level of culture and humanity that they now surpass almost every other people, also changed its geography. After winning the victory at his first assault, he had a channel cut fifteen *This was a bigger job* miles wide where the land joined the continent, and thus caused the sea *than digging across* to flow around the country. He put not only the natives to work at this *the Isthmus* [4] task, but all his own soldiers too, so that the vanquished would not think the labour a disgrace.[5] With the work divided among so many hands, the *Many hands make* project was finished quickly, and the neighbouring peoples, who at first *light work* had laughed at the folly of the undertaking, were struck with wonder and terror at its success.

[3] The Greek Gnostic Basilides (second century) postulated 365 heavens, and gave the name 'Abraxas' to the highest of them. The Greek letters that constitute the term have numerical equivalents summing to 365, but what 'Abraxas' actually means nobody knows. Erasmus refers to it several times; for him, as Dominic Baker-Smith says, it 'obviously means a far-fetched fantasy' (*More's 'Utopia'*, p. 55n).

The prototypes of Utopus are the legendary lawgivers of Greek tradition – Solon, Lycurgus, Pythagoras and others – who founded or regenerated polities.

[4] The Isthmus of Corinth joins the Peloponnesian peninsula to the rest of Greece. The failure of various attempts to excavate a canal across it made this difficult task proverbial.

[5] This is the first of several passages in *Utopia* stressing the dignity of labour. Frank and Fritzie Manuel observe that 'More's rehabilitation of the idea of physical labor was a milestone in the history of utopian thought, and was incorporated into all socialist systems' (*Utopian Thought in the Western World*, p. 127). The principal sources of this attitude are Christian; in particular, the monastic orders constituted a paradigm of a society in which all are workers. (Monasticism is the one European institution that the Utopians are said to admire (pp. 93–4), and such Utopian institutions as their uniform dress (pp. 49, 53) and common meals (p. 56) – generally, their communal way of life – recall the monastic rules.) By contrast, in classical political theory and practice manual labour was normally assigned to members of the lower orders (including especially slaves) and to women.

There are fifty-four cities[6] on the island, all spacious and magnificent, entirely identical in language, customs, institutions and laws. So far as the location permits, all of them are built on the same plan and have the same appearance. The nearest are twenty-four miles apart, and the farthest are not so remote that a person cannot travel on foot from one to another in a day.

The towns of Utopia

Likeness breeds concord

A middling distance between cities

Once a year each city sends three of its old and experienced citizens to Amaurot[7] to consider affairs of common interest to the island. Amaurot lies at the navel of the land, so to speak, and convenient to every other district, so it acts as a capital. Every city has enough ground assigned to it so that at least twelve miles of farmland are available in every direction, though where the cities are farther apart, their territories are much more extensive. No city wants to enlarge its boundaries, for the inhabitants consider themselves cultivators rather than landlords. At proper intervals all over the countryside they have houses furnished with farm equipment. These houses are inhabited by citizens who come to the country by turns. No rural household has fewer than forty men and women in it, besides two slaves bound to the land. A master and mistress, serious and mature persons, are in charge of each household, and over every thirty households is placed a single phylarch.[9] Each year twenty persons from each household move back to the city after completing a two-year stint in the country. In their place, twenty substitutes are sent out from town, to learn farm work from those who have already been in the country for a year and are therefore better skilled in farming. They, in turn, will teach those who come the following year. If all were equally untrained in farm work and new to it, they might harm the crops out of ignorance. This custom of alternating farm workers is the usual procedure, so that no one has to

Distribution of land

But today this is the curse of all countries[8]

Farming is the prime occupation

---

[6] Although the primary reference here is to the cities themselves, the word More uses – *civitas* – is the Latin equivalent of the Greek *polis*, 'city-state'. In fact each of the fifty-four Utopian *civitates* is, like the Greek *polis*, constituted of a central city and its surrounding countryside. Though federated, they also resemble the Greek city-states in functioning as largely independent political units. Throughout Book II, the concentration on the *civitas* is the most striking indication of More's debt to Greek political theory. In number, the Utopian cities match the number of counties in England and Wales – given as fifty-three in William Harrison's 1587 *Description of England* (ed. Georges Edelen (Ithaca, 1968), p. 86) – plus London.

[7] From *amauroton*, 'made dark or dim'.

[8] Although Utopia exists in the present, the glosses repeatedly refer to it as if it belonged to the distant past, like classical Greece and Rome.

[9] Greek *phylarchos*, 'ruler of a tribe'.

perform such heavy labour unwillingly for too long; but many of them who take a natural pleasure in farm life are allowed to stay extra years.

Farmers' jobs

The farm workers till the soil, feed the animals, procure wood and take their produce to the city by land or water, whichever is convenient. They

A notable way of hatching eggs

breed an enormous number of chickens by a most marvellous method. The farmers, not hens, keep the eggs alive and hatch them, maintaining them at an even, warm temperature.[10] As soon as they come out of the shell, the chicks recognise the humans and follow them around instead of their mothers.

Uses of the horse

They raise very few horses, and those full of mettle, which they keep only to exercise the young people in the art of horsemanship. For all the

Uses of oxen

work of ploughing and hauling they use oxen, which they agree are inferior to horses over the short haul, but which can hold out longer under heavy burdens, are less subject to disease (as they suppose), and besides can be kept with less cost and trouble. Moreover, when oxen are too old for work, they can be used for meat.

Food and drink

Grain they use only to make bread.[11] For they drink wine made of grapes, apple or pear cider, or simple water, which they sometimes boil with honey or liquorice, of which they have plenty. Although they know very well, down to the last detail, how much food each city and its surrounding

Method of planting

district will consume, they produce much more grain and cattle than they need for themselves, and share the surplus with their neighbours. Whatever goods the folk in the country need which cannot be had there, they request of the town magistrates, and, giving nothing in exchange, they get what they want without any trouble. They generally go to town once a month in any case, to observe the feast day. When harvest time approaches, the phylarchs in the country notify the town magistrates how many hands will be needed. The crowd of harvesters comes at just the

The advantage of collective labour

right time, and in about one day of good weather they can get in the whole crop.

THEIR CITIES, ESPECIALLY AMAUROT

If you know one of their cities you know them all, for they're exactly alike, except where geography itself makes a difference. So I will describe one of them, and no matter which. But what one rather than Amaurot, the

[10] It is not entirely clear what is meant here. Though artificial incubation is mentioned in Pliny's *Natural History* (x.lxxvi.154), it was not practised in More's time.

[11] I.e., they don't, like the English, use it to make beer and ale.

most worthy of all? – since its eminence is acknowledged by the other cities that send representatives to the senate there; besides which, I know it best because I lived there for five full years.

Description of Amaurot, principal city of Utopia

Well, then, Amaurot lies up against a gently sloping hill; the town is almost square in shape. From a little below the crest of the hill, its shorter side runs down two miles to the river Anyder;[12] its length along the river bank is somewhat greater. The Anyder rises from a small spring eighty miles above Amaurot, but other streams flow into it, two of them being pretty big, so that as it runs by Amaurot the river has grown to a width of about five hundred yards. It continues to grow even larger until at last, sixty miles farther along, it is lost in the ocean. In all this stretch between the sea and the city, and also for some miles above the city, the river is tidal, ebbing and flowing every six hours with a swift current. When the tide comes in, it fills the whole Anyder with salt water for about thirty miles, driving the fresh water back. Even above that, for several miles farther, the water is brackish; but higher up it gradually becomes free of salt, and the river is fresh as it runs through the city. When the tide ebbs, the river runs fresh and clean nearly all the way to the sea.

Description of the river Anyder

Just like the Thames in England

The two banks of the river at Amaurot are linked by a bridge, built not on wooden pillars and piles but on remarkable stone arches. It is placed at the upper end of the city farthest removed from the sea, so that ships can sail along the entire length of the city quays without obstruction.[13] There is also another stream, not particularly large but very gentle and pleasant, that gushes out of the hill on which the city is situated and, following the slope of the terrain, flows down through the centre of town and into the Anyder.[14] The inhabitants of Amaurot have walled around the head and source of this stream, which is somewhat outside the city, and joined it to the town proper, so that if they should be attacked the enemy would not be able to cut off and divert the stream, or poison it. Water from the stream is carried by tile pipes into various sections of the lower town. Where the terrain makes this impractical, they collect rain water in cisterns, which serve just as well.

Here too London is just like Amaurot

A source of drinking water

The town is surrounded by a thick, high wall, with many towers and battlements. On three sides it is also surrounded by a dry ditch, broad and

Fortified city walls

---

[12] From *anydros*, 'waterless'. The description of the Anyder and the situation of Amaurot correspond in detail to the Thames and London, except that the Thames rises about twice as far above London as the Anyder above Amaurot.

[13] This is an improvement on the situation of London Bridge, which was in the lower part of town.

[14] Except in its pleasantness, this second stream resembles London's Fleet Ditch.

deep and filled with thorn hedges; on its fourth side the river itself serves
as a moat. The streets are conveniently laid out both for use by vehicles
and for protection from the wind. Their buildings are by no means shabby.
Long unbroken rows of houses face each other down the whole block. The
housefronts along each block are separated by a street twenty feet wide.[15]
Behind the houses, a large garden – as long on each side as the block
itself – is hemmed in on all sides by the backs of the houses.

Every house has a front door to the street and a back door to the garden.
The double doors, which open easily with a push of the hand and close
again automatically, let anyone come in – so there is nothing private
anywhere. Every ten years they exchange the houses themselves by lot.[16]
The Utopians are very fond of these gardens of theirs.[17] They raise vines,
fruits, herbs and flowers, so well cared for and flourishing that I have
never seen any gardens more productive or elegant than theirs. They
keep interested in gardening, partly because they delight in it, and also
because of the competition among the blocks, which challenge one another
to produce the best gardens. Certainly you will not easily find anything
else in the whole city more useful or more pleasant to the citizens. And
from that fact it appears that the city's founder must have made such
gardens a primary object of his consideration.

They say that from the beginning the whole city was planned by Utopus
himself, but that he left to posterity matters of adornment and improvement such as he saw could not be perfected in one man's lifetime. Their
records began 1,760 years ago[19] with the conquest of the island, were
diligently compiled, and are carefully preserved in writing. From these

Marginal notes:
- Streets, of what sort
- Buildings
- Gardens next to the houses
- This smacks of Plato's community
- *(handwritten: Reminiscent of Plato)*
- Virgil also wrote in praise of gardens[18]

[15] Lavish, by sixteenth-century standards. Goodey observes that the layout of Amaurot is reminiscent of Roman urban planning: 'Twenty feet was the average width of Roman city streets,
which, again like Amaurotum, were bordered by fairly high-density housing blocks that
surrounded large courtyards used for recreation. As in Amaurotum, the rectangular block
pattern was the most evident feature of the Roman urban plan. In the Roman city this pattern
was broken only by the insertion of major public buildings, again a feature of the Utopian
city' ('Mapping "Utopia"', p. 29). The notable *difference* from Roman arrangements lies in
the fact that the Utopian courtyards are merged in the communal gardens.

[16] Cf. Plato, *Republic* V.416D: the Guardians 'shall have no private property beyond the barest
essentials . . . none of them shall possess a dwelling-house or other property to which all have
not the right of entry'. The Carthusian monks, among whom More sojourned for a few years,
regularly exchange dwellings.

[17] Apart from its obvious practical advantages, the Utopians' fondness for gardens may hint
at the connection of their way of life with Epicureanism. Early in life, Epicurus retired to a
house and garden given him by his disciples; and his school was called the Garden.

[18] In the *Georgics* (IV.116–48).

[19] Counting from 1516, this takes us back to 244 BC, when Agis IV became King of Sparta: he
was put to death for proposing egalitarian reforms. See Plutarch's 'Agis'; and R. J. Schoeck,

records it appears that the first houses were low, like cabins or peasant huts, built slapdash out of any sort of lumber, with mud-plastered walls. The roofs, rising up to a central point, were thatched with straw. But now their houses are all three storeys high and handsomely constructed; the outer sections of the walls are made of fieldstone, quarried rock or brick, and the space between is filled up with gravel and cement.[20] The roofs are flat and are covered with a kind of plaster that is cheap but formulated so as to be fireproof, and more weather-resistant even than lead. Glass (of which they have a good supply) is used in windows to keep out the weather; and they also use thin linen cloth treated with clear oil or gum so that it has the double advantage of letting in more light and keeping out more wind.[21]

Windows of glass or linen

THEIR OFFICIALS

Once a year, every group of thirty households elects an official, called the syphogrant in their ancient language,[22] but now known as the phylarch. Over every group of ten syphogrants with their households there is another official, once called the tranibor but now known as the head phylarch. All the syphogrants, two hundred in number,[23] elect the governor. They take an oath to choose the man they think best qualified; and then by

In the Utopian tongue 'tranibor' means 'chief official'

'More, Plutarch, and King Agis: Spartan history and the meaning of *Utopia*', *Philological Quarterly*, 35 (1956), 366–75; rpt *Essential Articles for the Study of Thomas More*, pp. 275–80.

[20] The housing of modern Amaurot is considerably more impressive than that of early sixteenth-century London, where dwellings were normally of timber and of at most two storeys.

[21] Glass windows were uncommon in England. Oiled linen, sheets of horn and lattices of wicker or wood were used instead.

[22] 'Syphogrant' appears to be constructed from Greek *sophos* ('wise') – or perhaps *sypheos* ('of the sty') – plus *gerontes* ('old men'). For 'tranibor' (below), the etymology seems to be *traneis* or *tranos* ('clear', 'plain', 'distinct') plus *boros* ('devouring', 'gluttonous'). Although Hythloday says that these terms have been displaced by the more unambiguously respectful 'phylarch' and 'protophylarch' (translated as 'head phylarch'), in the remainder of his account he invariably uses the 'older' terms. 'Phylarch' occurs twice before this passage, but never again; 'protophylarch' occurs only this once.

The Utopian form of government is republican: syphogrants are elected by the households, and the syphogrants of each city elect – and can remove – the governor (below), as well as the class of scholars, from which all high officials are chosen (p. 52). The particular republic that the Utopian arrangements would be most likely to call to mind was Venice, whose 'mixed' constitution combined the institutions of Doge (the elected head of government), Senate and Grand Council. The famous stability of this constitution was thought to be owed to its embodiment of Plato's view (*Laws* III.691D–693E, IV.712B–E) that the soundest form of government was an amalgam of monarchy, aristocracy and democracy. See Skinner, *The Foundations of Modern Political Thought*, 1, 139–42.

[23] Because there are 6,000 families in each city (p. 54), with thirty families per syphogrant.

A notable way of electing officials

Tyranny hateful to the well-ordered commonwealth

A quick ending to disputes, which now are endlessly and deliberately prolonged

No abrupt decisions

Would that the same rules prevailed in our modern councils

This is the old saying, 'to sleep on a decision'

Agriculture is everyone's business, though now we put it off on a despised few

secret ballot they elect the governor from among four men commended to the senate by the people of the four sections of the city.[24] The governor holds office for life, unless he is suspected of aiming at a tyranny. Though the tranibors are elected annually, they are not changed for light or casual reasons. All their other officials hold office for a single year only.

The tranibors meet to consult with the governor every other day, more often if necessary: they discuss affairs of state and settle disputes between private parties (if there are any, and there are very few), acting as quickly as possible. The tranibors always invite two syphogrants to the senate chamber, different ones every day. There is a rule that no decision can be made on a matter of public business unless it has been discussed in the senate on three separate days. It is a capital offence to make plans about public business outside the senate or the popular assembly. The purpose of these rules, they say, is to prevent governor and tranibors from conspiring together to alter the government and enslave the people. Therefore all matters which are considered important are first laid before the assembly of syphogrants. They talk the matter over with the households they represent, consult among themselves, and then report their recommendation to the senate. Sometimes a question is brought before the general council of the whole island.

The senate also has a standing rule never to debate a matter on the same day that it is first introduced but to put it off till the next meeting. This they do so that a man will not blurt out the first thought that occurs to him, and then devote all his energies to defending his own proposals, instead of considering the common interest. They know that some men have such a perverse and preposterous sense of shame that they would rather jeopardise the general welfare than their own reputation by admitting they were short-sighted in the first place. They should have had enough foresight at the beginning to speak with consideration rather than haste.

THEIR OCCUPATIONS

Farming is the one job at which everyone works, men and women alike, with no exception.[25] They are trained in it from childhood, partly in the

[24] While each city has a governor, there is no governor over the whole island, so that when the national council meets at Amaurot (p. 43) there's nobody for it to advise – no executive.

[25] Agriculture gets the same heavy emphasis in *Utopia* as it did in sixteenth-century Europe, where most of the populace had to work at providing a subsistence. A great deal of this work was hard, monotonous and unappealing – and thus required careful apportioning in an egalitarian society.

schools, where they learn theory, partly through field trips to nearby farms, which make something like a game of practical instruction.[26] On these trips they don't just observe, but frequently pitch in and get a workout by doing the jobs themselves.

Besides farm work (which, as I said, everybody performs), each person is taught a particular trade of his own, such as wool-working, linen-making, masonry, metal-work or carpentry. No other craft is practised by any considerable number of them.[27] Their clothing – which is, except for the distinction between the sexes and between married and unmarried persons, the same throughout the whole island and throughout one's lifetime, and which is by no means unattractive, does not hinder bodily movement and serves for warm as well as cold weather – this clothing, I say, each family makes for itself.

Trades taught to satisfy need, not greed

A uniform dress code

Every person (and this includes women as well as men) learns one of the trades I mentioned. As the weaker sex, women practise the lighter crafts, such as working in wool or linen; the other, heavier jobs are assigned to the men. Ordinarily, the son is trained to his father's craft, for which most feel a natural inclination. But if anyone is attracted to another occupation, he is transferred by adoption into a family practising that trade. Both his father and the authorities take care that he is assigned to a grave and responsible householder. After someone has mastered one trade, if he wants to learn another he gets the same permission. When he has learned both, he pursues the one he likes better, unless the city needs one more than the other.[28] ← A bit different than Plato.

No citizen without a trade

Everyone to learn the trade for which his nature fits him

The chief and almost the only business of the syphogrants is to take care and see to it that no one sits around in idleness, and to make sure that everyone works hard at his trade. But no one has to be exhausted with endless toil from early morning to late at night like a beast of burden. Such wretchedness, really worse than slavery, is the common lot of workmen

The idle are expelled from the commonwealth

---

[26] Both Plato (*Laws* I.643B–C, VII.797A–B) and Aristotle (*Politics* VII.xvii.5) stress the educational potential of games. In particular, Plato says that a 'man who intends to be a good farmer must play [in childhood] at farming' (*Laws* I.643C).

[27] One would have thought that considerable numbers would also have been employed making such things as pottery, harness, bread and books, or in mining or the merchant marine. Presumably all professionals – doctors, for example – are drawn from the class of scholars (p. 52).

[28] The fact that all Utopians have at least two occupations (agriculture and one of the crafts), and in some cases three, brings them into implicit conflict with Plato, who strongly insists that in a well-ordered commonwealth each individual would have one and only one profession (*Republic* II.370A–C, 374A–D; *Laws* VIII.846D–E).

almost everywhere except in Utopia.[29] Of the twenty-four equal hours into which they divide the day and the night, the Utopians devote only six to work. They work three hours before noon, when they go to lunch. After lunch, they rest for two hours, then go to work for another three hours. Then they have supper, and about eight o'clock (counting the first hour after noon as one) they go to bed, and sleep eight hours.

Workmen not to be overtasked

The other hours of the day, when they are not working, eating or sleeping, are left to each person's individual discretion, provided that free time is not wasted in roistering or sloth but used properly in some chosen occupation. Generally these intervals are devoted to intellectual activity. For they have an established custom of giving daily public lectures before dawn;[30] attendance at these lectures is required only of those who have been specifically chosen to devote themselves to learning, but a great many other people of all kinds, both men and women,[31] gather to hear them. Depending on their interests, some go to one lecture, some to another. But if anyone would rather devote his spare time to his trade, as many do who are not suited to the intellectual life, this is not prohibited; in fact, such persons are commended as specially useful to the commonwealth.

The pursuit of learning

After supper, they devote an hour to recreation, in their gardens during the summer, or during winter in the common halls where they have their meals. There they either play music or amuse themselves with conversation. They know nothing about gambling with dice or other such foolish and ruinous games, but they do play two games not unlike chess. One is a battle of numbers, in which one number captures another. The other is a game in which the vices fight a battle against the virtues. The game is ingeniously set up to show how the vices oppose one another, yet combine against the virtues; then, what vices oppose what virtues, how they try to assault them with open force or undermine them indirectly through trickery, how the defences of the virtues can break the strength of the vices or skilfully elude their plots; and finally, by what means one side or the other gains the victory.

Entertainment at supper

But now dicing is the sport of princes

Their games are useful too

---

[29] In England, for example, an 'Act concerning Artificers & Labourers', 1514–15, made exorbitant demands upon the time of workmen: daybreak to nightfall from mid-September to mid-March; before 5 a.m. to between 7 and 8 p.m. from mid-March to mid-September (*The Statutes of the Realm*, III (1822), 124–6).

[30] In the universities of More's time, lectures normally began between 5 and 7 a.m.

[31] Humanists were pioneers in forwarding the education of women. Celibate Erasmus was greatly impressed by the erudite daughters of his married fellow humanists, including Margaret More. See 'The Abbot and the learned lady' among Erasmus' *Colloquies*, trans. Craig R. Thompson (Chicago, 1965), pp. 217–23.

But at this point you may get a wrong impression if we don't go back and consider one matter more carefully. Because they allot only six hours to work, perhaps you might think the necessities of life would be in scant supply. This is far from the case. Their working hours are ample to provide not only enough but more than enough of the necessities and even the conveniences of life. You will easily appreciate this if you consider how large a part of the population in other countries lives without doing any work at all. In the first place, hardly any of the women, who are a full half *Kinds of idlers* of the population, work;[32] or, if they do, then as a rule their husbands lie snoring in bed. Then there is a great lazy gang of priests and so-called religious.[33] Add to them all the rich, especially the landlords, who are commonly called gentlemen and nobles. Include with them their retainers, *Noblemen's* that cesspool of worthless swashbucklers. Finally, reckon in with these the *bodyguards* sturdy and lusty beggars who feign some disease as an excuse for their idleness. You will certainly find that all the things which satisfy the needs *A very shrewd* of mortals are produced by far fewer hands than you had supposed. *observation*

And now consider how few of those who do work are doing really essential things. For where money is the measure of everything, many vain and completely superfluous trades are bound to be carried on simply to *Plato* satisfy luxury and licentiousness. Suppose the multitude of those who now work were limited to a few trades and set to producing just those commodities that nature really requires.[34] They would be bound to produce so much that prices would drop and the workmen would be unable to make a living. But suppose again that all the workers in useless trades were put to useful ones, and that the whole crowd of languid idlers (each of whom consumes as much as any two of the workmen who provide what he consumes) were assigned to productive tasks – well, you can easily see how little time would be enough and more than enough to produce all the goods that human needs and conveniences call for – yes, and human pleasure too, as long as it is true and natural pleasure.

[32] A strange statement, in view of the fact that women had the same, or heavier, domestic duties in the sixteenth century as in the twenty-first. In Utopia, they are responsible for some at least of these duties – cooking, childcare (pp. 56–7) – in addition to practising a craft and taking their turn at farm work. Numerous problems, such as who does the laundry, who cleans the house, who tends the garden, are solved by the simple expedient of not mentioning them.

[33] I.e., members of the various religious orders.

[34] The notion that a well-ordered commonwealth would not countenance trades other than those that supply legitimate human needs is traceable to Plato (*Republic* II.372D–373D). Plutarch says that Lycurgus, the lawgiver of Sparta, 'banished the unnecessary and superfluous arts' ('Lycurgus' IX.3).

The experience of Utopia makes this perfectly apparent. For there, in the whole city and its surrounding countryside barely five hundred of those men and women whose age and strength make them fit for work are exempted from it.[35] Among these are the syphogrants, who by law are free *Not even officials* not to work; yet they don't take advantage of the privilege, preferring to set *dodge work* a good example to their fellow citizens. Some others are also permanently exempted from work so that they may devote themselves to study, but only on the recommendation of the priests[36] and through a secret vote of the syphogrants. If any of these scholars disappoints the hopes they had for him, he is sent packing, to become a workman again. On the other hand, it happens not infrequently that a craftsman devotes his leisure so earnestly to study, and makes such progress by his diligence, that he is released from his craft and promoted to the order of learned men. From this scholarly *Only the learned* class are chosen ambassadors, priests, tranibors and the governor himself, *hold public office* who used to be called Barzanes, but in their modern tongue is known as Ademus.[37] Since almost all the rest of the populace is neither idle nor engaged in useless trades, it is easy to see why they produce so much in such a short working day.

Apart from all this, they have it easier because in most of the necessary crafts they need less labour than people elsewhere do. First of all, building *Avoiding expense* and repairing houses everywhere demands the constant labour of many *in building* men, because what a father has built, his thriftless heir lets fall into ruin; and then his successor has to reconstruct, at great expense, what could have been kept up at a very small charge. Even more, when a man has built a splendid house at vast cost, someone else may think he has better taste, let the first house fall to ruin, and then build another one somewhere else for just as much money. But among the Utopians, where everything has been well-ordered and the commonwealth properly established, building a new house on a new site is a rare event. They are not only quick to repair deterioration but foresighted in preventing it. The result is that their buildings last for a very long time with minimum repairs; and workmen

The idea can now be added to [handwritten marginal note, partially legible]

---

[35] Two hundred of these are syphogrants; presumably the governor, the twenty tranibors and the thirteen priests (p. 98) are also exempt. The rest must be scholars, and the ambassadors drawn from their ranks.

[36] The priests are in charge of the education of children (p. 99).

[37] 'Barzanes': probably Hebrew *bar*, 'son of', plus *Zanos*, Doric poetic form of the genitive of Zeus. A potent Chaldean magician named Mithrobarzanes figures in Lucian's 'Menippus', which More had translated. 'Ademus': Greek α-privative plus *demos*, 'people': hence 'Peopleless'.

of that sort sometimes have so little to do that they are set to shaping timber and squaring stone for prompt use in case of future need.

Consider, too, how little labour their clothing requires. Their work clothes are unpretentious garments made of leather or pelts, which last seven years. When they go out in public, they cover these rough work clothes with a cloak. Throughout the entire island, these cloaks are of the same colour, which is that of natural wool.[38] As a result, they not only need less woollen cloth than people anywhere else, but what they do need is also less expensive. Even so, they use linen cloth most, because it requires least labour. They like linen cloth to be white and wool cloth to be clean; but they do not value fineness of texture. Everywhere else a man may not be satisfied with four or five woollen cloaks of different colours and as many silk shirts – or if he's a bit of a fop, even ten are not enough. But there everyone is content with a single cloak, and generally wears it for two years. There is no reason why he should want any more garments, for if he had them, he would not be better protected against the cold, nor would he appear the least bit more fashionable.

How to do so in clothing

Since there is an abundance of everything – as a result of everyone working at useful trades and the trades requiring less work – they sometimes assemble great numbers of people to work on the roads, if any need repairs. And when there is no need even for this sort of work, then they very often proclaim a shorter work day, since the magistrates never force their citizens to perform useless labour. The chief aim of their constitution is that, as far as public needs permit, all citizens should be free to withdraw as much time as possible from the service of the body and devote themselves to the freedom and culture of the mind. For in that, they think, lies the happiness of life.

SOCIAL RELATIONS

Now it would be well to explain how the citizens behave towards one another, the nature of their social relations and their system of distributing goods.

[38] More's letter to Erasmus of *c.* 4 December 1516 – in which he reports a daydream of being King of Utopia – identifies this garment as a Franciscan habit (*Selected Letters*, p. 85). The Carthusians, with whom More lived for some years (Introduction, p. xiv), wore garments of undyed wool. The biographical sketch of More that Erasmus included in a letter to Ulrich von Hutten says that 'Simple clothes please . . . [More] best, and he never wears silk or scarlet or a gold chain, except when it is not open to him to lay it aside' (*CWE*, VII, 18).

Each city, then, consists of households, the households consisting generally of blood-relations. When the women grow up and are married, they move into their husbands' households. On the other hand, male children and grandchildren remain in the family, and are subject to the oldest member, unless his mind has started to fail from old age, in which case the next oldest takes his place. To keep the cities from becoming too sparse or too crowded, they take care that each household (there are six *The number of* thousand of them in each city, exclusive of the surrounding countryside) *citizens* should have no fewer than ten nor more than sixteen adults. They cannot, of course, regulate the number of minor children in a family.[39] The limit on adults is easily observed by transferring individuals from a household with too many into a household with too few. But if a city has too many people, the extra persons serve to make up the shortage of population in other cities. And if the population throughout the entire island exceeds the quota, they enrol citizens out of every city and plant a colony under their own laws on the mainland near them, wherever the natives have plenty of unoccupied and uncultivated land. Those natives who want to live with the Utopians are adopted by them. When such a merger occurs, the two peoples gradually and easily blend together, sharing the same way of life and customs, much to the advantage of both. For by their policies the Utopians make the land yield an abundance for all, though previously it had seemed too poor and barren even to support the natives. But those who refuse to live under their laws they drive out of the land they claim for themselves; and against those who resist them, they wage war. They think it is perfectly justifiable to make war on people who leave their land idle and waste yet forbid the use and possession of it to others who, by the law of nature, ought to be supported from it.[40]

If for any reason the population of one city shrinks so sharply that it cannot be made up without reducing others below their quota, the

---

[39] If an average household includes thirteen adults, then there are approximately 78,000 adults per city. Those on two-year tours of agricultural duty may or may not be included. Allowing for children and slaves, the population of each Utopian city must be in excess of 100,000, making them larger than all but the greatest European cities of the time.

The closest parallel to the Utopian arrangements is found in Plato's *Laws* (V.740A–741A), where the ideal figure of 5,040 households for the polis is maintained by relocating children, manipulating the birthrate and establishing colonies.

[40] On the law of nature, see p. 113n. A fundamental principle of this law is that all things are common; from this it follows that, as Surtz says, 'a nation may take possession of wasteland necessary for its survival' (*CW*, IV, 416). Similar arguments were applied to colonisation of the New World – to which, as Baker-Smith observes, the Utopians' proceedings bear 'a painful similarity' (*More's 'Utopia'*, p. 186).

numbers are restored by bringing people back from the colonies. This has happened only twice, they say, in their whole history, both times in consequence of a frightful plague. They would rather let their colonies disappear than allow any of the cities on their island to get too small.

But to return to the communal life of the citizens. The oldest of every household, as I said, is the ruler. Wives act as servants to their husbands, children to their parents, and generally the younger to their elders.[41] Every city is divided into four equal districts, and in the middle of each district is a market for all kinds of commodities. Whatever each household produces is brought here and stored in warehouses, each kind of goods in its own place. Here the head of every household looks for what he or his family needs, and carries off what he wants without any sort of payment or compensation. Why should anything be refused him? There is plenty of everything, and no reason to fear that anyone will claim more than he needs. For why would anyone be suspected of asking for more than is needed, when he knows there will never be any shortage? Fear of want, no doubt, makes every living creature greedy and rapacious, and man, besides, develops these qualities out of sheer pride, which glories in getting ahead of others by a superfluous display of possessions. But this sort of vice has no place whatever in the Utopian scheme of things.

Next to the marketplaces of which I just spoke are the food markets, where people bring all sorts of vegetables, fruit and bread. Fish, meat and poultry are also brought there from designated places not far outside the city, where running water can carry away all the blood and refuse. Bondsmen do the slaughtering and cleaning in these places: citizens are not allowed to do such work.[42] The Utopians feel that slaughtering our fellow creatures gradually destroys the sense of compassion, the finest sentiment of which our human nature is capable. Besides, they don't allow anything dirty or filthy to be brought into the city, lest the air become tainted by putrefaction and thus infectious.

Every square block has its own spacious halls, equally distant from one another, and each known by a special name. In these halls live the

Thus they eliminate crowds of idle servants

The sources of greed

Filth and refuse spread disease in cities

By butchering beasts we learn to slaughter men

---

[41] This patriarchy finds strong support in innumerable classical, Biblical and later texts. See, for example, Aristotle, *Politics* I.xii.1–2, and Ephesians 5:22–6:4. The Utopians are perhaps especially interested in reinforcing it as a way of countering the disruptive effects supposed to be entailed in communism (cf. pp. 38–9).

[42] The bondsmen (Latin *famuli*), who are mentioned only here, should possibly be distinguished from the slaves (Latin *servi*) who are referred to several times. But on p. 71 Hythloday notes that the Utopians have assigned hunting 'to their butchers, who, as I said before, are all slaves' (*servi*).

syphogrants. Thirty families are assigned to each hall – fifteen from each side of it – to take their meals in common.[43] The stewards of all the halls meet at a fixed time in the market and requisition food according to the number of persons for whom each is responsible.

Caring for the sick

But first consideration goes to the sick, who are cared for in public hospitals. Every city has four of these, built at the city limits slightly outside the walls, and spacious enough to appear like little towns. The hospitals are large for two reasons: so that the sick, however numerous they may be, will not be packed closely and uncomfortably together, and also so that those with contagious diseases, such as might pass from one to the other, can be isolated. These hospitals are well ordered and supplied with everything needed to cure the patients, who are nursed with tender and watchful care. Highly skilled physicians are in constant attendance. Consequently, though nobody is sent there against his will, still there is hardly anyone in the whole city who would not rather be treated for an illness at the hospital than at home.

The germ theory of disease?

When the hospital steward has received the food prescribed for the sick by their doctors, the best of the remainder is fairly divided among the halls according to the number in each, except that special regard is paid to the governor, the high priest and the tranibors, as well as to ambassadors and foreigners, if there are any. In fact, there are very few; but when they do come, they have certain furnished houses assigned to them. At

Meals in common, mixing all groups

the hours of lunch and supper, a brazen trumpet summons the entire syphogranty to assemble in their hall, except for those who are bedridden in the hospitals or at home. After the halls have been served with their

Note how freedom is granted everywhere, lest people act under compulsion

quotas of food, nothing prevents an individual from taking home food from the marketplace. They realise that no one would do this without good reason. For while it is not forbidden to eat at home, no one does it willingly, because it is not thought proper; and besides, it would be stupid to work at preparing a worse meal at home when there is an elegant and sumptuous one near at hand in the hall.

In this hall, slaves do all the particularly dirty and heavy chores. But

Women prepare the meals

planning the meal, as well as preparing and cooking the food, is carried out by the women alone, with each family taking its turn. Depending on

[43] According to Plutarch, Lycurgus instituted the common messes of Sparta as part of his plan 'to attack luxury . . . and remove the thirst for wealth' ('Lycurgus' x). For similar reasons the institution was incorporated into the ideal commonwealths of Plato and Aristotle (*Republic* III.416E; *Politics* VII.x.10).

the number, they sit down at three or more tables. The men sit with their backs to the wall, the women on the outside, so that if a woman has a sudden qualm or pain, such as occasionally happens during pregnancy, she may get up without disturbing the others and go off to the nurses.

A separate dining room is assigned to the nurses and infants, with a plentiful supply of cradles, clean water and a warm fire. Thus the nurses may lay the infants down, or remove their swaddling clothes before the fire and let them renew their strength by playing. Each child is nursed by its own mother, unless death or illness prevents. When that happens, the wives of the syphogrants quickly find a nurse. The problem is not difficult: any woman who can volunteers more willingly than for any other service, since everyone applauds her kindheartedness, and the child itself regards its nurse as its natural mother.

Unlike in Plato's Republic. Honour and praise incite people to act properly. Christian value.

Children under the age of five sit together in the nurses' den. All other minors, among whom they include boys and girls up to the age of marriage, either wait on table, or, if not old and strong enough for that, stand by in absolute silence. Both groups eat whatever is handed to them by those sitting at the table, and have no other set time for their meals.

Raising the young

At the middle of the first table sits the syphogrant with his wife. This is the place of greatest honour, and from this table, which is placed at the highest level of the hall and crosswise to the other tables, the whole gathering can be seen. Two of the eldest sit next to them – for the seating is always by groups of four. But if there is a church in the district, the priest and his wife sit with the syphogrant so as to preside. On both sides of them sit younger people, next to them older people again, and so through the hall: thus those of about the same age sit together, yet are mingled with others of a different age. The reason for this, as they explain it, is that the dignity of the aged, and the respect due to them, may restrain the younger people from improper freedom of words or gestures, since nothing said or done at table can pass unnoticed by the old, who are present on every side.

Priest before prince. But now even bishops act as servants to royalty

Young mixed with old

Dishes of food are not served down the tables in order from top to bottom, but all the old persons, who are seated in conspicuous places, are served first with the best food, and then equal shares are given to the rest. The old people, as they feel inclined, give their neighbours a share of those delicacies which were not plentiful enough to go around. Thus due respect is paid to seniority, yet everyone enjoys some of the benefits.

Respect for the elderly

Nowadays even monks scarcely do this

They begin every lunch and supper with some reading on a moral topic,[44] but keep it brief lest it become a bore. Taking their cue from this, the elders introduce proper topics of conversation, but not gloomy or dull

Table talk

ones. They never monopolise the conversation with long monologues, but are eager to hear what the young people say. In fact, they deliberately draw them out, in order to discover the natural temper and quality of each one's mind, as revealed in the freedom of mealtime talk.

Modern physicians condemn this practice

Their lunches are light, their suppers more generous, because lunch is followed by work, supper by rest and a night's sleep, which they think particularly helpful to good digestion. No evening meal passes without

Music at mealtimes

music, and the dessert course is never scanted; they burn incense and scatter perfume, omitting nothing which will cheer up the diners. For

Innocent pleasures are not to be rejected

they are somewhat inclined to think that no kind of pleasure is forbidden, provided harm does not come of it.

This is the pattern of life in the city; but in the country, where they are farther removed from neighbours, they all eat in their own homes. No family lacks for food since, after all, whatever city-dwellers eat comes originally from those in the country.

THE TRAVELS OF THE UTOPIANS

Any individuals who want to visit friends living in another city, or simply to see the place itself, can easily obtain permission from their syphogrants and tranibors, unless there is some need for them at home. They travel together in groups, taking a letter from the governor granting leave to travel and fixing a day of return. They are given a wagon and a public slave to drive the oxen and look after them, but unless women are in the company they dispense with the wagon as a burden and a hindrance. Wherever they go, though they take nothing with them, they never lack for anything, because they are at home everywhere. If they stay more than a day in one place, each one practises his trade there, and is kindly received by his fellow artisans.

Anyone who takes upon himself to leave his district without permission, and is caught without the governor's letter, is treated with contempt, brought back as a runaway, and severely punished. If he is bold enough to try it a second time, he is made a slave. Anyone who is eager to stroll

---

[44] Humanists were fond of this ancient social custom – which, as the gloss implies, lingered longest in the monasteries. Thomas Stapleton says it was the practice at More's table (*The Life and Illustrious Martyrdom of Sir Thomas More*, p. 89).

about his own district is not prevented, provided he first obtains his father's permission and his spouse's consent. But wherever he goes in the countryside, he gets no food until he has completed either a morning's or an afternoon's stint of work.[45] On these terms he may go where he pleases within his own district, yet be just as useful to the city as if he were in it.

So you see that nowhere is there any chance to loaf or any pretext for evading work; there are no wine-bars, or ale-houses, or brothels; no chances for corruption; no hiding places; no spots for secret meetings. Because they live in the full view of all, they are bound to be either working at their usual trades or enjoying their leisure in a respectable way. Such customs must necessarily result in plenty of life's good things, and since they share everything equally, it follows that no one can ever be reduced to poverty or forced to beg.

O sacred society, worthy of imitation, even by Christians!

Equality for all results in enough for each

In the senate at Amaurot (to which, as I said before, three representatives come every year from each city), they first determine where there are shortages and surpluses, and promptly satisfy one district's shortage with another's surplus. These are outright gifts; those who give get nothing in return from those who receive. Though they give freely to one city asking for nothing in return, they get what they need from another to which they gave nothing. Thus the whole island is like a single family.[46]

The commonwealth is nothing but a kind of extended family

After they have accumulated enough for themselves – and this they consider to be a full two-years' store, because next year's crop is always uncertain – then they export their surpluses to other countries: great quantities of grain, honey, wool, flax, timber, scarlet and purple dyestuffs, hides, wax, tallow and leather, as well as livestock. One seventh of all these things they give freely to the poor of the importing country, and the rest they sell at moderate prices. In exchange they receive not only such goods as they lack at home (in fact, about the only important thing they lack is iron) but immense quantities of silver and gold. They have been carrying on trade for a long time now, and have accumulated a greater supply of the precious metals than you would believe possible. As a result, they now care very little whether they sell for cash or on credit, and most payments to them actually take the form of promissory notes. However, in all such transactions, they never trust individuals but insist that the foreign city become officially responsible. When the day of payment comes, the city

Utopian business dealings

Nowhere do they fail to be mindful of their community

---

[45] The Utopians in this rule agree with St Paul: II Thessalonians 3:10.

[46] According to Plutarch, Lycurgus, returning from a journey just after harvest, and seeing 'the heaps of grain standing parallel and equal to one another, . . . said to them that were by: "All Laconia looks like a family estate newly divided among many brothers"' ('Lycurgus' VIII.4).

How money can be useful

collects the money from private debtors, puts it into the treasury, and enjoys the use of it till the Utopians claim payment. Most of it, in fact, is never claimed. The Utopians think it is hardly right to take what they don't need away from people who do need it. But if there is a need to lend some part of the money to another nation, then they call it in – as they do also when they must wage war. This is the only reason that they keep such an immense treasure at home, as a protection against extreme peril or sudden emergency. They use it above all to hire, at extravagant rates of pay, foreign mercenaries, whom they would much rather risk in battle

Better to avoid war by bribery or guile than to wage it with great loss of human blood

than their own citizens. They know very well that for large enough sums of money many of the enemy's soldiers themselves can be bought off or set at odds with one another, either openly or secretly.

For this reason, therefore, they have a vast treasure in reserve, but they do not keep it like a treasure. I'm really quite ashamed to tell you how they do keep it, because you probably won't believe me; I would not

O crafty fellow!

have believed it myself if someone else had simply told me about it, but I was there and saw it with my own eyes. As a general rule, the more different anything is from what the listeners are used to, the harder it is to believe. But considering that all their other customs are so unlike ours, a sensible judge will perhaps not be surprised that they treat gold and silver quite differently from the way we do. After all, they never do use money among themselves, but keep it only for a contingency that may or may not actually arise. So in the meanwhile they keep gold and silver (of which money is made) in such a way that no one will value them beyond

As far as utility goes, gold is inferior to iron

what the metals themselves deserve. Anyone can see, for example, that iron in itself is far superior to either;[47] men could not live without iron, by heaven, any more than without fire or water. But Nature granted to gold and silver no function with which we cannot easily dispense. Human folly has made them precious because they are rare. In contrast, Nature, like a most indulgent mother, has placed her best gifts out in the open, like air, water and the earth itself; vain and unprofitable things she has hidden away in remote places.

And so, if in Utopia gold and silver were kept locked up in some tower, smart fools among the common people might concoct a story that the governor and senate were out to cheat ordinary folk and get some advantage for themselves. Of course, the gold and silver might be put into plate-ware and such handiwork, but then they see that in case of necessity the

---

[47] More expresses the same view *in propria persona* in two works of 1534: *A Dialogue of Comfort against Tribulation* (*CW*, XII, 207); *A Treatise upon the Passion* (*CW*, XIII, 8).

people would not want to give up articles on which they had begun to fix their hearts – only to melt them down for soldiers' pay. To avoid these problems they thought of a plan which conforms with the rest of their institutions as sharply as it contrasts with our own. Unless one has actually seen it working, their plan may seem incredible, because we prize gold so highly and are so careful about guarding it. While they eat from earthenware dishes and drink from glass cups, finely made but inexpensive, their chamber pots and all their humblest vessels, for use in the common halls and even in private homes, are made of gold and silver.[48] Moreover, the chains and heavy shackles of slaves are also made of these metals. Finally, criminals who are to bear the mark of some disgraceful act are forced to wear golden rings in their ears and on their fingers, golden chains around their necks, and even golden headbands. Thus they hold up gold and silver to scorn in every conceivable way. As a result, if they had to part with their entire supply of these metals, which other people give up with as much agony as if they were being disembowelled, no one would feel it any more than the loss of a penny.

[margin note: O magnificent scorn for gold! Looking down for Gold the mark of infamy riches.]

They pick up pearls by the seashore, and also diamonds and garnets from certain cliffs, but never go out of set purpose to look for them.[49] If they happen to find some, they polish them and give them as decorations to the children, who feel proud and pleased with such ornaments during the early years of childhood. But when they have grown a bit older and notice that only small children like this kind of toy, they lay them aside. Their parents don't have to say anything; they simply put these trifles away out of shame, just as our children, when they grow up, put away their marbles, baubles and dolls.

[margin note: Gems the playthings of children]

These customs so different from those of other people also produce a quite different cast of mind: this never became clearer to me than it did in the case of the Anemolian[50] ambassadors, who came to Amaurot while I was there. Because they came to discuss important business, the national council had assembled ahead of time, three citizens from each city. The

[margin note: A neat tale How gay.]

[48] Tacitus reports of the ancient Germans (whose 'primitive' society he admires in various respects) that 'One may see among them silver vessels... treated as of no more value than earthenware' (*Germania* 5). Vespucci notes the native Americans' indifference to gold and gems (*Four Voyages*, p. 98), as does the explorer Pietro Martire d'Anghiera (1457–1526), who tells of a tribe that 'used kitchen and other common utensils made of gold' (*De Orbe Novo* [*On the New World*], trans. Francis A. MacNutt, 2 vols. (New York and London, 1912; rpt New York, 1970), I, 221).

[49] Similarly, Tacitus reports of the ancient Britons that though their sea produces pearls, 'they are gathered only when thrown up on shore' (*Agricola* 12).

[50] From *anemolios*, 'windy'.

ambassadors from nearby nations, who had visited Utopia before and knew the local customs, understood that fine clothing was not respected in that land, silk was despised, and gold a badge of contempt; therefore they always came in the very plainest of their clothes. But the Anemolians, who lived farther off and had had fewer dealings with them, had heard only that they all dressed alike and very simply; so they took for granted that their hosts had nothing to wear that they didn't put on. Being themselves rather more proud than wise, they decided to dress as elegantly as the very gods, and dazzle the eyes of the poor Utopians with the splendour of their garb.

And so the three ambassadors made a grand entry with a suite of a hundred attendants, all in clothing of many colours, and most in silk. Being noblemen at home, the ambassadors were arrayed in cloth of gold, with heavy gold chains round their necks, gold earrings, gold rings on their fingers and sparkling strings of pearls and gems hanging on their caps. In fact, they were decked out in all the articles which in Utopia are used to punish slaves, shame wrongdoers or entertain infants. It was a sight to see how they strutted when they compared their finery with the dress of the Utopians, who had poured out into the streets. But it was just as funny to see how wide they fell of the mark, and how far they were from getting the consideration they thought they would get. Except for a very few Utopians who for some good reason had visited foreign countries, all the onlookers considered this splendid pomp a mark of disgrace. They therefore bowed to all the humblest of the party as lords, and took the ambassadors, because of their golden chains, to be slaves, passing them by without any reverence at all. You might have seen children, who had themselves thrown away their pearls and gems, nudge their mothers when *O what a craftsman!* they saw the ambassadors' jewelled caps and say, 'Look at that big lout, mother, who's still wearing pearls and jewels as if he were a little boy!' But the mother, in all seriousness, would say, 'Quiet, son, I think he is one of the ambassadors' fools.'

Others found fault with the golden chains as useless because they were so flimsy any slave could break them, and so loose that he could easily shake them off and run away anywhere he wanted, foot-loose and fancy-free.

But after the ambassadors had spent a couple of days among the Utopians, they saw the immense amounts of gold which were as thoroughly despised there as they were prized at home. They saw too that more gold and silver went into making chains and shackles for a single runaway slave than into costuming all three of them. Somewhat ashamed and crestfallen, they put away all the finery in which they had strutted so arrogantly – especially after they had talked with the Utopians enough to learn their customs and opinions.[51]

They marvel that any mortal can take pleasure in the dubious sparkle of a tiny little jewel or gemstone, when he has a star, or the sun itself, to look at. They are amazed at the madness of any man who considers himself a nobler fellow because he wears clothing of specially fine wool. No matter how fine the thread, they say, a sheep wore it once, and still was nothing but a sheep.[52] They are surprised that gold, a useless commodity in itself, is everywhere valued so highly that man himself, who for his own purposes conferred this value on it, is considered far less valuable than the gold – so much so that a dunderhead who has no more brains than a post, and who is as vicious as he is foolish, should command a great many wise and good men, simply because he happens to have a big pile of gold coins. Yet if this master should lose his money to the lowest rascal in his household (as can happen by chance or through some legal trick – for the law can produce reversals as violent as Fortune herself), he would soon become the servant of his servant, as if he were personally attached to the coins, and a mere appendage to them. Even more than this, they are appalled at those people who practically worship a rich man, though they neither owe him anything nor are under his thumb in any way. What impresses them is simply the fact that the man is rich. Yet all the while they know he is so mean and grasping that as long as he lives not a single little penny out of that great mound of money will ever come their way.

These and the like attitudes the Utopians have picked up partly from their upbringing, since the institutions of their commonwealth are completely opposed to such folly, partly from instruction and good books. For though not many people in each city are excused from labour and assigned to scholarship full-time (these are persons who from childhood have given evidence of excellent character, unusual intelligence and devotion to learning), every child gets an introduction to good literature, and

*'Dubious'
because the
gems are fake,
or their glitter
is feeble and
scanty*

*How true and
how apt!*

*How much wiser
are the Utopians
than the ruck
of Christians*

---

[51] The story of the Anemolian ambassadors owes something to Lucian's 'The Wisdom of Nigrinus', in which a visiting millionaire makes a fool of himself by stalking around Athens in a purple robe: 'with his crowd of attendants and his gay clothes and jewelry, ... [he] expected to be looked up to as a happy man. But they thought the creature unfortunate, and undertook to educate him ... His gay clothes and his purple gown they stripped from him very neatly by making fun of his flowery colours, saying "Spring already?" "How did that peacock get here?" "Perhaps it's his mother's" and the like' (sect. 13).

[52] The source is Lucian's 'Demonax' (sect. 41). More repeated the idea years later (1534) in *A Treatise upon the Passion* (*CW*, XIII, 8).

throughout their lives many people, men and women alike, devote the free time I've mentioned to reading.

Training and studies of the Utopians
They study all the branches of learning in their native tongue,[53] which is not deficient in terminology or unpleasant in sound and adapts itself as well as any to the expression of thought. This same language, or something close to it, is diffused through much of that part of the world, except that everywhere else it is corrupted to various degrees.

Before we came there the Utopians had never so much as heard about a single one of those philosophers[54] whose names are so celebrated in *Music, dialectic and* our part of the world. Yet in music, dialectic, arithmetic and geometry[55] *mathematics* they have found out just about the same things as our great men of the past. But while they equal the ancients in almost all subjects, they are far from matching the inventions of our modern logicians. In fact they have *The passage seems a* not discovered even one of those elaborate rules about restrictions, am- *bit satiric* plifications and suppositions which young men here study in the *Parva logicalia*.[56] They are so far from being able to speculate on 'second intentions'[57] that not one of them was able to see 'man-in-general', though we pointed straight at him with our fingers, and he is, as you well know, colossal and bigger than any giant.[58] On the other hand, they have learned

[53] Perhaps More intends an implicit contrast with Europe, where Latin rather than the vernaculars was the language of schools.

[54] As the following sentences indicate, 'philosophers' is used here in the old, broad sense that includes those learned in the natural and mathematical sciences as well as students of metaphysics and moral philosophy.

[55] Music, arithmetic and geometry, together with astronomy (below), constitute the advanced division – the *quadrivium* – of the traditional Seven Liberal Arts. Dialectic joins with grammar and rhetoric to constitute the elementary division – the *trivium*. Grammar and rhetoric would be encompassed in the Utopians' study of 'good literature'.

[56] Probably the *Parva logicalia* (*Little Logicbook*) of Peter of Spain (d. 1277), though more than one textbook bore this name. More mounts a sustained attack on the 'modern logicians' (i.e., scholastic dialecticians) in his long open letter to the Dutch theologian and philologist Maarten van Dorp, composed in the same year (1515) in which he wrote Book II of *Utopia*. In the letter, More suggests that the *Parva logicalia* is 'so called probably because it contains little logic': 'it is worth having a look at its chapters on so-called suppositions, on ampliations, restrictions, and appellations, and everywhere else, to see all of the pointless and even false little precepts it does contain' (*CW*, XV, 29). On the technical terms, see the discussion in Daniel Kinney's introduction to the letter (XV, liv–lv).

[57] 'First intentions' are the direct apprehensions of things; 'second intentions' are purely abstract conceptions, derived from considering the relations of first intentions.

[58] The Utopians' blindness to 'man-in-general' (i.e., man as a 'universal') makes them just opposite to the scholastic philosophers mocked by Erasmus' Folly, who, 'though ignorant even of themselves and sometimes not able to see the ditch or stone lying in their path, either because most of them are half-blind or because their minds are far away, . . . still boast that they can see ideas, universals, separate forms, prime matters, quiddities, ecceities' (*CWE*, XXVII, 126).

to plot expertly the courses of the stars and the movements of the heavenly bodies. To this end they have devised a number of different instruments by which they compute with the greatest exactness the course and position of the sun, the moon and the other stars that are visible in their area of the sky. As for the conjunctions and oppositions of the planets and that whole deceitful business of divination by the stars, they have never so much as dreamed of it.[59] From long experience in observation, they are able to forecast rains, winds and other changes in the weather. But as to the causes of the weather, of the tides in the sea and its saltiness, and, finally, the origins and nature of the heavens and the earth, they have various opinions. To some extent they treat of these matters as our ancient philosophers did, but they are also like them in disagreeing with one another. So too, when they propose a new theory they differ from our ancient philosophers and yet reach no consensus at all among themselves.

The study of the stars

Yet these astrologers are revered by Christians to this day

Physics the most uncertain study of all

In matters of moral philosophy, they carry on the same arguments as we do. They inquire into the goods of the mind and goods of the body and external goods.[60] They ask whether the name of 'good' can be applied to all three, or whether it refers only to goods of the mind.[61] They discuss virtue and pleasure, but their chief concern is what to think of human happiness, and whether it consists of one thing or of more.[62] On this point, they seem rather too much inclined to the view which favours pleasure, in which they conclude that all or the most important part of human happiness consists.[63] And what is more surprising, they seek support for

Ethics

Higher and lower goods

Supreme goods

The Utopians consider honest pleasure the measure of happiness

---

[59] More wrote a number of Latin poems ridiculing judicial astrology (see *CW*, III, Part II, 133–7, 159, 167, 215–17).

[60] This threefold classification of goods appears in Plato (*Laws* III.697B, V.743E) but is especially associated with Aristotle (*Nicomachean Ethics* I.viii.2, *Politics* VII.i.3–4) and Aristotelian tradition. Of course the Utopians have never heard of Plato, Aristotle or any other European philosopher, and one point of the account of Utopian philosophy is that natural reason will lead earnest, ingenious thinkers to the same set of problems and positions at any time and place. The other, main point is to argue that the moral norms derivable from reason are consistent with those of Christianity.

[61] The first position is especially that of the Aristotelians, the second that of the Stoics.

[62] The topics of virtue and pleasure are linked especially in discussions – like Cicero's *On the Supreme Good and Evil* – of the relative merits of Stoic and Epicurean ethics. The idea that happiness is the end of life is axiomatic in all the major philosophical schools; whether it depends on one thing or more than one depends on how many *goods* there are.

[63] I.e., the Utopians are inclined to the Epicurean position. The remark launches a long passage that constitutes, as Surtz points out (*The Praise of Pleasure*, pp. 9–11), a praise of pleasure reminiscent of Erasmus' praise of folly. The praise of pleasure, and of Epicurus, had an important precedent in Lorenzo Valla's *On the True and False Good* (1444–9), which in its original version (1431) was called *On Pleasure*. Valla's work furthered the gradual, qualified humanist rehabilitation of Epicurus that began with Petrarch and Boccaccio and in which

First principles of
philosophy to be
sought in religion
this comfortable opinion from their religion, which is serious and strict, indeed almost stern and forbidding. For they never discuss happiness without joining to the rational arguments of philosophy certain principles drawn from religion. Without these religious principles, they think that reason by itself is weak and defective in its efforts to investigate true happiness.

Utopian theology

The religious principles they invoke are of this nature: that the soul is immortal, and by God's beneficence born for happiness; and that after this

The immortality of the soul, about which nowadays no small number even of Christians have their doubts.[64]

life, rewards are appointed for our virtues and good deeds, punishments for our sins. Though these are indeed religious principles, they think that reason leads us to believe and accept them.[65] And they add unhesitatingly that if these beliefs were rejected, no one would be so stupid as not to feel that he should seek pleasure, regardless of right and wrong. His only care would be to keep a lesser pleasure from standing in the way of a greater one, and to avoid pleasures that are inevitably followed by pain.[66] They

(after Valla) the Florentine philosophers Marsilio Ficino and Pico della Mirandola, as well as Erasmus, played a part: these writers pointed out that, contrary to popular opinion, Epicurus did not mean by 'pleasure' mere sensuality. See, in addition to Surtz, D. C. Allen, 'The rehabilitation of Epicurus and his theory of pleasure in the early Renaissance' (*Studies in Philology*, 41 (1944), 1–15); Edgar Wind, *Pagan Mysteries in the Renaissance*, pp. 48–71; Logan, *The Meaning of More's 'Utopia'*, pp. 144–7, 154–63; and *The Cambridge History of Renaissance Philosophy*, pp. 374–86. Vespucci's observation about the native Americans may also be relevant: 'Since their life is so entirely given over to pleasure, I should style it Epicurean' (*Four Voyages*, p. 97; see also *New World*, p. 6).

[64] The immortality of the soul, formulated as a dogma of the Church by the Lateran Council of 1513, was the subject of much philosophical discussion in the fifteenth and sixteenth centuries. For an overview, see Paul Oskar Kristeller, *Renaissance Thought and Its Sources* (New York, 1979), pp. 181–96.

[65] Thomistic theology supports this view. As Surtz observes, Aquinas maintains that 'man, without supernatural grace, can come to the knowledge...of moral and religious truths, such as the existence and perfections of God, the immortality and spirituality of the soul, the duties of man toward his Creator, and the punishments and rewards of the future life' ('Interpretations of *Utopia*', *Catholic Historical Review*, 38 (1952), 163). In *A Dialogue Concerning Heresies* (1529), More says that 'all the whole number of the old philosophers...found out by nature and reason that there was a god either maker or governor or both of all this whole engine of the world' (*CW*, VI, 73).

Since Epicurus maintained the indifference of the gods and the mortality of the soul, these principles sharply distinguish Utopian philosophy from classical Epicureanism and lead the Utopians to a view of the good life similar to the Christian view.

[66] This is the first of three citations of Epicurus' rules for choosing between competing pleasures (see Introduction, p. xxviii). The rules find perhaps their most influential statement in Cicero's dialogue *On the Supreme Good and Evil*, where the Epicurean Torquatus explains that 'The wise man always holds...to this principle of selection: he rejects pleasures to secure other greater pleasures, or else he endures pains to avoid worse pains' (I.x.33; cf. I.x.36). Another formulation occurs in a letter of Epicurus quoted by Diogenes Laertius: 'since pleasure is

think you would have to be actually crazy to pursue harsh and painful virtue, give up the pleasures of life, and suffer pain from which you can expect no advantage. For if there is no reward after death, you have no compensation for having passed your entire existence without pleasure, that is, miserably.[67]

Not every pleasure is desirable, neither is pain to be sought, except for the sake of virtue

To be sure, they think happiness is found, not in every kind of pleasure, but only in good and honest pleasure. Virtue itself, they say, draws our nature to pleasure of this sort, as to the supreme good. There is an opposed school which declares that virtue is itself happiness.[68]

They define virtue as living according to nature; and God, they say, created us to that end. When an individual obeys the dictates of reason in choosing one thing and avoiding another, he is following nature.[69] Now above all reason urges us to love and venerate the Divine Majesty to whom we owe our existence and our capacity for happiness. Secondly, nature prescribes that we should lead a life as free of anxiety and as full of joy as possible, and that we should help all others – because of our natural fellowship – toward that end. The most hard-faced eulogist of virtue and the grimmest enemy of pleasure, while he invites you to toil and sleepless nights and mortification, still admonishes you to relieve the poverty and distress of others as best you can. It is especially praiseworthy, they think, when we provide for the comfort and welfare of our fellow creatures. Nothing is more humane (and humanity is the virtue most proper to human beings) than to relieve the misery of others, remove all sadness from their lives, and restore them to enjoyment, that is, pleasure.

This is like Stoic doctrine

our first and native good, for that reason we do not choose every pleasure whatsoever, but ofttimes pass over many pleasures when a greater annoyance ensues from them' (*Lives of Eminent Philosophers* X.129). The Utopians accept these rules of selection, but recognise that their application leads to quite different conclusions about the good life depending on whether religious principles are factored into the individual's calculations.

[67] The Utopians, that is, reject the claim that purely rational and mundane considerations provide sufficient sanction for moral behaviour. In this respect, too, they differ from Epicurus, who thought that the mental pleasure of moral actions and the fear of detection in wrongdoing provided adequate incentives to virtue (cf. Diogenes Laertius X.131–2).

[68] This second position is that of the Stoics, who declared that virtue constitutes happiness, whether it leads to pleasure or not – indeed, that a man who is enduring great misery may derive happiness from his knowledge of his own virtuous behaviour. As the following marginal gloss points out, the Utopians' *definition* of virtue is also Stoic. See, for example, Cicero, *On the Supreme Good and Evil* III.ix.31.

[69] Throughout the ensuing discussion, 'reason' has the sense of 'right reason' – the faculty that, according to a conception passed on by the Stoics to the Middle Ages and the Renaissance, enables human beings to distinguish right and wrong with instinctive clarity; that is, to apprehend the natural law.

Well, then, why doesn't nature equally invite all of us to do the same thing for ourselves? Either a joyful life (that is, one of pleasure) is a good thing, or it isn't. If it isn't, then you should not help anyone to it – indeed, you ought to take it away from everyone you can, as being harmful and deadly to them. But if you are allowed, indeed obliged, to help others to such a life, why not first of all yourself, to whom you owe no less favour than to anyone else? For when nature prompts you to be kind to your neighbours, she does not mean that you should be cruel and merciless to yourself. Thus, they say, nature herself prescribes for us a joyous life, in other words, pleasure, as the goal of all our actions; and living according to her rules is to be defined as virtue. But as nature bids mortals to make one another's lives cheerful, as far as they can – and she does so rightly, for no one is placed so far above the rest that he is nature's sole concern, and she cherishes equally all those to whom she has granted the same form – so she repeatedly warns you not to seek your own advantage in ways that cause misfortune to others.

But now some people cultivate pain as if it were the essence of religion, rather than incidental to performance of a pious duty or the result of natural necessity – and thus to be borne, not pursued

Consequently, they think that one should abide not only by private agreements but by those public laws which control the distribution of vital goods, such as are the very substance of pleasure. Any such laws, when properly promulgated by a good king, or ratified by the common consent of a people free of tyranny and deception, should be observed. So long as they are observed, to pursue your own interests is prudent; to pursue the public interest as well is pious; but to pursue your own pleasure by depriving others of theirs is unjust. On the other hand, to decrease your own pleasure in order to augment that of others is a work of humanity and benevolence, which never fails to reward the doer over and above his sacrifice. You may be repaid for your kindness, and in any case your consciousness of having done a good deed, and recalling the affection and good will of those whom you have benefited, gives your mind more pleasure than your body would have drawn from the things you forfeited. Finally, as religion easily persuades a well-disposed mind to believe, God will requite the loss of a brief and transitory pleasure here with immense and never-ending joy in heaven. And so they conclude, after carefully considering and weighing the matter, that all our actions, including even the virtues exercised within them, look toward pleasure as their happiness and final goal.[70]

Contracts and laws

Mutual assistance

A form of Hedonism

---

[70] This is Epicurus' view, as reported by Diogenes Laertius: 'we choose the virtues too on account of pleasure and not for their own sake' (X.138).

By pleasure they understand every state or movement of body or mind *What pleasure is* in which we find delight according to the behests of nature.[71] They have good reason for adding that the desire is according to nature. By following our senses and right reason we may discover what is pleasant by nature: it is a delight that does not injure others, does not preclude a greater pleasure, and is not followed by pain. But all pleasures which are against nature, and which men agree to call 'delightful' only by the emptiest of fictions (as if *False pleasures* one could change the real nature of things just by changing their names), do not, they have decided, really make for happiness; in fact, they say such pleasures often preclude happiness. And the reason is that once they have taken over someone's mind, they leave no room for true and genuine delights, and they completely fill the mind with a false notion of pleasure. For there are a great many things which have no genuine sweetness in them but are for the most part actually bitter – yet which, through the perverse enticement of evil desires, are not only considered very great pleasures but are even included among the primary reasons for living.

Among the pursuers of this false pleasure, they include those whom I mentioned before, the people who think themselves finer folk because *Mistaken pride* they wear finer clothes. On this one point, these people are twice mistaken: *in fancy dress* first in supposing their clothes better than anyone else's, and then in thinking themselves better. As far as a garment's usefulness goes, why is fine woollen thread better than coarse? Yet they strut about and think their clothes make them more substantial, as if they were exalted by nature herself, rather than their own fantasies. Therefore, honours they would never have dared to expect if they were plainly dressed they demand as rightfully due to their fancy suit, and they grow indignant if someone passes them by without showing special respect.

Isn't it the same kind of stupidity to be pleased by empty, merely cer- *Foolish honours* emonial honours? What true or natural pleasure can you get from some-one's bent knee or bared head? Will the creaks in your own knees be eased thereby, or the madness in your head? The phantom of false pleasure is illustrated by others who are pleasantly mad with delight over their own blue blood, flatter themselves on their nobility, and gloat over all the long *Empty nobility* line of rich ancestors they happen to have (and wealth is the only sort of nobility these days), and especially over their ancient family estates.

---

[71] Both Plato (*Philebus* 36C–52B) and Aristotle (*Nicomachean Ethics* I.viii.II, VII.v.I) acknowledge the importance to the good life of physical as well as mental pleasures and distinguish between true pleasures – which are 'pleasant by nature' – and false ones. The ensuing discussion relies heavily on their arguments.

Even if these ancestors have left them no estates to inherit, or if they've squandered all of their inheritance, they don't consider themselves a bit less noble.[72]

The silliest pleasure of all: gemstones

In the same class they put those people I described before, who are captivated by jewels and gemstones, and think themselves divinely happy if they get a good specimen, especially of the sort that happens to be fashionable in their country at the time – for not every country nor every era values the same kinds. But collectors will not make an offer for a stone till it's taken out of its gold setting, and even then they will not buy unless the dealer guarantees and gives security that it is a true and genuine stone. What they fear is that their eyes will be deceived by a counterfeit. But why should a counterfeit give any less pleasure, if, when you look at it, your eyes cannot distinguish it from a genuine gem? Both should be of equal value to you – no less so, by heaven, than they would be to a blind man.[73]

Popular opinion gives gems their value or takes it away

What about those who pile up money, not for any real purpose, but just to look at it? Do they feel a true pleasure, or aren't they simply deluded by a show of pleasure? Or what about those with the opposite vice, who hide away gold they will never use and perhaps never even see again? In their anxiety not to lose it, they actually do lose it. For what else happens when you deprive yourself, and perhaps all other people too, of a chance to use your gold, by burying it in the ground? And yet, when you've hidden your treasure away, you are overjoyed, as if your mind were now at ease. Suppose someone stole it, and you died ten years later, knowing nothing of the theft. During all those ten years, what did it matter to you whether the money was stolen or not? In either case, it was equally useless to you.[74]

A strange fancy, and much to the point

To these foolish pleasures they add gambling, which they have heard about, though they've never tried it, as well as hunting and hawking. What pleasure can there be, they say, in throwing dice on a playing-table? If there were any pleasure in the action, wouldn't doing it over and over again make one tired of it? What pleasure can there be in listening to the barking and howling of dogs – isn't that rather a disgusting noise? Is any

Dicing

Hunting

---

[72] This passage – like the catalogue of false pleasures as a whole – is close in substance and tone to *The Praise of Folly*. Folly comments on 'those who are no better than the humblest worker but take extraordinary pride in an empty title of nobility' (*CWE*, XXVII, 116).

[73] There are similar sentiments in More's *Treatise upon the Passion* (*CW*, XIII, 8) and *The Last Things* (*c.* 1522) (*CW*, I, 130). Erasmus' Folly tells how More 'made his new bride a present of some jewels which were copies, and . . . persuaded her that they were not only real and genuine but also of unique and incalculable value' (*CWE*, XXVII, 118).

[74] There is a very similar passage in More's *Dialogue of Comfort* (*CW*, XII, 210).

more pleasure felt when a dog chases a hare than when a dog chases a dog? If what you like is fast running, there's plenty of that in both cases; they're just about the same. But if what you really want is slaughter, if you want to see a creature torn apart under your eyes – you ought to feel nothing but pity when you see the little hare fleeing from the hound, the weak creature tormented by the stronger, the fearful and timid beast brutalised by the savage one, the harmless hare killed by the cruel hound. And so the Utopians, who regard this whole activity of hunting as unworthy of free men, have accordingly assigned it to their butchers, who, as I said before, are all slaves. In their eyes, hunting is the lowest thing even butchers can do. In the slaughterhouse, their work is more useful and honest, since there they kill animals only out of necessity; whereas the hunter seeks nothing but his own pleasure from killing and mutilating some poor little creature. Taking such relish in the sight of slaughter, even if only of beasts, springs, in their opinion, from a cruel disposition, or else finally produces cruelty, through the constant practice of such brutal pleasures.[75]

Yet today this is the chosen art of our court- divinities

Common opinion considers these activities, and countless others like them, to be pleasures; but the Utopians say flatly they have nothing at all to do with real pleasure, since there's nothing naturally pleasant about them. They often please the senses, and in this they are like pleasure, but that does not alter their view. The enjoyment doesn't arise from the nature of the experience itself but from the perverse habits of the mob, which cause them to mistake the bitter for the sweet, just as pregnant women whose taste has been distorted sometimes think pitch and tallow taste sweeter than honey. A person's taste may be depraved by disease or by custom, but that doesn't change the nature of pleasure or of anything else.

Morbid tastes of pregnant women

They distinguish several classes of pleasures which they confess to be genuine, attributing some to the mind and others to the body. Those of the mind are knowledge and the delight that arises from contemplating the truth, the gratification of looking back on a well-spent life, and the unquestioning hope of happiness to come.

Classes of true pleasure

---

[75] In one of More's Latin poems (*CW*, III, Part II, 123), a hunter 'looks on and smiles' as his hound tears a rabbit to pieces: 'Insensate breed, more savage than any beast, to find cruel amusement in bitter slaughter!' Similarly, Folly satirises those who 'declare they take unbelievable pleasure in the hideous blast of the hunting horn and baying of the hounds … All they achieve by this incessant hunting and eating wild game is their own degeneration – they're practically wild beasts themselves' (*CWE*, XXVII, 112–13). By contrast, hunting is praised as good exercise and good practice for war by Plato (*Laws* VII.823B–824B) and other classical and later writers, including many of More's and Erasmus' fellow humanists.

Bodily pleasures   Pleasures of the body they also divide into two classes. The first is that which fills the senses with immediate delight. Sometimes this happens when bodily organs that have been weakened by natural heat are restored with food and drink; sometimes it happens when we eliminate some excess in the body, as when we move our bowels, generate children, or relieve an itch somewhere by rubbing or scratching it. Now and then pleasure arises, not from restoring a deficiency or discharging an excess, but from something that affects and excites our senses with a hidden but unmistakable force, and attracts them to itself. Such is the power of music.

The second kind of bodily pleasure they describe as nothing but the calm and harmonious state of the body, its state of health when undisturbed by any disorder. Health itself, when not oppressed by pain, gives pleasure, without any external excitement at all. Even though it appeals less directly to the senses than the gross gratifications of eating and drinking, many
To enjoy anything, one needs good health still consider this to be the greatest pleasure of all. Most of the Utopians regard it as the foundation and basis of all the pleasures, since by itself alone it can make life peaceful and desirable, whereas without it there is no possibility of any other pleasure. Mere absence of pain, without positive health, they regard as insensibility, not pleasure.

Some have maintained that a stable and tranquil state of health is not really a pleasure, on the ground that the presence of health cannot be felt except in contrast to its opposite. The Utopians (who have considered the matter thoroughly) long ago rejected this opinion. Quite the contrary, they nearly all agree that health is crucial to pleasure. Since pain is inherent in disease, they say, and pain is the bitter enemy of pleasure just as disease is the enemy of health, then pleasure must be inherent in quiet good health. Whether pain is the disease itself or just an accompanying effect makes, they think, no real difference, since the effect is the same either way. Indeed, whether health is itself a pleasure or simply the cause of pleasure (as fire is the cause of heat), the fact remains that those who have stable health must also have pleasure.

When we eat, they say, what happens is that health, which was starting to fade, takes food as its ally in the fight against hunger. While our health gains strength, the simple process of returning vigour gives us pleasure and refreshment. If our health feels delight in the struggle, will it not rejoice when the victory has been won? When at last it is happily restored to its original strength, which was its aim all through the conflict, will it at once become insensible and fail to recognise and embrace its own good? The idea that health cannot be felt they consider very far from the truth.

What man, when he's awake, can fail to feel that he's in good health – except one who isn't? Is anyone so torpid and dull that he won't admit health is agreeable and delightful to him? And what is delight except pleasure under another name?

Among the various pleasures, then, they seek primarily those of the mind, and prize them most highly. The foremost mental pleasure, they believe, arises from practice of the virtues and consciousness of a good life.[76] Among pleasures of the body, they give first place to health. As for eating, drinking and other delights of that sort, they consider them desirable, but only for the sake of health. They are not pleasant in themselves, but only as ways to withstand the insidious encroachments of sickness. A wise man would rather escape sickness altogether than have a medicine against it; he would rather prevent pain than find a palliative. And so it would be better not to need this kind of pleasure at all than to be assuaged by it.

Anyone who thinks happiness consists of this sort of pleasure must confess that his ideal life would be one spent in an endless round of hunger, thirst and itching, followed by eating, drinking, scratching and rubbing. Who can fail to see that such an existence is not only disgusting but miserable? These pleasures are certainly the lowest of all, as they are the most adulterated – for they never occur except in connection with the pains that are their contraries.[77] Hunger, for example, is linked to the pleasure of eating, and by no equal law, since the pain is sharper and lasts longer; it precedes the pleasure, and ends only when the pleasure ends with it. So they think pleasures of this sort should not be highly rated, except insofar as they are necessary to life. Yet they enjoy these pleasures too, and acknowledge gratefully the kindness of Mother Nature, who coaxes her children with enticing delight to do what in any case they must

---

[76] The formulation is from Cicero, who in *On Old Age* maintains that 'the most suitable defences of old age are the principles and practice of the virtues, which, if cultivated in every period of life, bring forth wonderful fruits at the close of a long and busy career, not only because they never fail you even at the very end of life . . . but also because it is most delightful to have the consciousness of a life well spent and the memory of many deeds worthily performed' (III.9).

The idea that pleasures can be ranked is found in both Plato (*Philebus* 57A–59D, 61D–E) and Aristotle (*Nicomachean Ethics* X.v.6–7). Both assert the superiority of mental pleasures to bodily ones (as does Epicurus: Diogenes Laertius X.137), but differ from the Utopians in regarding philosophic contemplation as the highest mental pleasure (*Republic* IX.583A; cf. 585D–586C; *Nicomachean Ethics* X.vii.1–viii.8).

[77] There is a similar passage in More's 1533 treatise *The Answer to a Poisoned Book* (*CW*, XI, 32). The idea that the restorative pleasures are contaminated by being mixed with the opposite pains comes directly from the *Philebus* (46C–D), as does the notion of a life given over to itching and scratching (46D, 47B; cf. *Gorgias* 494B–D).

do from necessity. How wretched life would be if the daily diseases of hunger and thirst had to be overcome by bitter potions and drugs, like some other diseases that afflict us less often!

Beauty, strength and agility, as special and pleasant gifts of Nature, they joyfully cherish. The pleasures of sound, sight and smell they also pursue as the agreeable seasonings of life, recognising that Nature intended them to be the particular province of man. No other kind of animal contemplates with delight the shape and loveliness of the universe, or enjoys odours (except in the way of searching for food), or distinguishes harmonious from dissonant sounds. But in all their pleasures, they observe this rule, that the lesser shall not interfere with the greater, and that no pleasure shall carry pain with it as a consequence. If a pleasure is dishonourable, they think it will inevitably lead to pain.

Moreover, they think it is crazy for a man to despise beauty of form, to impair his strength, to grind his agility down to torpor, to exhaust his body with fasts, to ruin his health and to scorn all other natural delights, unless by so doing he can more zealously serve the welfare of others or the common good. Then indeed he may expect a greater reward from God. But otherwise to inflict pain on oneself without doing anyone any good – simply to gain the empty and shadowy appearance of virtue, or to be able to bear with less distress adversities that may never come – this they consider to be absolutely crazy, the token of a mind cruel to itself as well as most ungrateful to Nature – as if, to avoid being in her debt, it is rejecting all her gifts.

Note this and note it well

This is the way they think about virtue and pleasure. Human reason, they think, can attain to no truer conclusions than these, unless a revelation from heaven should inspire men with holier notions. In all this, I have no time now to consider whether they are right or wrong, and don't feel obliged to do so. I have undertaken only to describe their principles, not to defend them. But of this I am sure, that whatever their principles are, there is not a more excellent people or a happier commonwealth anywhere in the whole world.

The happiness of the Utopians, and a description of them

In body they are nimble and vigorous, and stronger than you would expect from their stature, though they're by no means tiny. Their soil is not very fertile, nor their climate of the best, but they protect themselves against the weather by temperate living, and improve their soil by industry, so that nowhere do grain and cattle flourish more plentifully, nowhere are people's bodies more vigorous or less susceptible to disease. There you can not only observe that they do all the things farmers usually do to improve poor soil by hard work and technical knowledge, but you can see a forest which they tore up by the roots with their own hands and moved to another site. They did this not so much for the sake of better growth but to make transport easier, by having wood closer to the sea, the rivers, or the cities themselves. For grain is easier than wood to carry by land over a long distance.

The people are easy-going, cheerful, clever, and like their leisure. They can stand heavy labour when it is useful, but otherwise they are not very fond of it. In intellectual pursuits they are tireless. When they heard from us about the literature and learning of the Greeks (for we thought that, except for the historians and poets, there was nothing in Latin that they would value), it was wonderful to behold how eagerly they sought to learn Greek through our instruction. We therefore began to read with them, at first more to avoid seeming lazy than out of any expectation they would profit by it. But after a short trial, their diligence immediately convinced us that ours would not be wasted. They picked up the forms of letters so easily, pronounced the language so aptly, memorised it so quickly, and began to recite so accurately, that it seemed like a miracle. Most of our pupils were established scholars, of course, picked for their unusual ability and mature minds; and they studied with us, not just of their own free will, but at the command of the senate. Thus in less than three years they had perfect control of the language, and could read the best authors fluently, unless the text was corrupt. I have a feeling they picked up Greek more easily because it was somewhat related to their own tongue. Though their language resembles Persian in most respects, I suspect their race descends from the Greeks because, in the names of cities and in official titles, they retain some vestiges of the Greek tongue.

The usefulness of the Greek tongue

The Utopians' wonderful aptitude for learning

But now clods and blockheads are assigned to learning, while the best minds are corrupted by pleasures

Before leaving on the fourth voyage I placed on board, instead of merchandise, a good-sized packet of books; for I had resolved not to return at all rather than come home soon. Thus they received from me most of Plato's works and more of Aristotle's, as well as Theophrastus' book *On Plants*,[78] though the latter, I'm sorry to say, was somewhat mutilated. During the voyage I carelessly left it lying around, a monkey got hold of it, and from sheer mischief ripped out a few pages here and there and tore them up. Of the grammarians they have only Lascaris, for I did not

---

[78] Theophrastus was a pupil of Aristotle. His views were still current in the Renaissance.

take Theodorus with me, nor any dictionary except that of Hesychius; and they have Dioscorides.[79] They are very fond of Plutarch's writings, and delighted with the witty persiflage of Lucian.[80] Among the poets they have Aristophanes, Homer and Euripides, together with Sophocles in the small typeface of the Aldine edition.[81] Of the historians they possess Thucydides and Herodotus, as well as Herodian.[82]

As for medical books, a comrade of mine named Tricius Apinatus[83] brought with him some small treatises by Hippocrates, and the *Microtechne* of Galen.[84] They were delighted to have these books because, even though there is hardly a country in the world that needs medicine less, still it is

Medicine the most useful of studies nowhere held in greater honour, since they consider a knowledge of it one of the finest and most useful parts of philosophy.[85] They think that when, with the help of philosophy, they explore the secrets of nature, they

Contemplation of nature are gratifying not only themselves but the author and maker of nature. They suppose that like other artists he created this beautiful mechanism of the world to be admired – and by whom, if not by man, who is alone in being able to appreciate so great a thing? Therefore he is bound to prefer a careful observer and sensitive admirer of his work before one who, like a brute beast, looks on such a grand and wonderful spectacle with a stupid and inert mind.

Once stimulated by learning, the minds of the Utopians are wonderfully quick to seek out those various skills which make life more agreeable. Two inventions, to be sure, they owe to us: the art of printing and the manufacture of paper. At least they owe these arts partly to us, though

[79] Constantinus Lascaris and Theodorus Gaza wrote Renaissance grammars of Greek. The Greek dictionary of Hesychius (fifth century AD?) was first printed in 1514. Dioscorides (first century AD) wrote a treatise on drugs and herbs (not properly a dictionary), which was printed in 1499.

[80] 'Plutarch's writings' presumably includes the *Moral Essays* as well as the *Parallel Lives* of eminent Greeks and Romans. For Lucian, see Introduction, pp. xx–xxi.

[81] The first modern edition of Sophocles was that of Aldus Manutius in 1502. The house of Aldus, where Erasmus lived and worked for a while, was distinguished both for its list of Greek and Latin works and for its contributions to the art of book design.

[82] Thucydides and Herodotus (both fifth century BC) are the great historians of classical Greece. Herodian (c. 175–250 AD) wrote a history of the Roman emperors of the second and third centuries.

[83] A learned joke (in keeping with Hythloday's own name) based on a passage in the *Epigrams* of Martial. Martial says of one set of his poems that *Sunt apinae tricaeque*: 'They're trifles and toys' (XIV.i).

[84] Hippocrates (fifth century BC) and Galen (second century AD) were the most influential Greek medical writers. The *Microtechne* is a medieval summary of Galen's ideas.

[85] As earlier (p. 64), 'philosophy' is employed in its old, inclusive sense.

also in good measure to themselves. While we were showing them the books printed on paper in Aldine letters, we talked about what paper is made of and how letters are printed, though without going into details, for none of us had had any practical experience of either skill. But with great sharpness of mind they immediately conceived how to do it. While previously they had written only on vellum, bark and papyrus, they now undertook to make paper and print with type. Their first attempts were not altogether successful, but with practice they soon mastered both arts. They became so proficient that, if they had the texts of the Greek authors, they would have no lack of volumes. But now they have no more than those I mentioned – which, however, they have reprinted in thousands of copies.

Any sightseer coming to their land who has some special intellectual gift, or who has travelled widely and knows about many countries, is sure of a warm welcome. That is why we were received so kindly. Indeed they love to hear what is happening throughout the world. Few merchants, however, go there to trade. What could they import, except iron – or else gold and silver, which everyone would rather take home than send abroad? As for the export trade, they prefer to do their own transportation, instead of letting strangers come there to fetch the goods. By carrying their own cargoes, they are able to learn more about foreign countries on all sides and keep their own navigational skills from getting rusty.

SLAVES

The only prisoners of war the Utopians keep as slaves are those captured in wars they fight themselves.[86] The children of slaves are not born into slavery,[87] nor are any slaves obtained from foreign countries. They are either their own citizens, enslaved for some heinous offence, or else for-eigners who had been condemned to death in their own cities; the latter sort predominate. Sometimes the Utopians buy them at a low price; more often they ask for them, get them for nothing, and bring them home in considerable numbers. These kinds of slaves are not only kept constantly

The wonderful fairness of these people

---

[86] In classical times prisoners of war – civilians as well as soldiers – constituted a major source of slaves. By More's day there was general agreement that it was wrong for Christians to enslave Christian captives; but non-Christians – especially Africans and American Indians – were often regarded as a different matter. A later passage (p. 92) suggests that the Utopians enslave only the defenders of cities they have had to besiege.

[87] The non-hereditary character of Utopian slavery distinguishes it sharply from that of the classical world and from medieval serfdom.

at work, but are always fettered. The Utopians, however, deal more harshly with their own people than with the others, feeling that they are worse and deserve stricter punishment because they had an excellent education and the best of moral training, yet still couldn't be restrained from wrong-doing.[88] A third class of slaves consists of hard-working penniless drudges from other nations who voluntarily choose slavery in Utopia. Such people are treated with respect, almost as kindly as citizens, except that they are assigned a little extra work, on the score that they're used to it. If one of them wants to leave, which seldom happens, no obstacles are put in his way, nor is he sent off empty-handed.

The sick   As I said before, they care for the sick with great affection, neglecting nothing whatever in the way of medicine or diet which might restore them to health. Everything possible is done to mitigate the pain of those suffering from incurable diseases; and visitors do their best to console them by sitting and talking with them. But if the disease is not only incurable, but excruciatingly and unremittingly painful, then the priests and public officials come and remind the sufferer that he is now unequal

Deliberate death   to any of life's duties, a burden to himself and others; he has really outlived his own death. They tell him he should not let the pestilence prey on him any longer, but now that life is simply torture he should not hesitate to die but should rely on hope for something better; and since his life is a prison where he is bitterly tormented, he should escape from it on his own or allow others to rescue him from it.[89] This would be a wise act, they say, since for him death would put an end not to pleasure but to agony. In addition, he would be obeying the counsel of the priests, who are the interpreters of God's will; thus it would be a pious and holy act.[90]

Those who have been persuaded by these arguments either starve themselves to death of their own accord or, having been put to sleep, are freed from life without any sensation of dying. But they never force this step on a man against his will; nor, if he decides against it, do they lessen their

---

[88] For the same reason, Plato would punish lawbreakers among the citizens of his ideal commonwealth more severely than non-citizens who commit the same crime (*Laws* IX.854E).

[89] More was fond of the figure of the world as a prison. See his Latin poem no. 119 (*CW*, III, Part II, 167–9), *A Dialogue Concerning Heresies* (*CW*, VI, 259–77) and *The Last Things* (*CW*, I, 156–8).

[90] Though in the ancient world suicide was regarded as an honourable way out of deep personal and political difficulties, neither suicide nor euthanasia was (or is) acceptable in Catholic Christianity. More discusses the 'wicked temptation' of suicide at length in *A Dialogue of Comfort against Tribulation* (1534) (*CW*, XII, 122–57); and cf. Hythloday's earlier reference to God's prohibition of self-slaughter (p. 22).

care of him. The man who yields to their arguments, they think, dies an honourable death; but the suicide, who takes his own life without approval of priests and senate, him they consider unworthy of either earth or fire, and they throw his body, unburied and disgraced, into a bog.

Women do not marry till they are eighteen, nor men till they are twenty- *Marriages* two.[91] Clandestine premarital intercourse, if discovered and proved, brings severe punishment on both man and woman; and the guilty parties are forbidden to marry for their whole lives, unless the governor by his pardon remits the sentence. Also both the father and mother of the household where the offence was committed suffer public disgrace for having been remiss in their duty. The reason they punish this offence so severely is that they suppose few people would join in married love – with confinement to a single partner and all the petty annoyances that married life involves – unless they were strictly restrained from promiscuous intercourse.

In choosing marriage partners they solemnly and seriously follow a custom which seemed to us foolish and absurd in the extreme. Whether she be widow or virgin, the woman is shown naked to the suitor by a *Not very modest,* responsible and respectable matron; and similarly, some honourable man *but not so* *impractical either* presents the suitor naked to the woman. We laughed at this custom, and called it absurd; but they were just as amazed at the folly of all other peoples. When men go to buy a colt, where they are risking only a little money, they are so cautious that, though the animal is almost bare, they won't close the deal until saddle and blanket have been taken off, lest there be a hidden sore underneath.[92] Yet in the choice of a mate, which may cause either delight or disgust for the rest of their lives, men are so careless that they leave all the rest of the woman's body covered up with clothes and estimate her attractiveness from a mere handsbreadth of her person, the face, which is all they can see. And so they marry, running great risk of bitter discord, if something in either's person should offend the other.

---

[91] Canon law required that girls be at least twelve and boys at least fourteen at the time of marriage. In fact, even younger children were sometimes forced into marriage in Christian Europe.

[92] Plato's *Laws* commends with perfect seriousness a practice similar to the Utopians': 'when people are going to live together as partners in marriage, it is vital that the fullest possible information should be available ... Boys and girls must dance together at an age when plausible occasions can be found for their doing so, in order that they may have a reasonable look at each other; and they should dance naked, provided sufficient modesty and restraint are displayed by all concerned' (VI.771E–772A). J. S. Cummins suggests that the Utopian custom may have the purpose – hinted at in 'hidden sore' – of curbing the spread of syphilis, which had become a scourge in Europe (if not Utopia) by the time More wrote. See 'Pox and paranoia in Renaissance Europe', *History Today*, 38 (August 1988), 29.

Not all people are so wise as to concern themselves solely with character; and even the wise appreciate the gifts of the body as a supplement to the virtues of the mind. There's no doubt that a deformity may lurk under clothing, serious enough to alienate a man's mind from his wife when his body can no longer lawfully be separated from her. If some disfiguring accident takes place after marriage, each person must bear his own fate; but beforehand everyone should be legally protected from deception.

There is extra reason for them to be careful, because in that part of the world they are the only people who practise monogamy,[93] and because their marriages are seldom terminated except by death – though they

Divorce do allow divorce for adultery or for intolerably offensive behaviour. A husband or wife who is the aggrieved party in such a divorce is granted leave by the senate to take a new mate; the guilty party suffers disgrace and is permanently forbidden to remarry.[94] But they absolutely forbid a husband to put away his wife against her will and without any fault on her part, just because of some bodily misfortune; they think it cruel that a person should be abandoned when most in need of comfort; and they add that old age, since it not only entails disease but is a disease itself,[95] needs more than a precarious fidelity.

It happens occasionally that a married couple have incompatible characters, and have both found other persons with whom they hope to live more harmoniously. After getting approval of the senate, they may then separate by mutual consent and contract new marriages. But such divorces are allowed only after the senators and their wives have carefully investigated the case. Divorce is deliberately made difficult because they know that conjugal love will hardly be strengthened if each partner has in mind that a new marriage is easily available.

Violators of the marriage bond are punished with the strictest form of slavery. If both parties were married, both are divorced, and the injured parties may marry one another if they want, or someone else. But if one of the injured parties continues to love such an undeserving spouse, the marriage may go on, provided the innocent person chooses to share in the labour to which the slave is condemned. And sometimes it happens

---

[93] In this respect the Utopians resemble the ancient Germans as portrayed by Tacitus: 'the marriage tie with them is strict: you will find nothing in their character to praise more highly. They are almost the only barbarians who are content with a wife apiece' (*Germania* 17).

[94] Although the Church in More's day permitted separation in the case of adultery, it did not allow the injured party to remarry.

[95] The phrase comes from Terence's comedy *Phormio* (IV.i; l. 575).

that the repentance of the guilty and the devotion of the innocent party so move the governor to pity that he restores both to freedom. But a relapse into the same crime is punished by death.

No other crimes carry fixed penalties; the senate decrees a specific punishment for each misdeed, as it is considered atrocious or venial. Husbands chastise their wives and parents their children, unless the offence is so serious that public punishment is called for. Generally, the gravest crimes are punished with slavery, for they think this deters offenders just as much as getting rid of them by immediate capital punishment, and convict labour is more beneficial to the commonwealth. Slaves, moreover, contribute more by their labour than by their death, and they are permanent and visible reminders that crime does not pay. If the slaves rebel against their condition, then, since neither bars nor chains can tame them, they are finally put to death like wild beasts. But if they are patient, they are not left altogether without hope. When subdued by long hardships, if they show by their behaviour that they regret the crime more than the punishment, their slavery is lightened or remitted altogether, sometimes by the governor's prerogative, sometimes by popular vote. *The penalty for soliciting to lewdness*

Attempted seduction is subject to the same penalty as seduction itself. They think that a crime clearly and deliberately attempted is as bad as one committed, and that failure should not confer advantages on a criminal who did all he could to succeed.

They are very fond of fools, and think it contemptible to insult them.[96] There is no prohibition against enjoying their foolishness, and they even regard this as beneficial to the fools. If anyone is so solemn and severe that the foolish behaviour and comic patter of a clown do not amuse him, they don't entrust him with the care of such a person, for fear that one who gets not only no use from a fool but not even any amusement – a fool's only gift – will not treat him kindly. *Pleasure derived from fools*

To deride a person for being deformed or crippled is considered ugly and disfiguring, not to the victim but to the mocker, who stupidly reproaches the cripple for something he cannot help.

Though they think it a sign of weak and sluggish character to neglect one's natural beauty, they consider cosmetics a disgraceful affectation. From experience they have learned that no physical attractions recommend a wife to her husband so effectually as an upright character and a *Artificial beauty*

Assignment of punishments left to the magistracy

---

[96] More's household included a fool, Henry Patenson – who appears in Hans Holbein's sketch of the family.

respectful attitude. Though some men are captured by beauty alone, none are held except by virtue and compliance.

Citizens to be encouraged by rewards to do their duty

They not only deter people from crime by penalties, but they incite them to virtue by public honours. Accordingly, they set up in the marketplace statues of distinguished men who have served their country well, thinking thereby to preserve the memory of their good deeds and to spur on citizens to emulate the glory of their ancestors.

Running for office condemned

Any man who campaigns for a public office is disqualified for all of them. They live together in a friendly fashion, and their public officials are never arrogant or unapproachable. They are called 'fathers', and that indeed is

Magistrates held in honour

the way they behave. Because officials never extort respect from the people against their will, the people respect them spontaneously, as they should.

Dignity of the governor

The governor himself is distinguished from his fellow citizens not by a robe or a crown but only by the sheaf of grain he bears, as the sign of the high priest is a wax candle carried before him.[97]

Few laws

They have very few laws, for their training is such that very few suf-

like the U.S.

fice.[98] The chief fault they find with other nations is that even their infinite volumes of laws and interpretations are not adequate. They think it com-

The useless crowd of lawyers

pletely unjust to bind people by a set of laws that are too many to be read or too obscure for anyone to understand. As for lawyers, a class of men whose trade it is to manipulate cases and multiply quibbles, they exclude them entirely. They think it practical for each man to plead his own case, and say the same thing to the judge that he would tell his lawyer. This makes for less confusion and readier access to the truth. A man speaks his mind without tricky instructions from a lawyer, and the judge examines each point carefully, taking pains to protect simple folk against the false accusations of the crafty. This sort of plain dealing is hard to find in other nations, where they have such a mass of incomprehensibly intricate laws. But in Utopia everyone is a legal expert. For the laws are very few, as I said, and they consider the most obvious interpretation of any law to be the fairest. As they see things, all laws are promulgated for the single purpose of advising every man of his duty. Subtle interpretations admonish very few, since hardly anybody can understand them, whereas the more simple and apparent sense of the law is open to everyone. If laws are not

[97] Grain (suggesting prosperity) and candle (suggesting vision) symbolise the special function of each.

[98] The idea that good education obviates the need for an elaborate system of law is common in the literature of the ideal commonwealth. See, for example, Plato, *Republic* IV.425C–D; Plutarch, 'Lycurgus' XIII.1–2.

clear, they are useless; for simple-minded men (and most men are of this sort, and must be told where their duty lies), there might as well be no laws at all as laws which can be interpreted only by devious minds after endless disputes. The dull mind of the common man cannot understand such laws, and couldn't even if he studied them his whole life, since he has to earn a living in the meantime.

Some of their free and independent neighbours (the Utopians themselves previously liberated many of them from tyranny) have learned to admire the Utopian virtues, and now of their own accord ask the Utopians to supply magistrates for them. Of these magistrates, some serve for one year, others for five. When their term of office is over, they bring them home with honour and praise, and take back new ones to their country. These peoples seem to have settled on an excellent scheme to safeguard the commonwealth. Since the welfare or ruin of a commonwealth depends on the character of the officials, where could they make a more prudent choice than among those who cannot be corrupted by money? For money is useless to them when they go home, as they soon must, and they can have no partisan or factional feelings, since they are strangers in the city over which they rule. Wherever they take root in men's minds, these two evils, greed and faction, soon destroy all justice, which is the strongest bond of any society. The Utopians call these people who have borrowed magistrates from them their allies; others whom they have benefited they call simply friends.

While other nations are constantly making, breaking and renewing treaties, the Utopians make none at all with any nation. If nature, they say, doesn't bind man adequately to his fellow man, what good is a treaty? If a man scorns nature herself, is there any reason to think he will care about mere words? They are confirmed in this view by the fact that in that part of the world, treaties and alliances between princes are not generally observed with much good faith. *Treaties*

In Europe, of course, and especially in these regions where the Christian faith and religion prevail, the dignity of treaties is everywhere kept sacred and inviolable. This is partly because the princes are all so just and virtuous, partly also from the awe and reverence that everyone feels for the popes.[99] Just as the popes themselves never promise anything that they

---

[99] The European rulers of the time were in fact ruthless and casual violators of treaties. So also were two recent popes, Alexander VI and Julius II. Of the former, Machiavelli says admiringly that he 'never did anything else and never dreamed of anything else than deceiving men...Never was there a man more effective in swearing and who with stronger oaths

do not scrupulously perform, so they command all other princes to abide by their promises in every way. If someone declines to do so, by pastoral censure and sharp reproof they compel him to obey. They think, and rightly, that it would be shameful if people who are specifically called 'the faithful' acted in bad faith.

But in that new world, which is as distant from ours in customs and manners as by the distance the equator puts between us, nobody trusts treaties. The greater the formalities, the more numerous and solemn the oaths, the sooner the treaty will be broken. They easily find some defect in the wording, which often enough they deliberately inserted themselves. No treaty can be made so strong and explicit that a government will not be able to worm out of it, breaking in the process both the treaty and its own word. If such craft (not to call it deceit and fraud) were practised in private contracts, the politicians would raise a great outcry against both parties, calling them sacrilegious and worthy of the gallows. Yet the very same politicians think themselves clever fellows when they give this sort of advice to princes. Thus people are apt to think that justice is altogether a humble, plebeian virtue, far beneath the dignity of kings. Or else they conclude that there are two kinds of justice, one for the common herd, a lowly justice that creeps along the ground, hedged in everywhere and encumbered with chains; and the other, which is the justice of princes, much more majestic and hence more free than common justice, so that it can do anything it wants and nothing it doesn't want.[100]

This royal practice of keeping treaties badly there is, I suppose, the reason the Utopians don't make any; perhaps if they lived here they would change their minds. However, they think it a bad idea to make treaties at all, even if they are faithfully kept. A treaty implies that people divided by some natural obstacle as slight as a hill or a brook are joined by no bond of nature; it assumes they are born rivals and enemies, and are right in trying to destroy one another except when a treaty restrains them. Besides, they see that treaties do not really promote friendship; for both parties still retain the right to prey on one another, insofar as careless drafting has left the treaty without sufficient provisions against it. The Utopians think, on

confirmed a promise, but yet honored it less' (*The Prince*, chapter 18; trans. Allan Gilbert, in Niccolò Machiavelli, *The Chief Works and Others*, 3 vols. (Durham, N.C., 1958), I, 65).
[100] The idea that political morality differs from private, and the attendant notion that political necessity or *raison d'état* sometimes dictates policies that conflict with traditional morality, gained increasing acceptance in the late Middle Ages and the Renaissance. By the late fifteenth century, various Italian political writers were exploring the ways in which the virtues of a ruler might differ from those of ordinary people – explorations that culminated in Machiavelli.

the other hand, that no one should be considered an enemy who has done no harm, that the kinship of nature is as good as a treaty, and that men are united more firmly by good will than by pacts, by their hearts than by their words.

MILITARY PRACTICES

They utterly despise war as an activity fit only for beasts,[101] yet practised more by man than by any other animal. Unlike almost every other people in the world, they think nothing so inglorious as the glory won in battle. Yet on certain assigned days both men and women carry on vigorous military training, so they will be fit to fight should the need arise. But they go to war only for good reasons: to protect their own land, to drive invading armies from the territories of their friends, or to liberate an oppressed people, in the name of compassion and humanity, from tyranny and servitude.[102] They war not only to protect their friends from present danger, but sometimes to repay and avenge previous injuries. But they enter a conflict only if they themselves have been consulted in advance, have approved the cause, and have demanded restitution, but in vain, and only if they are the ones who begin the war. They take this final step not only when their friends have been plundered, but also, and even more fiercely, when their friends' merchants have been subjected to extortion anywhere in the world under the semblance of justice, either on the pretext of laws unjust in themselves or through the perversion of good laws.

This and no other was the cause of the war which the Utopians waged a little before our time on behalf of the Nephelogetes against the Alaopolitans.[103] Under pretext of right, a wrong (as they saw it) had been inflicted on some Nephelogete traders residing in Alaopolis. Whatever the rights and wrongs of the quarrel, it developed into a fierce war, to

---

[101] A false etymology derived Latin *bellum* ('war') from *belua* ('beast').

For the most part, the Utopians' attitudes toward war – basically pacifistic and thoroughly anti-chivalric – are similar to those of More and his humanist circle. For a full account, see R. P. Adams, *The Better Part of Valor*.

[102] In the background is the ancient distinction between just and unjust wars. (A key locus is Cicero, *On Moral Obligation* I.xi.34–xiii.40.) It is not clear, though, that More would have approved of all the 'good reasons' for war listed here. Erasmus allows that purely defensive wars are just (*Complaint of Peace*, CWE, XXVII, 314), but he endorses Cicero's remark (*Letters to His Friends* VI.vi.5) that 'an unjust peace is far preferable to a just war'. More's friend and mentor John Colet stated unequivocally – in a sermon before the king – that for Christians *no* war is just (*CWE*, VIII, 243).

[103] More Greek compounds: 'People Born from the Clouds' and 'Citizens of a Country without People'.

which, apart from the hostile forces of the two parties themselves, the neighbouring nations added their efforts and resources. Some prosperous nations were ravaged, others badly shaken. One trouble led to another, and in the end the Alaopolitans surrendered, and the Utopians (since they weren't involved on their own account) handed them over to be enslaved by the Nephelogetes – even though before the war the victors had not been remotely comparable in power to the Alaopolitans.

So sharply do the Utopians punish wrong done to their friends, even in matters of mere money; but they are not so strict in enforcing their own rights. When they are cheated out of their goods, so long as no bodily harm is done, their anger goes no further than cutting off trade relations with that nation till restitution is made. The reason is not that they care less for their own citizens than for their allies, but that the merchants of their friends, when they lose goods from their private stock, feel the loss more bitterly. The Utopian traders, by contrast, lose nothing but what belongs to the commonwealth, more particularly goods that were already abundant at home, even superfluous, since otherwise they wouldn't have been exported. Hence no one individual even notices the loss. So small an injury, which affects neither the life nor the livelihood of any of their own people, they consider it cruel to avenge by the deaths of many people. On the other hand, if one of their own is maimed or killed anywhere, whether by government decision or by a private citizen, they first send envoys to look into the circumstances; then they demand that the guilty persons be surrendered; and if that demand is refused, they are not to be put off, but at once declare war. Those who devoted themselves to doing injury are punished by death or slavery.

Victory dearly bought

The Utopians are not only troubled but ashamed when their forces gain a bloody victory, thinking it folly to pay too high a price even for the best goods. But if they overcome the enemy by skill and cunning, they exult mightily, celebrate a public triumph, and raise a monument as for a glorious exploit. They boast that they have really acted with manly and virile bravery when they have won a victory such as no animal except man could have achieved – a victory gained by strength of understanding. Bears, lions, boars, wolves, dogs and other wild beasts fight with their bodies, they say; and most of them are superior to us in strength and ferocity; but we outdo them all in intelligence and rationality.

The only thing they aim at, in going to war, is to secure what would have prevented the declaration of war, if the enemy had conceded it beforehand.

Or, if they cannot get that, they try to take such bitter revenge on those who provoked them that they will be afraid ever to do it again. These are their chief aims, which they try to achieve quickly, yet in such a way as to avoid danger rather than to win fame or glory.

As soon as war is declared, therefore, they have their secret agents simultaneously post many placards, each marked with their official seal, in the most conspicuous places throughout enemy territory. In these proclamations they promise immense rewards to anyone who will do away with the enemy prince. They offer smaller but still substantial sums for killing any of a list of other individuals whom they name. These are the persons whom they regard as most responsible, after the prince, for plotting aggression against them. The reward for an assassin is doubled for anyone who succeeds in bringing in one of the proscribed men alive. In fact, they even offer the same reward, plus a guarantee of personal safety, to any one of the proscribed men who turns against his comrades. As a result, the enemies of the Utopians quickly come to suspect all other mortals and even among themselves are neither trusting nor trustworthy, so that they live in the greatest fear and danger. They know very well that many of them, including especially their princes, have been betrayed by those in whom they placed complete trust – so effective are bribes as an incitement to crime. Hence the Utopians are lavish in their promises of bounty. Being well aware of the risks their agents must run, they make sure the payments are in proportion to the peril; thus they not only offer, but actually deliver, enormous sums of gold, as well as valuable landed estates in very secure locations on the territory of their friends.

Other nations condemn this custom of bidding for and buying the life of an enemy as the cruel villainy of a degenerate mind; but the Utopians consider it praiseworthy: wise, since it enables them to win tremendous wars without fighting any actual battles, and also merciful and humane, since it enables them, by the sacrifice of a few guilty men, to spare the lives of many innocent persons who would have died in the fighting, some on their side, some on the enemy's. They pity the mass of the enemy's soldiers almost as much as their own citizens, for they know common people do not go to war of their own accord, but are driven to it by the madness of princes.

If assassination does not work, they stir up dissensions by inciting the brother of the prince or some other member of the nobility to plot for the crown.[104] If internal discord dies down, they try to rouse up neighbouring peoples against the enemy by digging up ancient claims to dominion, of which kings always have an ample supply.

When they promise their resources to help in a war, they send money very freely, but commit their citizens very sparingly indeed. They hold their own people dear, and value one another so highly that they would not willingly exchange one of themselves for an enemy's prince. But gold and silver, all of which they keep for this purpose alone, they spend without hesitation; after all, they will continue to live just as well even if they expend the whole sum. Moreover, in addition to the wealth they have at home, they also have a vast treasure abroad since, as I said before, many nations owe them money. So they hire mercenary soldiers from everywhere, especially the Zapoletes.[105]

A people not so
unlike the Swiss These people live five hundred miles to the east of Utopia, and are rough, rude and fierce. The forests and mountains where they are bred are the kind of country they like: tough and rugged. They are a hard race, capable of standing heat, cold and drudgery, unacquainted with any luxuries, careless about their houses and their clothes; they don't till the fields but raise cattle instead. Most survive by hunting and stealing. These people are born for battle, which they seek out at every opportunity and eagerly embrace when they have found it. Leaving their own country in great numbers, they offer themselves for cheap hire to anyone in need of warriors. The only art they know for earning a living is the art which aims at death.

For the people who pay them, they fight with great courage and complete loyalty, but they will not bind themselves to serve for any fixed period of time. They take sides on such terms that if someone, even the enemy, offers them more money tomorrow, they will take his part; and the day after tomorrow, if a trifle more is offered to bring them back, they'll return to their first employers. Hardly a war is fought in which a good number of them are not engaged on both sides. Thus it happens every day that men who are united by ties of blood and have served together in friendship, but who are soon after separated into opposing armies, meet in battle. Forgetful of kinship and comradeship alike, they furiously run each other

---

[104] The stratagems of this paragraph compare interestingly with some of the recommendations of the corrupt privy councillors in Hythloday's imaginary strategy session (p. 29).

[105] As the following gloss points out, the Zapoletes (from Greek: 'busy sellers') resemble the Swiss, who provided Europe's most feared and hated mercenaries. Many Italian princes, as well as the French, hired Swiss mercenaries; and popes have Swiss guards to this day. Johann Froben, who printed the 1518 editions of *Utopia*, was Swiss himself and omitted the gloss.

through, driven to mutual destruction for no other reason than that they were hired for a paltry sum by opposing princes. They reckon up money so closely that they can easily be induced to change sides for an increase of only a penny a day. They have quickly picked up the habit of avarice, but none of the profit; for what they earn by blood-letting they immediately squander on debauchery of the most squalid sort.

Because the pay for their services is nowhere higher than what the Utopians offer, these people are ready to serve them against any mortals whatever. And the Utopians, as they seek out the best possible men for proper uses, hire these, the worst possible men, for improper uses. When the situation requires, they thrust the Zapoletes into the positions of greatest danger by offering them immense rewards. Most of them never come back to collect their stipend, but the Utopians faithfully pay off those who do survive, to encourage them to try it again. As for how many Zapoletes get killed, the Utopians never worry about that, for they think they would deserve very well of mankind if they could sweep from the face of the earth all the dregs of that vicious and disgusting race.[106]

After the Zapoletes, they employ as auxiliaries the soldiers of the people for whom they have taken up arms, and then squadrons of their other friends. Last, they add their own citizens, including some man of known bravery to command the entire army. They also appoint two substitutes for him, who hold no rank as long as he is safe. But if the commander is captured or killed, one of these two substitutes becomes his successor, and in case of a mishap to him, the third.[107] Thus, despite the many accidents of war, they ensure that the whole army will not be disorganised through loss of the general.

In each city, soldiers are chosen from those who have volunteered. No one is forced to fight abroad against his will, because they think a man who is naturally fearful will act weakly at best, and may even spread panic among his comrades. But if their own country is invaded they call to arms even the fearful (as long as they are physically fit), placing them on shipboard among braver men, or here and there along fortifications, where there is no place to run away. Thus shame at failing their countrymen,

---

[106] Sixteenth-century accounts of horrors perpetrated by mercenaries – including an account by More of the sacking of Rome in 1527 (*Dialogue Concerning Heresies, CW*, VI, 370–2) – help to explain the Utopians' genocidal policy toward the Zapoletes. In *The Education of a Christian Prince*, Erasmus says of mercenaries that 'there is no class of men more abject and indeed more damnable' (*CWE*, XXVII, 283). How the Utopians reconcile their employment of the Zapoletes with their aim of minimising bloodshed and plunder in war is unclear.

[107] This is a Spartan practice. See Thucydides, *The Peloponnesian War* IV.xxxviii.

the immediate presence of the enemy and the impossibility of flight often combine to overcome their fear, and they make a virtue out of sheer necessity.

Just as no man is forced into a foreign war against his will, so women are allowed to accompany their men on military service if they want to – not only not forbidden, but encouraged and praised for doing so. Each leaves with her husband, and they stand shoulder to shoulder in the line of battle; in addition, they place around a man his children and his blood- or marriage-relations, so that those who by nature have most reason to help one another may be closest at hand for mutual support. It is a matter of great reproach for either spouse to come home without the other, or for a son to return after losing a parent. The result is that if the enemy stands his ground, the hand-to-hand fighting is apt to be long and bitter, ending only when everyone is dead.

They take every precaution to avoid having to fight in person, so long as they can use mercenaries to wage war for them. But when they are forced to enter the battle, they are as bold in the struggle as they were prudent in putting it off as long as possible. In the first charge they are not fierce, but gradually as the fighting goes on they grow more determined, putting up a steady, stubborn resistance. Their spirit is so strong that they will die rather than yield ground. They are sure that everyone at home will be provided for, nor do they have any worry about the future of their families (for that sort of care often daunts the boldest courage); so their spirit is proud and unconquerable. Moreover, their skill in the arts of war gives them confidence; also they have been trained from infancy in sound principles of conduct (which their education and the good institutions of their society both reinforce), and that too adds to their courage. They don't hold life so cheap that they throw it away recklessly, nor so dear that they grasp it greedily at the price of shame when duty bids them give it up.

The enemy general to be most fiercely attacked, so as to end the war sooner

At the height of the battle, a band of the bravest young men, who have taken a special oath, devote themselves to seeking out the opposing general. They assail him directly, they lay secret traps for him, they hit at him from near and far. A long and continuous wedge of fresh men keep up the assault as the exhausted drop out. It rarely happens that they fail to kill or capture him, unless he takes flight.

When they win a battle, it never ends in a massacre, for they would much rather take prisoners than cut throats. They never pursue fugitives without keeping one line of their army drawn up under the colours. They

This is similar to Plato's idea that women should train along side men.

The killing of the general allows for less bloodshed.

are so careful of this that if they win the victory with this last reserve force (after the rest of their army has been beaten), they ordinarily let the enemy army escape instead of pursuing fugitives with their own ranks in disorder. They recall what has happened more than once to themselves: that when the enemy seemed to have the best of the day, had routed the main Utopian force, and, exulting in their victory, had scattered to round up runaways, a few Utopians held in reserve and watching their opportunity have suddenly attacked the dispersed and straggling enemy just when he felt safe and had lowered his guard. Thereby they changed the fortune of the day, snatched certain victory out of the enemy's hands, and, though conquered themselves, conquered their conquerors.

It is not easy to say whether they are more crafty in laying ambushes or more clever in avoiding them. You would think they are about to run away when that is the last thing in their minds; when they are really ready to retreat, you would never guess it. If they are outnumbered, or if the terrain is unsuitable, they shift their ground silently by night or get away by some stratagem; or if they withdraw by day, they do so gradually, and in such good order that they are as dangerous to attack then as if they were advancing. They fortify their camps thoroughly, with a deep, broad ditch, the earth being thrown inward;[108] the work is done not by labourers but by the soldiers themselves with their own hands. The whole army pitches in, except for an armed guard posted outside the ditch to prevent surprise attack. With so many hands at work, they complete great fortifications, enclosing wide areas with unbelievable speed.

Their armour is strong enough to stand up under blows but does not prevent free movement of the body; indeed, it doesn't even interfere with swimming, and swimming in armour is a normal part of their training. For long-range fighting they use arrows, which they shoot with great force and accuracy, from horseback as well as on foot. At close quarters they use not swords but battle-axes, which because of their sharp edge and great weight are lethal weapons, whether used to slash or thrust. They are very skilful in inventing machines of war, but carefully conceal them, since if they were made known before they were needed, they might prove ridiculous rather than useful.[109] Their first consideration in designing them is to make them easy to move and aim.

Kinds of weapons

---

[108] That is, to form a parapet.

[109] Perhaps because the enemy could prepare countermeasures or move out of range.

    The military devices of the Utopians are a patchwork of different notions from the common knowledge of the day. Their camps are fortified like Roman ones. Their reliance on archery

Truces

Truces made with the enemy they observe so religiously that they will not break them even if provoked. They do not ravage the enemy's territory or burn his crops; indeed, so far as possible, they avoid any trampling of the fields by men or horses, thinking they may use the grain themselves. Unless he is a spy, they injure no unarmed man. Cities that are surrendered to them they keep intact; even after storming a place, they do not plunder it, but put to death the men who prevented surrender, enslave the other defenders, and do no harm to civilians. If they find any inhabitants who recommended surrender, they give them a share in the property of the condemned. What is left they divide among their auxiliaries; for themselves, they never take any booty.

But nowadays the victors pay most of the expenses

After a war is ended they collect the cost of it, not from the allies for whose sake they undertook it, but from the conquered. They take as indemnity not only money, which they set aside to finance future wars, but also landed estates, from which they may enjoy forever a substantial annual income. They now have revenues of this sort in many different countries, acquired little by little in various ways, which have mounted to over seven hundred thousand ducats[110] a year. As managers of these estates, they send abroad some of their citizens to serve as collectors of revenue. Though they live on the properties in great style and conduct themselves like magnates, plenty of income is still left over to be put into the treasury, unless they lend it to the conquered nation. They often do the latter until they need the money, and it rarely happens that they call in the entire debt. They give some of the estates to those who have taken great risks at their instigation, as I mentioned before.

If any prince takes up arms and prepares to invade their land, they immediately send a powerful force to encounter him outside their own borders. For they don't like to wage war on their own soil, nor is any necessity so great as to bring them to allow foreign auxiliaries onto their island.

links them with the English – though their skill in shooting arrows from horseback recalls the ancient Parthians and Scythians. The 'machines' are presumably like Roman stone-throwers, battering rams and dart-hurlers; but the emphasis on their portability probably reflects contemporary experience with cannon, which were terribly hard to drag over the muddy roads of the time.

[110] Gold coins of this name were minted by several European countries. Four ducats of Burgundy, Venice or Hungary were roughly equivalent to an English pound; and the pound itself was worth several hundred times its value today.

THE RELIGIONS OF THE UTOPIANS

There are different forms of religion not only throughout the island but even within the individual cities. Some worship as a god the sun, others the moon, still others one of the planets. There are some who worship a man of past ages, conspicuous either for virtue or glory; they consider him not only a god but the supreme god. But the vast majority, and those by far the wiser ones, believe nothing of the kind: they believe in a single divinity, unknown, eternal, infinite, inexplicable, beyond the grasp of the human mind, and diffused throughout the universe, not physically, but in influence. Him they call their parent, and to him alone they attribute the origin, increase, progress, changes and ends of all things; they do not offer divine honours to any other.

Though all the others differ from this group in various particular beliefs, they agree with them in a single main head, that there is one supreme power, the maker and ruler of the universe. In their native tongue they all alike call him Mythra.[111] But the others differ from the main group in that they define this supreme power in various ways, everyone asserting that whatever he considers to be supreme is that one and only nature to whose divine majesty, by the consensus of all nations, the highest status of all is attributed. Gradually, though, they are all coming to forsake this mixture of superstitions and unite in that one religion which seems more reasonable than any of the others. And there is no doubt that the other religions would have disappeared long ago, had not whatever unlucky accident that befell anyone who was thinking of changing his religion been interpreted, out of fear, as a sign of divine anger, not chance – as if the deity who was being abandoned were avenging an insult against himself.

But after they heard from us the name of Christ, and learned of his teachings, his life, his miracles and the no less marvellous constancy of the many martyrs whose blood, freely shed, has drawn so many nations far and near into their religion, you would not believe how eagerly they assented to it, either through the secret inspiration of God or because Christianity seemed very like the sect that most prevails among them. But I think they were also much influenced by the fact that Christ approved of his followers' communal way of life,[112] and that among the truest groups of Christians *Monasteries*

---

[111] In ancient Persian religion, Mithra or Mithras, the spirit of light, was the supreme force of good in the universe. Recall that the Utopians' language 'resembles Persian in most respects' (p. 75).

[112] On the communist practice of the early Christians, see Acts 2:44–5 and 4:32–5.

the practice still prevails. Whatever the reason, no small number of them joined our religion, and were washed in the holy waters of baptism.

By that time, two of our group had died, and among us four survivors there was, I am sorry to say, no priest. So, though they received the other sacraments, they still lack those which in our religion can be administered only by priests.[113] They do, however, understand what these are, and eagerly desire them. In fact, they dispute warmly whether a man chosen from among themselves could receive the sacerdotal character[114] without the dispatch of a Christian bishop. Though they seemed about to elect such a person, they had not yet done so when I left.

Those who have not accepted Christianity make no effort to restrain others from it, nor do they criticise new converts to it. While I was there, only one of our communion was interfered with. As soon as he was baptised, he took upon himself to preach the Christian religion publicly, with more zeal than discretion. We warned him not to do so, but he began to work himself up to a pitch where he not only set our religion above the rest but roundly condemned all others as profane, leading their impious and sacrilegious followers to the hell-fires they richly deserved. After he had been preaching in this style for a long time, they arrested him. He was tried on a charge, not of despising their religion, but of creating a public disorder, convicted, and sentenced to exile. For it is one of their oldest rules that no one should suffer for his religion.

Men must be drawn to religion by praising it

Utopus had heard that before his arrival the natives were continually squabbling over religious matters, and he had observed that it was easy to conquer the whole country because the different sects were too busy fighting one another to oppose him. And so at the very beginning, after he had gained the victory, he prescribed by law that everyone may cultivate the religion of his choice, and strenuously proselytise for it too, provided he does so quietly, modestly, rationally and without insulting others. If persuasion fails, no one may resort to abuse or violence; and anyone who fights wantonly about religion is punished by exile or slavery.

Utopus laid down these rules not simply for the sake of peace, which he saw was being completely undermined by constant quarrels and implacable

---

[113] Of the seven sacraments, only baptism and matrimony can be conferred without a priest.
[114] In Catholic doctrine, a 'character' is 'a spiritual seal or stamp impressed on the soul by God to indicate the consecration of that soul to him in some official capacity' (George D. Smith, ed., *The Teaching of the Catholic Church*, 2nd edn (1952), p. 1030). Quoted in the note on the term at *CW*, IV, 520, where Surtz also points out that 'Consecration at the hands of a bishop was always deemed necessary, as is presupposed in More's letter to Giles' (above, p. 5).

hatreds, but he also thought such decrees would benefit religion itself. In such matters he was not at all quick to dogmatise, because he was uncertain whether God likes diverse and manifold forms of worship and hence inspires different people with different views. On the other hand, he was quite sure that it was arrogant folly for anyone to force conformity with his own beliefs on everyone else by threats or violence.[115] He easily foresaw that if one religion is really true and the rest are false, the truth will sooner or later emerge and prevail by its own natural strength, if men will only consider the matter reasonably and moderately. But if they try to decide things by fighting and rioting, since the worst men are always the most headstrong, the best and holiest religion in the world will be crowded out by foolish superstitions, like grain choked by thorns and briars. So he left the whole matter open, allowing each person to choose what he would believe. The only exception was a solemn and strict law against anyone who should sink so far below the dignity of human nature as to think that the soul perishes with the body, or that the universe is ruled by blind chance, not divine providence.[116]

Thus they believe that after this life vices will be punished and virtue rewarded. Anyone who denies this proposition they consider not even one of the human race, since he has degraded the sublimity of his own soul to the base level of a beast's wretched body. Still less will they count him as one of their citizens, since he would openly despise all the laws and customs of society, if not prevented by fear. Who can doubt that a man who has nothing to fear but the law, and no hope of life beyond the grave, will do anything he can to evade his country's laws by craft or to break them by violence, in order to gratify his own personal greed? Therefore a person who holds such views is offered no honours, entrusted with no offices, and given no public responsibility; he is universally regarded as low and torpid. Yet they do not punish him, because they are persuaded that no one can choose to believe by a mere act of the will. They do not compel him

---

[115] This was not the attitude More took a decade later, when he was involved in the prosecution of Protestants. In the *Dialogue Concerning Heresies*, he wrote that 'if it were now doubtful and ambiguous whether the church of Christ were in the right rule of doctrine or not, then were it very necessary to give them all good audience that could and would anything dispute on either party for or against it, to the end that if we were now in a wrong way, we might leave it and walk in some better' (*CW*, VI, 345–6). In Utopia, which has not had the Christian revelation, a high degree of religious toleration is appropriate; in England, the fact that the 'right rule of doctrine' was clearly established justified, so More believed, harsh suppression of dissenting views.

[116] The Utopians regard basic truths about immortality and divine providence as attainable by natural reason and as providing the only rational sanction for the life of virtue (pp. 66–7).

by threats to dissemble his views, nor do they tolerate in the matter any deceit or lying, which they detest as next door to deliberate malice. They do not forbid him to argue in favour of his opinion, except that he may not do so among the common people; but in the presence of priests and other important persons, in private, they not only permit but encourage it. For they are confident that in the end his madness will yield to reason.

A strange opinion about the souls of animals
There are others who err the other way, in supposing that animals have immortal souls,[117] though not comparable to ours in excellence nor destined to equal felicity. In fact, there is no small number of such people, because their view is not forbidden, since it is not wholly unreasonable and wicked.

Almost all the Utopians are absolutely convinced that human bliss after death will be enormous; thus they lament every individual's sickness, but mourn over a death only if they see that a person was torn from life anxiously and unwillingly. Such behaviour they take to be a very bad sign, as if the soul, despairing and conscious of guilt, dreaded death through some secret premonition of punishments to come. Besides, they suppose God can hardly be well pleased with the coming of one who, when he is summoned, does not come gladly, but is dragged off reluctantly and against his will. Such a death fills the onlookers with horror, and they carry the corpse out to burial in melancholy silence. Then, after begging God to have mercy on his spirit and to pardon his infirmities, they cover the body with earth. But when someone dies blithely and full of good hope, they do not mourn for him but carry the body cheerfully away, singing and commending the dead man's soul to God. They cremate[118] him in a spirit of reverence more than of grief, and erect in that place a column on which the dead man's honours are inscribed. After they have returned home, they talk of his character and deeds, and no part of his life is mentioned more frequently or more gladly than his joyful death.

They think that this remembrance of the dead person's probity inspires the living to behave virtuously and is the most acceptable form of honour to the dead. For they think that dead people are actually present among us, and hear what we say about them, though through the dullness of human sight they remain invisible. Given their state of bliss, the dead must be able to travel freely where they please, and it would be unkind of them to cast

---

[117] Some ancient philosophers – particularly the Pythagoreans, as a facet of their doctrine of the transmigration of souls – held the same view.

[118] Cremation was standard practice in most of the ancient world, but was not used by Christians before the nineteenth century.

off every desire of seeing those friends to whom in life they had been joined by mutual affection and charity. They think that after death charity, like other good qualities, is increased rather than diminished in good men; and thus they believe the dead come frequently among the living, to observe their words and acts.[119] Hence they go about their business the more confidently because of their trust in such protectors; and the belief that their forefathers are present keeps them from any secret dishonourable deed.

Fortune-telling and other vain, superstitious divinations, such as other peoples take very seriously, they have no part of and consider ridiculous. But they venerate miracles which occur without the help of nature, considering them direct and visible manifestations of the divinity. Indeed, they report that miracles often occur in their country. Sometimes in great and dangerous crises they pray publicly for a miracle, which they then anticipate with great confidence, and obtain.

They think the contemplation of nature and the reverence arising from it are a kind of worship acceptable to God. There are some people, however, and not just a few of them, who from religious motives neglect literary and scientific pursuits; but none of them is the least bit idle. They are determined to earn happiness after death only by their labours and *The active life* by doing good deeds for others. Some tend the sick; others repair roads, clean ditches, rebuild bridges, dig turf, sand or stones; still others fell trees and cut them up, and transport wood, grain or other commodities into the cities by wagon. They work for private citizens as well as for the public, and work even harder than slaves. With cheerful good will they undertake any task that is so rough, hard and dirty that most people refuse to tackle it because of the toil, tedium and frustration involved. While constantly engaged in heavy labour themselves, they procure leisure for others, yet claim no credit for it. They neither criticise the way others live nor boast of their own doings. The more they put themselves in the position of slaves, the more highly they are honoured by everyone.

These people are of two sects. The first are celibates who abstain not only from sex but also from eating meat, and some from any sort of animal food whatever. They completely reject all the pleasures of this life as harmful, and look forward only to the joys of the life to come, which they hope to

---

[119] In the *Dialogue Concerning Heresies*, More wrote of the saints that 'if their holy souls live, there will no wise man ween them worse, and of less love and charity to men that need their help, when they be now in heaven, than they had when they were here in earth . . . When saints were in this world at liberty and might walk the world about, ween we that in heaven they stand tied to a post?' (*CW*, VI, 211, 213).

merit by hard labour and all-night vigils. As they hope to attain it soon, they are cheerful and active in the here and now. The other kind are just as fond of hard work, but prefer to marry. They don't despise the comforts of marriage, but think that, as they owe nature their labour, so they owe children to their country. Unless it interferes with their labour, they avoid no pleasure. They eat meat, precisely because they think it makes them stronger for any sort of heavy work. The Utopians regard the second sort as more sensible, but the first sort as holier. If they chose celibacy over marriage and a hard life over a comfortable one on grounds of reason alone, they would be laughed at; but as these people profess to be motivated by religion, the Utopians respect and revere them. On no subject are they warier of jumping to conclusions than in this matter of religion. Such, then, are the people whom in their own language they call Buthrescas, a term which can be translated as 'the religious'.[120]

Their priests are of extraordinary holiness and therefore very few. In each city there are no more than thirteen, one for each church. In case of war, seven of them go out with the army, and seven substitutes are appointed to fill their places for the time being. When the regular priests come back, they all return to their former posts. Until the time when the extra priests succeed in an orderly fashion to the regular priests who have died, they serve as attendants to the high priest. For one of the priests has authority over the others. Like all other officials, priests are elected by secret popular vote, to avoid competition.[121] After election they are ordained by the college of priests.

They preside over divine worship, attend to religious matters, and act as censors of public morality; for a person to be summoned or brought before them for not living an honourable life is considered a great disgrace. As the duty of the priests is merely to counsel and advise, so correcting and punishing offenders is the duty of the governor and other officials, though the priests do exclude flagrant sinners from divine service. Hardly any punishment is more dreaded than this; the excommunicate suffers great infamy, and is secretly tortured by religious fear. Not even his body will be safe for very long, for unless he quickly convinces the priests of his repentance he will be seized and punished by the senate for impiety.

[120] 'Buthrescas' is another Greek compound, translated in the text. The constant, selfless industry of the Buthrescas embodies the monastic ideal (though in that ideal labour is combined with contemplation and prayer).

[121] They are elected from the class of scholars – whose members are nominated by the priests and elected by the syphogrants (p. 52).

The priests do the teaching of children and young people.[122] Instruction in morality and virtue is considered no less important than learning proper. They make every effort to instil in the pupils' minds, while they are still tender and pliable, principles useful to the commonwealth. What is planted in the minds of children lives on in the minds of grown men and serves greatly to strengthen the commonwealth; its decline can always be traced to vices that arise from wrong attitudes.[123]

Women are not debarred from the priesthood, but only a widow of advanced years is ever chosen, and it doesn't happen often. The wives of the male priests are the very finest women in the whole country.[124] *Female priests*

No official is more honoured among the Utopians than the priest, to such an extent that even if one of them commits a crime, he is not brought to court but left to God and his own conscience. They think it wrong to lay human hands on a man, however guilty, who has been specially consecrated to God, as a holy offering, so to speak. This custom is the easier for them to observe because their priests are so few and so carefully selected. For it rarely happens that a man chosen for his goodness and raised to high dignities solely because of his moral character will fall into corruption and vice. And even if such a thing should happen, human nature being as changeable as it is, no great harm to the public is to be feared, because the priests are so few and have no power beyond that which derives from their good repute. In fact, the reason for having so few priests is to prevent the order, now so highly esteemed, from being cheapened by numbers. Besides, they think it would be hard to find many men qualified for a dignity for which merely ordinary virtues are not sufficient. *Excommunication*[125]

But what a crowd of them we have!

Their priests are not more esteemed at home than abroad – the reason for which can easily be seen, I think, from the following account. Whenever their armies join in battle, the Utopian priests are to be found, a little removed from the fray but not far, wearing their sacred vestments and down on their knees. With hands raised to heaven, they pray first of all for peace, and then for victory for their own side, but without much

---

[122] Surely the priests only supervise the teaching. There are but thirteen of them per city, whereas each city includes a good many thousand children.

[123] The fundamental importance of education, including especially moral education, to the health of the commonwealth is the central tenet of the Greek treatments of the ideal commonwealth. See, e.g., Plato, *Republic* IV.424D–E, 425A; Aristotle, *Politics* V.vii.20, VIII.i.1–3.

[124] In *The Confutation of Tyndale's Answer* (1532–3), More took the standard position that the prohibition against female priests rests on divine revelation (*CW*, VIII, Part I, 260–1). Priestly celibacy, though, is a matter of ecclesiastical discipline rather than a divine decree (*ibid.*, 307).

[125] All four early editions place the gloss here, but it perhaps belongs three paragraphs earlier.

O priests far more holy than our own!

bloodshed on either part.[126] Should their side be victorious, they rush among the combatants and restrain the rage of their own men against the defeated. If any of the enemy see these priests and call to them, it is enough to save their lives; to touch the flowing robes of a priest will save all their property from confiscation. This custom has brought them such veneration among all peoples, and given them such genuine authority, that they have saved Utopians from the rage of the enemy as often as they have protected the enemy from Utopians. For it is well established that on some occasions, when the Utopian line had buckled, when the field was lost, and the enemy was rushing in to kill and plunder, the priests have intervened to stop the carnage and separate the armies, and an equitable peace has been devised and concluded. There was never anywhere a tribe so fierce, cruel and barbarous as not to hold their persons sacrosanct and inviolable.

Feast days observed by the Utopians

The Utopians celebrate the first and last days of every month, and likewise of each year, as feast days. They divide the year into months, which they measure by the orbit of the moon, just as they measure the year itself by the course of the sun. In their language, the first days are known as the Cynemerns and the last days as the Trapemerns,[127] which is to say 'First-feasts' and 'Last-feasts'. Their churches are beautifully

What their churches are like

constructed, finely adorned, and large enough to hold a great many worshippers. This is a necessity, since churches are so few.[128] The interiors are all rather dark, not from architectural ignorance but from deliberate policy; for the priests (they say) think that in bright light thoughts will go wandering, whereas a dim light concentrates the mind and aids devotion.

Though there are various religions in Utopia, all of them, even the most diverse, agree in the main point, which is worship of the divine nature; they are like travellers going to a single destination by different roads. So nothing is seen or heard in the churches that does not square with all the creeds. If any sect has a special rite of its own, that is celebrated in a private

---

[126] By contrast, Erasmus describes European clerics as 'often ... very firebrands of war' (*The Education of a Christian Prince*, CWE, XXVII, 286), and his Folly tells of German bishops who think it dishonourable to die anywhere but on the battlefield (*ibid.*, 140).

[127] More Greek compounds, literally meaning 'Dog-days' (or possibly 'Starting-days') and 'Turning-days'. A note in J. H. Lupton's edition explains that in ancient Greece the 'dog's day' was 'strictly the night between the old and new [months], when food was placed out at the cross-roads, and the barking of the dogs was taken as a sign of the approach of Hecate' (goddess of darkness and the underworld). It may be relevant that Solon, the legendary lawgiver of Athens, called the last day of each month the 'Old-and-New day' (Diogenes Laertius 1.58).

[128] Doubtless there are several shifts of worship, but even so the churches must be *very* large: there are thirteen of them in each city, and each city contains over 100,000 people (p. 54n.).

house; the public service is ordered by a ritual which in no way derogates from any of the private services. Therefore in the churches no images of the gods are seen, so that each person may be free to form his own image of God according to his own religion, in any shape he pleases.[129] They do not invoke God by any name except Mythra. Whatever the nature of the divine majesty may be, they all agree to refer to it by that single word, and their prayers are so phrased that anyone can say them without offending his own sect.

They meet in their churches, therefore, on the evening of 'Last-feast', and while still fasting they thank God for their prosperity during the month or year just ending. Next day, which is 'First-feast', they all flock to the churches in the morning to pray for prosperity and happiness in the month or year just beginning. But on the day of 'Last-feast', at home, before they go to church, wives kneel before their husbands and children before their parents, to confess their sins of commission or of negligence, and beg forgiveness for their offences. Thus if any cloud of anger or resentment has arisen in the family, it is dispersed, and they can attend the sacrifices with clear and untroubled minds – for they are too scrupulous to worship with a rankling conscience.[130] If they are aware of hatred or anger toward anyone, they do not attend the sacrifices till they have been reconciled and have cleansed their hearts, for fear of some swift and terrible punishment. *The Utopians' confession* *But among us the worst sinners try to crowd closest to the altar*

As they enter the temple they separate, men going to the right side and women to the left.[131] Then they take their seats so that the males of each household are placed in front of the head of that household, while the womenfolk are directly in front of the mother of the family. In this way they ensure that all of everyone's public behaviour is supervised by the same person whose authority and discipline direct him at home. They take great care that the young are everywhere placed in the company of their elders.

[129] In one way or another, Utopian religion answers or somehow satisfies many of the complaints of the religious reformers of More's time – including complaints about idolatry and superstitious practices, ecclesiastical wealth and corruption, and censorship of expression on religious matters.

[130] Cf. Christ's injunction: 'if thou bring thy gift to the altar, and there rememberest that thy brother hath ought against thee; Leave there thy gift before the altar, and go thy way; first be reconciled to thy brother, and then come and offer thy gift' (Matthew 5:23–4). The Catholic institution of confession to priests is not paralleled in Utopia. More pointed out to his daughter Margaret that 'in Greece before Christ's days they used not confession, no more the men then, than the beasts now' (*The Correspondence of Sir Thomas More*, ed. Elizabeth F. Rogers (Princeton, 1947), p. 520).

[131] Separation of the sexes in church had been customary since the early Christian centuries.

For if children were trusted to the care of other children, they might spend in infantile foolery the time they should devote to developing a religious fear of the gods, which is the greatest and almost the only incitement to virtue.

They slaughter no animals in their sacrifices, and do not think that a merciful God, who gave life to all creatures that they might live, will be gratified with slaughter and bloodshed. They burn incense, scatter perfumes and display a great number of candles – not that they think these practices profit the divine nature in any way, any more than human prayers do; but they like this harmless kind of worship. They feel that sweet smells, lights and other such rituals somehow elevate the human mind and lift it with a livelier devotion towards the adoration of God.

In church the people all wear white. The priest wears robes of various colours, wonderful for their workmanship and decoration, though not made of especially costly materials. The robes have no gold embroidery nor any rare gems sewn on them, but are decorated with the feathers of different birds so skilfully woven together that the value of the handiwork far exceeds the cost of the richest materials.[132] Also, certain symbolic mysteries are hidden in the patterning of the feathers on the robes, the meaning of which is carefully taught by the priests. These messages serve to remind them of God's benefits toward them, and of the piety they owe in turn to God, as well as of their duty to one another.

As the priest in his robes appears from the vestibule, the people all fall to the ground in reverence. The stillness is so complete that the scene strikes one with awe, as if a divinity were actually present. After remaining in this posture for a little while, they rise at a signal from the priest. Then they *Utopian music* sing hymns to the accompaniment of musical instruments, most of them quite different in shape from those seen in our part of the world. Many of them produce sweeter tones than ours, but others are not even comparable. In one respect, however, they are beyond doubt far ahead of us, because all their music, both vocal and instrumental, renders and expresses natural feelings and perfectly matches the sound to the subject.[133] Whether the words of the prayer are supplicatory, cheerful, serene, troubled, mournful or angry, the music represents the meaning through the contour of the melody so admirably that it stirs up, penetrates and inflames the minds

---

[132] The choice of feathers for the vestments may reflect Vespucci's observation that the native Americans' riches 'consist of variegated birds' feathers' (*Four Voyages*, p. 98).

[133] Surtz points out that Hythloday's dissatisfaction with the increasingly elaborate church music of his time was shared by many other intellectuals (*CW*, IV, 555–6).

of the hearers. Finally, the priest and the people together recite certain fixed forms of prayer, so composed that what they all repeat in unison each individual can apply to himself.

In these prayers each one acknowledges God to be the creator and ruler of the universe and the author of all good things. He thanks God for the many benefits he has received, and particularly for the divine favour which placed him in the happiest of commonwealths and inspired him with religious ideas which he hopes are the truest. If he is wrong in this, and if there is some sort of society or religion more acceptable to God, he prays that God will, in his goodness, reveal it to him, for he is ready to follow wherever he leads. But if their form of society is the best and their religion the truest, then he prays that God will keep him steadfast, and bring other mortals to the same way of life and the same religious faith – unless, indeed, there is something in this variety of religions which delights his inscrutable will.

Then he prays that after an easy death God will take him to himself, how soon or late it is not for him to say. But if it please God's divine majesty, he asks to be brought to him soon, even by the hardest possible death, rather than be kept away from him longer, even by the most prosperous of earthly careers. When this prayer has been said, they prostrate themselves on the ground again; then after a little while they rise and go to lunch. The rest of the day they pass in games and military training.

Now I have described to you as accurately as I could the structure of that commonwealth which I consider not only the best but indeed the only one that can rightfully claim that name. In other places men talk all the time about the commonwealth, but what they mean is simply their own wealth; here,[134] where there is no private business, every man zealously pursues the public business. And in both places people are right to act as they do. For elsewhere, even though the commonwealth may flourish, there are very few who do not know that unless they make separate provision for themselves, they may perfectly well die of hunger. Bitter necessity, then, forces them to think that they must look out for themselves rather than for the people, that is, for other people. But here, where everything belongs to everybody, no one need fear that, so long as the public warehouses are filled, anyone will ever lack for anything for his own use. For the distribution of goods is not niggardly; no one is poor there, there are no beggars, and though no one owns anything, everyone is rich.

[134] Hythloday speaks as if he were still in Utopia.

For what can be greater riches than to live joyfully and peacefully, free from all anxieties, and without worries about making a living? No man is bothered by his wife's querulous complaints, no man fears poverty for his son, or worries about a dowry for his daughter. Everyone can feel secure of his own livelihood and happiness, and of his whole family's as well: wife, sons, grandsons, great-grandsons, great-great-grandsons, and that whole long line of descendants that the gentry are so fond of contemplating. Indeed, even those who once worked but can no longer do so are cared for just as well as those who are still working.

At this point, I'd like to see anyone venture to compare this equity of the Utopians with the justice that prevails among other nations – among whom I'll be damned if I can discover the slightest trace of justice or fairness. What kind of justice is it when a nobleman, a goldsmith,[135] a moneylender, or someone else who makes his living by doing either nothing at all or something not especially necessary for the commonwealth, gets to live a life of luxury and grandeur, while in the meantime a labourer, a carter or a carpenter or a farmer works so hard and so constantly that even beasts of burden would scarcely endure it? Although this work of theirs is so necessary that no commonwealth could survive for a year without it, they earn so meagre a living and lead such miserable lives that beasts would really seem to be better off. Beasts do not have to work every minute, and their food is not much worse; in fact they like it better, and besides, they do not have to worry about their future. But workingmen must not only sweat without reward or gain in the present but agonise over the prospect of a penniless old age. Their daily wage is inadequate even for present needs, so there is no possible chance of their saving today for their declining years.

Now isn't this an unjust and ungrateful commonwealth? It lavishes rich rewards on so-called gentry, goldsmiths and the rest of that crew, who don't work at all or are mere parasites, purveyors of empty pleasures. And yet it makes no proper provision for the welfare of farmers and colliers, labourers, carters and carpenters, without whom the commonwealth would simply cease to exist. After society has taken the labour of their best years, when they are worn out by age, sickness and utter destitution, then the thankless commonwealth, forgetting all their sleepless nights

---

[135] In addition to being the creators of objects that are, from the Utopian point of view, worthless, goldsmiths often functioned as bankers. As the inclusion of moneylenders in this list suggests, the idea that lending money at interest constituted sinful usury remained strong in More's time – though the sentence also makes it clear that the practice was firmly established.

and services, throws them out to die a miserable death. What is worse, the rich constantly try to grind out of the poor part of their daily wages, not only by private swindling but by public laws. Before, it appeared to be unjust that people who deserve most from the commonwealth should receive least. But now, by promulgating law, they have transmuted this perversion into justice.[136] When I consider and turn over in my mind the various commonwealths flourishing today, so help me God, I can see in them nothing but a conspiracy of the rich, who are advancing their own interests under the name and title of the commonwealth.[137] They invent ways and means to keep, with no fear of losing it, whatever they have piled up by sharp practice, and then they scheme to oppress the poor by buying their toil and labour as cheaply as possible. These devices become law as soon as the rich, speaking for the commonwealth – which, of course, includes the poor as well – say they must be observed.

Reader, note well!

And yet when these insatiably greedy and evil men have divided among themselves all the goods which would have sufficed for the entire people, how far they remain from the happiness of the Utopian republic, which has abolished not only money but with it greed! What a mass of trouble was cut away by that one step! What a thicket of crimes was uprooted! Everyone knows that if money were abolished, fraud, theft, robbery, quarrels, brawls, altercations, seditions, murders, treasons, poisonings and a whole set of crimes which are avenged but not prevented by the hangman would at once die out. At the very moment when money disappeared, so would fear, anxiety, worry, toil and sleepless nights. Even poverty, the one condition which has always seemed to need money, would immediately decline if money were entirely abolished.

Consider, if you will, this example. Take a barren year of failed harvests, when many thousands of people have been carried off by famine. If at the end of the scarcity the barns of the rich were searched, I dare assert that enough grain would be found in them to have kept all those who died of starvation and disease from even realising that a shortage ever existed – if only it had been divided among them. So easily might people get the necessities of life if that blessed money, that marvellous invention which is supposed to provide access to what we need to live, were not in fact

---

[136] Russell Ames suggests that there is a particular reference to legislation of recent Parliaments, completed in 1515, 'which re-enacted the old statutes against laborers while removing clauses unfavorable to employers' (*Citizen Thomas More and His Utopia* (Princeton, 1949), p. 128).

[137] Many readers have seen an allusion here to the judgement of St Augustine: 'if justice is left out, what are kingdoms but great robber bands?' (*The City of God* IV.iv).

the only barrier to our getting it. Even the rich, I'm sure, understand this. They must know that it's better to have enough of what we really need than an abundance of superfluities, much better to escape from our many present troubles than to be burdened with great masses of wealth. And in fact I have no doubt that every man's perception of where his true interest lies, along with the authority of Christ our Saviour (whose wisdom could not fail to recognise the best, and whose goodness would not fail to counsel it), would long ago have brought the whole world to adopt the laws of this *A striking phrase* commonwealth, were it not for one single monster, the prime plague and begetter of all others – I mean Pride.

Pride measures her prosperity not by what she has but by what others lack. Pride would not deign even to be made a goddess if there were no wretches for her to sneer at and domineer over. Her good fortune is dazzling only by contrast with the miseries of others; she displays her riches to torment and tantalise the poverty of others. Pride is a serpent from hell that twines itself around the hearts of men, acting like a suckfish[138] to draw and hold them back from choosing a better way of life.

Pride is too deeply fixed in human nature to be easily plucked out. So I am glad that the Utopians at least have been lucky enough to achieve this republic which I wish all mankind would imitate. Through the plan of living which they have adopted, they have laid the foundations of a commonwealth that is not only very happy but also, so far as human prescience can tell, likely to last forever. Now that they have torn up the seeds of ambition and faction at home, along with most other vices, they are in no danger from internal strife, which alone has destroyed the prosperity of many cities that seemed eminently secure. As long as they preserve harmony at home, and keep their institutions healthy, they can never be overcome or even shaken by all the envious princes of neighbouring countries, who have often attempted their ruin, but always in vain.

When Raphael had finished his story, I was left thinking that not a few of the laws and customs he had described as existing among the Utopians were really absurd. These included their methods of waging war, their religious practices, as well as other customs of theirs; but my chief objection was to the basis of their whole system, that is, their communal living and their moneyless economy. This one thing alone utterly subverts all the

[138] The remora has a suction plate atop its head, by which it attaches itself to the underbelly of larger fish or the hulls of ships. Impressed by the tenacity of its grip, the ancients fabled that it could impede ships in their course.

nobility, magnificence, splendour and majesty which (in the popular view) are the true ornaments and glory of any commonwealth.[139] But I knew that Raphael was tired with talking, and I was not sure he could take contradiction in these matters, particularly when I recalled that he had reproached certain people who were afraid they might not appear knowing enough unless they found something to criticise in the ideas of others. So with praise for their way of life and his account of it, I took him by the hand and led him in to supper. But first I said that we would find some other time for thinking of these matters more deeply, and for talking them over in more detail. Would that this would happen some day!

Meantime, while I can hardly agree with everything he said (though he is a man of unquestionable learning and enormous experience of human affairs), yet I freely confess that in the Utopian commonwealth there are very many features that in our own societies I would wish rather than expect to see.

END OF BOOK II.

THE END OF THE AFTERNOON DISCOURSE OF
RAPHAEL HYTHLODAY ON THE LAWS AND
INSTITUTIONS OF THE ISLAND OF UTOPIA,
HITHERTO KNOWN TO BUT FEW,
AS RECORDED BY THE MOST DISTINGUISHED
AND LEARNED MAN, MASTER THOMAS MORE,
CITIZEN AND UNDERSHERIFF OF LONDON.

---

[139] The view of 'More' is consistent with the Aristotelian position of his earlier speech against communism (pp. 38–9). Aristotle insists on the connection between nobility and wealth (*Politics* IV.viii.9, V.i.7), defines magnificence as 'suitable expenditure on a great scale' (*Nicomachean Ethics* IV.ii.1), and in general stresses the necessary connection between money and the exercise of virtue. These views were influential in the Renaissance, when, for example, the writers of advice books for rulers regarded magnificence and majesty as among the most important princely virtues. In both books of *Utopia*, however, Hythloday's remarks have suggested a radically opposed conception of the 'ornaments and glory' of a commonwealth.

Ancillary materials from
the early editions

THOMAS MORE TO HIS FRIEND PETER GILES, WARMEST GREETINGS[1]

My dear Peter, I was absolutely delighted with the judgement of that very sharp fellow you recall, who posed this dilemma regarding my *Utopia*: if the story is offered as fact (says he) then I see a number of absurdities in it; but if it is fiction, then I think More's usual good judgement is wanting in some matters. I'm very much obliged to this man, whoever he may be (I suspect he is learned, and I see he's a friend). His frank judgement gratified me more than any other reaction I've seen since my book appeared. First of all, led on by fondness either for me or for the work itself, he did not give up in the middle, but read my book all the way through. And he didn't read carelessly or quickly, as priests read the divine office – those who read it at all – but slowly and carefully in order to consider the different points thoughtfully. Then, having selected certain elements to criticise, and not very many of them, he says that he approves, not rashly but deliberately, of all the rest. Finally, he implies in his very words of criticism higher praise than those who set out to compliment the book on purpose. For he shows clearly how well he thinks of me when he expresses disappointment in a passage that is not as precise as it should be – whereas I would think myself lucky if I had been able to set down just a few things out of many that were not altogether absurd.

Still, if I in my turn can deal as frankly with him as he with me, I don't see why he should think himself so acute (or, as the Greeks say, so 'sharp-sighted') just because he has noted some absurdities in the institutions of the Utopians, or caught me putting forth some not sufficiently

---

[1] This second letter of More to Giles appeared only in the 1517 edition, where it immediately followed the text of Book II. The identity of the 'very sharp fellow' (below) is unknown – if indeed More didn't invent him.

practical ideas about the constitution of a republic. Aren't there any absurdities elsewhere in the world? And did any one of all the philosophers who have offered a pattern of a society, a ruler, or a private household set down everything so well that nothing ought to be changed? Actually, if it weren't for the great respect I retain for certain highly distinguished names, I could easily produce from each of them a number of notions which I can hardly doubt would be universally condemned as absurd.

But when he questions whether the book is fact or fiction, I find *his* usual good judgement wanting. I do not deny that if I had decided to write of a commonwealth, and a tale of this sort had come to my mind, I might not have shrunk from a fiction through which the truth, like medicine smeared with honey, might enter the mind a little more pleasantly. But I would certainly have softened the fiction a little, so that, while imposing on vulgar ignorance, I gave hints to the more learned which would enable them to see what I was about. Thus, if I had merely given such names to the governor, the river, the city and the island as would indicate to the knowing reader that the island was nowhere, the city a phantom, the river waterless and the governor without a people,[2] it wouldn't have been hard to do, and would have been far more clever than what I actually did. If the veracity of a historian had not actually required me to do so, I am not so stupid as to have preferred those barbarous and meaningless names of Utopia, Anyder, Amaurot and Ademus.

But I see, my dear Giles, some men are so suspicious that in their circumspect sagacity they can hardly be brought to believe what we simpleminded and credulous fellows wrote down of Hythloday's story. Lest my personal credibility among these people be shaken, not to speak of my reputation as a historian, I am glad I can say of my brainchild what Mysis, in Terence's play, says about Glycerium's boy, to keep him from being thought a changeling: 'By all the gods, I am glad that some ladies of rank were present at his birth.'[3] Similarly, it's my good fortune that Raphael told his story, not just to you and me, but to a great many other men, of the utmost gravity and unquestioned probity. I don't know whether he told them more and greater things, but I'm sure he told them no fewer and no less important things than he told us.

---

[2] This is of course precisely what the names mean.   [3] *The Lady of Andros* IV.iv; ll. 770–1.

But if the doubters are not satisfied even with these witnesses, let them consult Hythloday himself, for he is still alive. I recently heard from some travellers out of Portugal that on the first day of last March he was still healthy and vigorous as ever. And so let them ask him for the truth, or let them dig it out of him with their questions. I only want them to understand that I answer only for my own work, not for anyone else's credibility. Farewell to you, my dear Peter, to your charming wife and clever little daughter – to all, my wife sends her very best wishes.

ERASMUS OF ROTTERDAM TO HIS VERY DEAR FRIEND JOHANN FROBEN, THE FATHER OF HIS GODSON, GREETINGS[1]

While heretofore I have always thought extremely well of all of my friend More's writings, yet I rather mistrusted my own judgement because of the very close friendship between us. But when I see all the learned unanimously subscribe to my opinion, and esteem even more highly than I the divine wit of this man, not because they love him better but because they see more deeply into his merits, I am wholly confirmed in my opinion and no longer shrink from saying openly what I feel. How admirably would his fortunate disposition have stood forth if his genius had been nurtured in Italy![2] If he had devoted his whole energy to the service of the Muses, maturing gradually, as it were, towards his own proper harvest! As a youth, he toyed with epigrams, many written when he was only a lad. He has never left Britain except a couple of times to serve his prince as an

---

[1] In a letter of *c.* 20 September 1516, More told Erasmus he was anxious that *Utopia* 'be handsomely set off with the highest of recommendations, if possible, from several people, both intellectuals and distinguished statesmen' (*Selected Letters*, p. 76). Erasmus complied, in spades. The practice of publishing books with buttressing commendations was common then as now, but the amount of ancillary material in *Utopia* is unusual. The letters and poems are valuable, though, in indicating how *Utopia* struck the humanist readers for whom More appears primarily to have intended it. This and the following letters, poems and other materials are given in the order in which they appear in the edition of March 1518. Most of them preceded the text, but three items were printed at the end.

It is interesting that Erasmus' own tribute – which implies some reservations – did not appear until this third edition of the book. The addressee, Johann Froben (*c.* 1460–1527), was the distinguished printer whose Basel shop produced the edition and its November successor.

[2] I.e., in the centre of humanist learning.

ambassador to Flanders.[3] Apart from the cares of a married man and the responsibilities of his household, apart from his official post and floods of legal cases, he is distracted by so many and such important matters of state business that you would marvel he finds any free time at all for books.

For this reason I am sending you his *Exercises*[4] and his *Utopia*, so that, if you think proper, their appearance under your imprint may commend them to the world and to posterity. For the authority of your firm is such that a book is sure of pleasing the learned as soon as it is known to issue from the house of Froben. Farewell to you, to your excellent father-in-law,[5] your dear wife, and your delightful children. Make sure that Erasmus, the little son we share in common, and who was born among books, is educated in the best of them.

Louvain, 25 August 1517

GUILLAUME BUDE TO THOMAS LUPSET OF ENGLAND, GREETINGS[6]

Most learned of young men, Lupset, you have left me enormously in your debt by presenting me with the *Utopia* of Thomas More, and thereby introducing me to an extremely amusing and profitable book. In fact, you had recently asked me to do what on my own account I was more than ready to do – that is, to read over the six books of Galen, *On Protecting One's Health*, which the physician Thomas Linacre, a man equally skilled

---

[3] Actually More had visited the Universities of Louvain and Paris in 1508 (see *Selected Letters*, p. 17). The Flanders missions were the one during which he began *Utopia* (1515) and another in 1517.

[4] The *Exercises* (*Progymnasmata*) were a series of rival translations by More and the grammarian William Lily: both men made Latin versions of the same Greek epigrams. The *Exercises* were bound with *Utopia* in the Froben editions, along with a second series of epigrams by More and a collection of poems by Erasmus.

[5] Wolfgang Lachner, a bookseller who played an important part in Froben's business.

[6] While studying in Paris in 1517, Thomas Lupset (*c.* 1498-1530) supervised the printing of two of Thomas Linacre's translations of works by Galen (the great medical authority of classical Greece), and of the second edition of *Utopia*. He also made the acquaintance of Budé (1468-1540), the foremost French humanist of the time. Budé's lengthy epistle, which typifies humanist rhetoric at its most florid, was first published in the 1517 edition. Erasmus described the letter as an 'elegant preface' for More's book (*CWE*, v, 326), and he made a point of getting it into the Basel editions.

in both languages, lately translated from the extant originals, endowing them with Latinity – or rather bestowing them on Latinity – in such a way that if all the works of this author (who all by himself, in my view, comprehends the entire science of medicine) were turned into such Latin, the medical profession would then not need to know Greek. I consider your lending to me for so long a time the manuscripts of Linacre an act of the highest generosity; I believe I profited immensely from my first hasty reading of them, and I promise myself even richer rewards from the printed volume which you are just now busily ushering through the presses of this city. For this reason I already thought myself sufficiently in your debt; and now, as an appendix or supplement to your former gift, you send me the *Utopia* of More, a man of the keenest wit, the most agreeable temper and the most profound experience in judging human affairs.

I took his book with me to the country and kept it in my hands as I bustled about, in constant activity, supervising the various workmen (for you no doubt know, or have at least heard, that for two years now I have been absorbed in business connected with my country house); but when I read it I was so fascinated with learning about and reflecting on the customs of the Utopians that I almost forgot and even dismissed entirely the management of my household affairs. What nonsense, I thought, is all this bustle over maintaining a household, this whole business of constantly accumulating more and more!

And yet this appetite, like a hidden parasite rooted in our flesh from birth, preys on the whole human race – there is no one who does not see and understand that fact. I might almost say we are bound to admit that this is the real end of legal training and the profession of the civil law: to make each man act with ingrained and calculated malice towards the neighbour to whom he is linked by ties of citizenship and sometimes of blood. He is always grabbing something, taking it away, extorting it, suing for it, squeezing it out, breaking it loose, gouging it away, twisting it off, snatching it, snitching it, filching it, pinching it, pilfering it, pouncing on it – partly with the tacit complicity of the laws, partly with their direct sanction, he carries off what he wants and makes it his own.

This is particularly frequent in those countries where the two codes of law, called civil and canonical, exercise their double jurisdiction more widely. Everyone knows that through their precedents and institutions the opinion has solidified that only men skilled in the ways – or perhaps just the wiles – of the law, only those who set snares for unwary citizens, artists of the legal phrase or fraud, contrivers of complicated contracts, fosterers of litigation, exponents of a perverse, confused and unjust justice – only such men as these are to be thought the high priests of justice and equity. They only are qualified to say peremptorily what is just and good, they only have the authority and power to decide (a much greater matter) what each and every man should have, what he should not have, how much he can have and how long he can keep it; and all of this is accepted by a public opinion vitiated by illusions. Because they are bleary-eyed almost to the point of blindness, most men tend to think an individual has received full justice to the extent that he has satisfied the requirements of the law or received what the law allots him.

But if we measured our rights by the norm of truth and the prescriptions of evangelical simplicity, nobody is so dull or senseless as not to recognise, and (if pressed) to admit, that there are enormous differences. Justice is as remote from what is dispensed by papal decrees (both today and for a long time past), and real equity is as distant from what is expressed through civil laws and royal decrees, as the rule established by Christ, founder of our human condition, and observed by his disciples, is distant from the decrees and regulations of those who think the perfection of human happiness and the ultimate good are to be found in the gold-bags of Croesus and Midas.[7] So much so that if you now mean by justice what it used to mean in days gone by, that is, the power which gives to each his due,[8] you must either conclude it has no public existence at all or else we shall have to confess that it is (excuse the expression) like the servant girl who doles out the kitchen supplies. And this is true whether you regard the behaviour of our modern rulers or the relations between our fellow citizens and fellow countrymen.

Of course some argue that our modern law derives from an ancient and authentic code (which they call the law of nature), according to which the stronger a man is the more goods he should have, and the more goods he has the more authority he should exercise over his fellow citizens.[9]

---

[7] Proverbially rich men of antiquity.

[8] Cf. Cicero, *On the Supreme Good and Evil* V.xxiii.65; and Justinian, *Digests* I.1.10.

[9] The idea that there is an unchanging, universally valid body of natural law, which human beings apprehend by reason and instinct, was a central concept of legal and political theory from classical antiquity to the nineteenth century. Since human equality was normally regarded as a fundamental precept of natural law, the doctrine that might makes right could be derived from it only by a perverse understanding. The 'law of nations' (below) signifies the body of legal principles common to different peoples: what is universally practised, but

The result of this logic is that it is now an accepted principle of the law of nations that men who are of no practical use whatever to their fellow citizens and countrymen – so long as they can keep everyone else tied up in contractual knots and complicated testamentary clauses (matters which appear to the ignorant multitude, no less than to those humanistic scholars who live as retired and disinterested seekers after truth, as a vulgar combination of Gordian-knot tricks and common charlatanry surely not to be admired) – such men, it is now agreed, should have incomes equal to a thousand ordinary citizens, equal to a whole city, or even more. And they also acquire an honourable reputation, as wealthy men, worthy men, magnificent entrepreneurs. This happens in every age, under any customs and institutions and among any peoples who have decided that a man should have supreme power and authority in the degree that he has built up the biggest possible private fortune for himself and his heirs. And the process is cumulative, since his descendants and their descendants strive to build up their inheritance by one gigantic increment after another – meanwhile cutting off stringently all their connections and relatives by marriage, birth or blood.

But the founder and controller of all property, Christ, left his followers a Pythagorean rule of mutual charity and community property; not only so, but he confirmed it unmistakably when Ananias was sentenced to death for violating the rule of community property.[10] By this arrangement, Christ seems to me to have undermined – at least among his own disciples – all that body of civil and the more recent canon law worked out in so many vast volumes. Yet this is the law which we see now holding the fort of wisdom and ruling over our destinies.

The island of Utopia, however, which I hear is also called Udepotia,[11] is said (if the story is to be believed) to have imbibed, by marvellous good fortune, both in its public and its private life, truly Christian customs and authentic wisdom, and to have kept them inviolate even to this day. It has done so by holding tenaciously to three divine institutions: equality of all good and evil things among the citizens (or, if you prefer, full and complete

not necessarily consonant with natural justice. For a clear exposition of the development and relation of these concepts, see R. W. Carlyle and A. J. Carlyle, *A History of Mediaeval Political Theory in the West*, 6 vols. (1903–36), I, especially 33–44.

[10] Pythagoras was believed to have instituted a communal life among his followers. On the communism of the early Christians, see Acts 2:44–5. When Ananias sold a possession and 'kept back part of the price', Peter reproached him and he fell dead (Acts 5:1–5).

[11] From Greek *oudepote*, 'never'.

citizenship for all); a fixed and unwavering dedication to peace and tranquillity; and utter contempt for gold and silver. These three principles are the dragnets (so to speak) which sweep up all swindles, impostures, tricks, wiles and underhanded deceptions. Would that the gods, by their divine power, could cause these three pillars of Utopian policy to be fixed by the bolts of strong and settled conviction in the minds of all mortals. You would promptly witness the withering away of pride, greed, idiot competition and almost all the other deadly weapons of our hellish adversary. The immense weight of all those legal volumes, which occupy so many brilliant and solid minds for their whole lifetimes, would suddenly turn to empty air, the paper food for worms or used to wrap parcels in shops.

By all the gods above, I wonder what special holiness protected the Utopians, so that their island alone was shielded for so many centuries from the assaults, either stealthy or violent, of avarice and cupidity? What prevented those enemies from driving out justice and modesty under an onslaught of shameless effrontery? Would that almighty God, in his infinite goodness, had dealt as kindly with those regions which embrace and take their title from his most holy name! Surely avarice, the vice which now depraves and debases so many minds which might otherwise have been keen and vigorous, would then depart forever, and the golden age of Saturn[12] would return. One might even assert that Aratus and the other old poets were mistaken when they said Justice had fled the earth, and gave her a place in the zodiac.[13] For if we believe Hythloday, she must have remained on the island of Utopia and not yet have gone to heaven.

In fact, I have discovered, after investigating the matter, that Utopia lies outside the bounds of the known world. Perhaps it is one of the Fortunate Isles,[14] near neighbour to the Elysian Fields. As More himself

---

[12] Saturn ruled over the first and best of the mythological Four Ages of Man, an era of peace and happiness that ended when he was deposed by his son Jupiter.

[13] According to the Greek poet Aratus (fl. third century BC), the goddess of Justice, Astraea, who is identified with the constellation Virgo, departed earth in the face of mounting human wickedness.

[14] In classical culture, the Fortunate Isles, or Islands of the Blest, were the eternal paradise of heroes. They were thought to be situated – like Utopia – in the remotest west. The Isles were sometimes loosely identified with the Elysian Fields, that part of Hades where the virtuous pass eternity in the favourite pursuits of their former lives.

says, Hythloday has not yet told exactly where it is to be found. Though it is divided into a number of different cities, they are all united or confederated in a single society named Hagnopolis,[15] a nation content with its own customs and possessions, blessedly innocent, leading a celestial life, as it were – lower than heaven, indeed, but far above the smoke and stir of this known world, which – among men's constant squabbles, as violent and bitter as they are silly and futile – is being swept down a whirling cataract to the abyss.

Our knowledge of this island we owe to Thomas More, who in our time made known this model of the happy life and rule for living well. The actual discovery he attributes to Hythloday, to whom he assigns the whole thing. Thus, if Hythloday is the architect of the Utopian nation, the founder of its customs and institutions from which he has borrowed and brought home for us the very pattern of a happy life, More certainly is its adorner, who has bestowed on the island and its holy institutions the grace of his style, the polish of his diction. He it is who has shaped the city of the Hagnopolitans to the standard of a model and a general rule, and added all those touches which give beauty, order and authority to a magnificent work. And yet he claims as his part of the task only the role of a humble artisan. Evidently he made scruple of asserting too great a role in the book, lest Hythloday have grounds for complaint that More had prematurely plucked and pre-empted the glory due to him, which he might have had if he himself had chosen to write up his travels. *He feared, of course, that Hythloday, who was living of his own free will on the island of Udepotia, might some day return, and be angry and vexed at More's unfairness in leaving him only the husks of credit for his discovery. Such a conviction is characteristic of wise and virtuous men.*[16]

While More himself is a man of weight whose word carries great authority, I am bound to give him full credit on the word of Peter Giles of Antwerp. Though I do not know Giles personally – apart from commendations that have reached me of his learning and character – I love him because he is the sworn and intimate friend of Erasmus, a most distinguished man who has contributed so much to every sort of literary study, whether sacred or profane. With him I have long been in correspondence, with him I have long been on terms of close friendship.

---

[15] Holy City, or City of the Saints.   [16] Budé wrote the italicised passage in Greek.

Farewell, my dearest Lupset, and as soon as you can convey my greetings, whether in person or by letter, to Linacre, that pillar of the British name in all that concerns good learning; by now, I hope, he is no more yours than ours. He is one of the very few men whose good opinion I should be glad, if possible, to earn. When he was here, he made the very deepest and most favourable impression on me and on Jean Du Ruel, my friend and fellow student.[17] His excellent learning and careful diligence I shall always especially admire and strive to imitate.

Give my best regards also to More, either by letter, as I said before, or in person. He is a man whose name, in my opinion, and as I have often said, stands high in the ledgers of Minerva;[18] I particularly love and revere him for what he has written about this island of the New World, Utopia. Our own age and ages to come will discover in his narrative a seedbed, so to speak, of elegant and useful concepts from which they will be able to borrow practices to be introduced into their own several nations and adapted for use there. Farewell.

Paris, 31 July [1517]

SIX LINES ON THE ISLAND OF UTOPIA WRITTEN BY ANEMOLIUS,[19] POET LAUREATE, AND NEPHEW TO HYTHLODAY BY HIS SISTER

'No-Place' was once my name, I lay so far;
But now with Plato's state I can compare,
Perhaps outdo her (for what he only drew
In empty words I have made live anew
In men and wealth, as well as splendid laws):
'The Good Place'[20] they should call me, with good cause.

---

[17] Like Linacre, Du Ruel was a physician and translator.
[18] The Roman goddess of wisdom and the arts, identified with the Greek goddess Athena.
[19] From Greek *anemolios*: 'windy'. The real author of the poem is not known.
[20] The word translated here is *eutopia*, from Greek *eu-* ('happy', 'fortunate') plus *topos* ('place').

MAP OF UTOPIA[21]

[21] The map is the work of the Dutch painter Ambrosius Holbein, brother of the much better-known Hans Holbein the Younger. The 1516 edition had a cruder map, by an unknown hand.

THE UTOPIAN ALPHABET[22]

a b c d e f g h i k l m n o p q r s t u x y
Ọⵙⵕⵔⵔⵙⵕⵕⵕⵕⵕⵕⵕⵕⵕⵕ

A QUATRAIN IN THE UTOPIAN LANGUAGE

Vtopos ha Boccas peula chama.
ⴹⵕⵔⴹⵕⵕⵔⵕⵕⵔⵕⵕⵔⵕⵕⵔⵕⵕ
polta chamaan
ⵔⵕⵕⵔⵕⵕⵔ·
Bargol he maglomí baccan
ⴹⵕⵕⵔⵕⵕⵔⵕⵕⵔⵕⵕⵔ
ſoma gymnoſophaon
ⵕⵕⵔⵕⵕⵔⵕⵕⵔⵕⵕⵔ·
Agrama gymnoſophon labarem
ⵕⵕⵔⵕⵕⵔⵕⵕⵔⵕⵕⵔⵕⵕ
bacha bodamilomin
ⵕⵕⵔⵕⵕⵔⵕⵕⵔⵕⵕⵔ·
Voluala barchin heman la
ⵕⵕⵔⵕⵕⵔⵕⵕⵔⵕⵕⵔ
lauoluola dramme pagloni.
ⵕⵕⵔⵕⵕⵔⵕⵕⵔⵕⵕⵔ·

A LITERAL TRANSLATION OF THESE VERSES

The commander Utopus made me, who was once not an island, into
an island. I alone of all nations, without philosophy, have portrayed for
mortals the philosophical city. Freely I impart my benefits; not unwillingly
I accept whatever is better.

---

[22] Peter Giles was evidently responsible for this page (see p. 121). The sample of the
Utopian language, which reveals affinities with Greek and Latin, has enough internal con-
sistency to suggest that it was worked out with some care. See the discussion in *CW*,
IV, 277–8. The Utopian quatrain is followed by a stilted Latin quatrain that purports to
translate it.

TO THE MOST DISTINGUISHED GENTLEMAN, MASTER JEROME DE BUSLEYDEN, PROVOST OF AIRE AND COUNCILLOR TO THE CATHOLIC KING CHARLES, PETER GILES OF ANTWERP SENDS GREETINGS:[23]

Most eminent Busleyden, the other day Thomas More (who, as you very well know from your intimate acquaintance with him, is one of the great ornaments of our age) sent me his *Island of Utopia*. It is a place known so far to only a few men, but which should be known by everyone, as going far beyond Plato's Republic. It is particularly interesting because it has been so vividly described, so carefully depicted and brought before our very eyes, by a man of such great eloquence. As often as I read it, I seem to see even more than when I heard the actual words of Raphael Hythloday – for I was present at his discourse quite as much as More himself. As a matter of fact, Hythloday himself showed no mean gifts of expression in setting forth his topic; it was perfectly plain that he wasn't just repeating what he had heard from other people but was describing exactly what he had seen close at hand with his own eyes and experienced in his own person, over a long period of time. I consider him a man with more knowledge of nations, peoples and business than even the famous Ulysses. Such a man as this has not, I think, been born in the last eight hundred years; by comparison with him, Vespucci seems to have seen nothing at all. Apart from the fact that we naturally describe what we have seen better than what we have only heard about, the man had a particular skill in explaining things. And yet when I contemplate the same matters as sketched by More's pen, I am so affected by them that I sometimes seem to be living in Utopia itself. I can scarcely believe, by heaven, Raphael saw as much in the five years he lived on the island as can be seen in More's description. That description contains, in every part of it, so many wonders that I don't know what to marvel at first or most. Perhaps it should be the accuracy of his splendid memory, which could recite almost word for word so many different things

[23] This letter dedicates *Utopia* to Busleyden and also gives Giles a chance to talk about the book and his own role in its creation. The Burgundian Busleyden (*c.* 1470–1517) was a prominent statesman and patron of learning. His dignities included the office of Provost of St Peter's Church at Aire and membership in the council of Charles, Prince of Castile, who inherited the title 'the Catholic' (along with the throne of Aragon) at the death of his grandfather Ferdinand II in 1516. More met Busleyden in 1515 and wrote three flattering epigrams about him and his fine house. He was particularly interested in having an opinion about *Utopia* from Busleyden, whom he regarded as ideally combining learning, virtue and practical experience (*Selected Letters*, pp. 80, 76). For Busleyden's commendation of *Utopia*, see pp. 122–5.

that he had only heard; or else his good judgement, which traced back to sources of which the common man is completely ignorant the evils that arise in commonwealths and the blessings that could arise in them. Or finally I might marvel at the strength and amplitude of his language, in which he has gathered together so much matter and presented it in a Latin both pure and vigorous. This is all the more remarkable in a man distracted, as he is, by a mass of public business and private concerns. But of course none of this will surprise you, most erudite Busleyden, since you have already learned from your intimate acquaintance with him to appreciate the more-than-human, the almost-divine genius of the man.

For the rest, I can add nothing to what he has written. Only I did see to it that the book included a quatrain written in the Utopian tongue, which Hythloday showed to me after More had gone away. I've prefixed to it the alphabet of the Utopians, and also added to the volume some marginal notes.[24]

As for More's difficulties about locating the island, Raphael did not try in any way to suppress that information, but he mentioned it only briefly and in passing, as if saving it for another occasion. And then an unlucky accident caused both of us to miss what he said. For while Raphael was speaking of it, one of More's servants came in to whisper something in his ear; and though I was listening, for that very reason, more intently than ever, one of the company, who I suppose had caught cold on shipboard, coughed so loudly that some of Raphael's words escaped me. But I will never rest till I have full information on this point and can give you not just the general location of the island but its exact latitude – provided only our friend Hythloday is safe and sound.

For we hear various stories about him, some people asserting that he died on the way home, others that he got home but could not bear the ways of his countrymen, retained his old hankering for Utopia, and so made his way back there.[25]

It's true, of course, that the name of this island is not to be found among the cosmographers, but Hythloday himself had an elegant answer for that. For, he said, either the name that the ancients gave it was later changed, or else they never discovered the island at all. Nowadays we find all sorts

---

[24] Giles here seems to claim credit for the marginal glosses in *Utopia*. On the title page of the 1517 edition, however, they are attributed to Erasmus. Perhaps both contributed glosses; or perhaps the 1517 edition is wrong.

[25] Cf. More's second letter to Giles, which says (p. 110) that Hythloday is alive and well and living in Portugal.

of lands turning up that the old geographers never mentioned. But what's the point of piling up these arguments authenticating the story, when we already have it on the word of More himself?

His uncertainty about having the book published I attribute to his modesty, and very creditable it is. But on many scores it seems to me a work that should not be suppressed any longer; on the contrary, it eminently deserves to be sent forth into the hands of men, especially as commended to the world by the patronage of your name. Nobody knows More's good qualities better than you do, and no one is better suited than you to serve the commonwealth with good counsels. At this work you have laboured for many years, earning the highest praise for wisdom as well as integrity. Farewell, then, you Maecenas[26] of learning and ornament of our era.

Antwerp, 1 November 1516

JEROME DE BUSLEYDEN TO THOMAS MORE, GREETINGS[1]

For you, my most distinguished friend More, it was not enough to have devoted all your care, labour and energy to the interest and advantage of individuals: such is your goodness and liberality that you must bestow them on the public at large. You saw that this service of yours, however great it might be, would deserve more favour, gain more gratitude, and aim at greater glory, the more widely it was diffused, the more people shared in it and were benefited by it. This is what you've always tried to do on other occasions, and now with remarkable felicity you've attained it again – I mean by that afternoon's discussion which you have written down and published, about the right and proper constitution (which everyone must long for) of the Utopian republic.

It is a delightful description of a wonderful establishment, replete with profound erudition and a consummate knowledge of human affairs. Both

---

[26] Maecenas was the patron of Virgil, Horace and other Roman writers; and is often, as here, the type of the patron.

[1] This and the two following items appeared as prefatory materials in the 1516 edition. For the editions of 1517 and 1518, they were moved to the back of the book. On Busleyden, see p. 120n. His letter came directly to Erasmus, who had solicited it, with a covering note making it clear that Busleyden wrote out of esteem for Erasmus (*CWE*, IV, 483). Like Budé (pp. 111–17), the wealthy Busleyden singles out Utopian communism for special praise.

qualities meet in this work so equally and so congenially that neither yields
to the other, but both contend on an even footing. You enjoy such a wide
range of learning and such profound experience that whatever you write
comes from full experience, and whatever you decide to say carries a full
weight of learning.[2] A rare and wonderful happiness! And all the more
remarkable in that it withdraws itself from the multitude and imparts
itself only to the few – to such, above all, as have the candour to wish,
the erudition to understand, the trustworthiness to put into practice and
the authority to judge in the common interest as honourably, accurately
and practically as you do now. For you do not consider yourself born for
yourself alone, but for the whole world; and so by this splendid work
you have thought it worth your while to place the whole world in your
debt.

You could hardly have accomplished this end more effectually and correctly than by setting before rational men this pattern of a commonwealth,
this model and perfect image of proper conduct. And the world has never
seen a model more perfect than yours, more soundly established or fully
executed or more desirable. It surpasses and leaves far behind the many
celebrated commonwealths of which so much has been said, those of
Sparta, Athens and Rome. Had they been founded under the same aus-
pices as your commonwealth and governed by the same institutions, laws,
regulations and customs, certainly they would not now be fallen, levelled
to the ground and extinguished – alas! – beyond all hope of rebirth. On
the contrary, they would now be intact, fortunate and prosperous, leading a happy existence – mistresses of the world, besides, and dividing a
far-flung empire, by land and by sea.

Feeling pity for the pitiable fate of these commonwealths, you feared
lest others, which now hold supreme power, should undergo the same fate;
so you drew the portrait of a perfect commonwealth, one which devoted
its energies less to setting up laws than to forming the very best men to
administer them. And in this they were absolutely right; for without good
rulers, even the best laws (if we take Plato's word for it)[3] would be nothing
but dead letters. It is according to the pattern of such rulers as these –
models of probity, specimens of good conduct, images of justice – that
the whole existence and proper character of any commonwealth should

---

[2] 'More' praises Hythloday, and Hythloday praises Cardinal Morton, in very similar terms
(pp. 13–14, 15).
[3] E.g., *Laws* VI.751B–C.

be imagined. What is needed is prudence in the rulers, courage in the military, temperance in the private citizenry and justice in all.[4]

Since the nation you praise so lavishly is clearly formed on these principles, no wonder if it seems not only a challenge to many nations but an object of reverence to all peoples and an achievement to be celebrated among future generations. Its great strength lies in the fact that all squabbles over private property are removed, and no one has anything of his own. Instead, everyone has everything in common for the sake of the common good, and thus every action and each decision, whether public or private, trifling or important, is not directed by the greed of the many or the lusts of the few, but is aimed solely at upholding one uniform rule of justice, equality and community solidarity. Where the common good is fully respected, there is necessarily a clean sweep of everything that might serve as torch, kindling or fuel for ambition, luxury, envy and injustice. These are vices into which men are sometimes pushed against their will, and to their own immense and incomparable loss, by private property or lust for gain or that most miserable of passions, ambition. From these sources there frequently spring up mental quarrels, martial clashes and wars worse than civil,[5] which not only completely destroy the flourishing state of supremely happy republics but cause their previous glories, their past triumphs, rich prizes and proud spoils taken from defeated enemies to be utterly obliterated.

If my thoughts on this point should be less than absolutely convincing, only consider the swarm of perfectly reliable witnesses I can call to my support – I mean the many great cities destroyed in times past, the states crushed, the republics beaten down, the villages fired and consumed. Today not only are there scarcely any remains or vestiges of those great calamities – not even the names of the places are reliably preserved by any history, however far back it reaches.

Such terrible downfalls, devastations, disasters and other calamities of war our commonwealths (if we have any) could easily escape if they would only adapt themselves exactly to the Utopian pattern not swerving from

---

[4] Prudence (or wisdom), courage, temperance and justice are the four cardinal virtues of Greek and Roman ethics. Busleyden's remark summarises the main argument of Book IV of the *Republic* (especially 427D–434C).

[5] 'Wars worse than civil' ('Bella plus quam civilia', as in Busleyden's Latin) is the opening phrase of Lucan's *Pharsalia*, an epic poem on the civil war between Pompey and Caesar.

it, as people say, by a hair's breadth. If they act so, the result will fully convince them how much they have profited by the service you have done them; especially since in this way they will have learned to keep their republic healthy, unharmed and victorious. Their debt to you, their most ready and willing saviour, will be no less than what is rightly owed to a man who has saved not just one citizen of a country, but the entire country itself.

Farewell for now. May you continue to prosper, ever contriving, carrying out and completing new plans which will bring long life to the commonwealth, and to yourself immortality. Farewell, most learned and humane More, supreme ornament of your Britain and of this world of ours.

From my house at Mechlin, 1516

GERARD GELDENHOUWER ON UTOPIA[6]

If pleasure you seek, good reader, it's here;
If profit, no book is more suited to teach;
If both – on this island, both will appear
To sharpen at once both your thoughts and your speech:
    Here the springs both of good and of ill are set forth
    By More, London's star of incomparable worth.

CORNELIS DE SCHRIJVER TO THE READER[7]

You seek new monsters from the world new-found?
New ways of life, drawing on different springs?
The source of human virtue? The profound
Evil abyss? The void beneath all things?
    Read here what's traced by More's ingenious pen,
    More, London's pride, and Britain's first of men.

---

[6] The Dutch humanist Geldenhouwer (1482–1542) assisted the printer Dirk Martens in the production of many books, including the first edition of *Utopia*.

[7] De Schrijver (*c.* 1482–1558), a Latin poet of wide reputation, settled in Antwerp by 1515, where he became a close associate of Peter Giles.

BEATUS RHENANUS[1] TO WILLIBALD PIRCKHEIMER,
COUNCILLOR TO THE EMPEROR MAXIMILIAN AND
CITY COUNCILLOR OF NUREMBERG, GREETINGS

... Well, just as these toys[2] serve to display More's wit and notable erudition, so the keenness of his judgement in practical affairs comes brilliantly clear in *Utopia*. Of that, I need say only a few words in passing, because the book has already been praised as it deserves in a splendid preface by that most rigorous of scholars Budé, who is an incomparable exponent of the higher learning, as well as a giant, even unique, genius of French letters. More's book contains principles of a sort not to be found in Plato, Aristotle, or even in the Pandects of your Justinian.[3] Its teachings are perhaps less philosophical than those others, but they are more Christian. And yet (if you'd like to hear, with the favour of the Muses, a good story), when the subject of *Utopia* came up here lately in a gathering of various important men, and when I praised it, one foolish fellow said More deserved no more credit than a paid scribe, who simply writes down what other people say after the fashion of a pen-pusher (so they call him), who may sit in a meeting, but expresses no ideas of his own. Everything in the book, he said, came from the mouth of Hythloday; all More did was write it down. And for that More deserved no more credit than attaches to making a good transcript. And there was no lack of those who gave this simpleton high marks as a man of shrewd insights. *Now, don't you admire the sly wit of More, who can bamboozle men like these, not just ordinary dolts but men of standing and trained theologians at that?...*[4]

Basel, 23 February 1518

[1] The son of a Rheinau butcher named Bild, Beatus Rhenanus (1485–1547), like other humanists, took a new Latin name to go with his classical learning. Under this cheerful sobriquet ('Beatus' means 'happy', 'blessed'), he assisted Erasmus in the publication of many of his works, in addition to pursuing scholarly enterprises of his own. He supervised the printing of the 1518 editions of *Utopia*, which also included epigrams by More, William Lily and Erasmus, and supplied this dedicatory epistle, of which we print only the part dealing with *Utopia*. The addressee, Willibald Pirckheimer (1470–1530), was a Nuremberg patrician distinguished both as a man of affairs and as a scholar.
[2] I.e., the epigrams.
[3] The Pandects or Digests of Roman law were compiled under the Emperor Justinian in the sixth century AD. 'Your' Justinian because of Pirckheimer's legal studies and practice.
[4] Beatus wrote the italicised passage in Greek.

JEAN DESMAREZ OF CASSEL TO MASTER PETER GILES, GREETINGS[1]

I have read the *Utopia* of your friend More, along with his *Epigrams* – whether with more pleasure or admiration, I do not know. How happy is Britain, which now blossoms forth with talents of such eminence that they rival those of antiquity! And how lumpish are we,[2] duller than lead, if we cannot be roused to compete for the same sort of praise by examples so near at hand. 'It is shameful to keep silent', says Aristotle, 'while Isocrates still speaks'.[3] We should feel disgraced to devote ourselves only to pleasure-seeking and money-making, when the British, who live at the ends of the earth, are bringing forth, thanks to the favour and generosity of their princes, learning in such profusion. Although the Greeks and Italians used to have almost a monopoly of good learning, Spain too has some eminent names among the ancients of whom she boasts; Scythia, savage though she is, has her Anacharsis;[4] Denmark her Saxo Grammaticus; France her Budé. Germany has many men famous for learning, England has very many, and those among the most distinguished. For what must we think of the others, if More is so outstanding – and this despite his youth, the distraction of his many other public and private concerns,[5] and the fact that literature is far from being his primary vocation? Only we, of all people, seem satisfied to scratch our skins and stuff our moneybags. Indeed, even we are shaking off our torpor and preparing to take part in this glorious contest, in which it is no shame to be beaten and splendid to be victorious. Many examples provoke us to it, on all sides; so does our admirable Prince Charles,[6] who rewards nothing more generously than learning combined with virtue, while the great Maecenas and patron of

---

[1] Desmarez (d. 1526) was public orator and professor at the University of Louvain. His letter and poem (below) appeared among the prefatory materials in the editions of 1516 and 1517. Erasmus was not deterred by his long friendship with Desmarez from authorising Beatus Rhenanus to omit both productions from the 1518 editions (*CWE*, V, 229).

[2] I.e., we of the Low Countries.

[3] The remark, which is attributed to Aristotle by Quintilian (*The Education of the Orator* III.i.14), paraphrases a line in Euripides' lost play *Philoctetes*. Isocrates was the pre-eminent orator of Aristotle's time.

[4] Anacharsis (fl. sixth century BC) was a Scythian sage, famed less for his wisdom than for the fact that, among the Scythians, any sage was conspicuous. Saxo Grammaticus (fl. thirteenth century) wrote *Gesta Danorum*, a history of his native land.

[5] This phrase, which seems to be adapted from a very similar one in Giles's letter to Busleyden (p. 121), is one of several indications of the derivative nature of Desmarez's letter.

[6] Prince Charles of Castile.

all good pursuits, Jean Le Sauvage,[7] Chancellor of Burgundy, also urges us forward.

Let me warmly encourage you, most learned Peter Giles, to have *Utopia* published as soon as possible; in it can be seen, as in a mirror, everything that relates to the proper establishment of a commonwealth. I could wish that, just as the Utopians have begun to accept our religion, we might adopt their system of ordering the commonwealth. Perhaps the change might easily be made if a number of distinguished and persuasive theologians were sent to that island; they would invigorate the faith of Christ, which is already springing up there, and then bring back to us their customs and institutions.

Utopia owes a great debt to Hythloday for making known this land which ought not to have remained obscure; it owes an even greater debt to the most learned More, whose skilful pencil has drawn it for us so vividly. In addition to both of them, not the least part of the thanks must be shared with you, who will make public both Hythloday's conversation and More's report of it – to the no small delight of future readers, and their even greater profit, if they weigh the details prudently.

Utopia has so stirred my spirit that, though long a stranger to the Muses, I have invoked them anew[8] – with what success you must be the judge.

Farewell, most courteous Peter Giles, you who are both practitioner and patron of good letters.

From my house at Louvain, 1 December [1516]

Poem on the New Island of Utopia by the Same John Desmarez,
Public Orator at Louvain

> The men of Rome were brave; the lofty Greeks
> Famous for eloquence; Sparta's men were strict;
> The Germans, tough; the honest Marseillais
> Noted for probity; urbane and witty men
> Flourished in Attica; Africans were deep.

---

[7] Le Sauvage (1455/7–1518) held several key offices under the young Charles V. He was one of the statesmen whose response to *Utopia* More told Erasmus he was particularly eager to know (*Selected Letters*, p. 80).
[8] I.e., in the following verses.

France bred religious saints; the British men
Were world-wide famous for munificence.
   The virtues have their special homes; what here
Abounds is somewhere else in short supply.
Only one isle, Utopia, displays to men
The sum of all the virtues in one place.

Index[1]

Abraxa 42
Achorians 30
Ackroyd, Peter xiiin.
action vs. contemplation: and counsel
xviii–xix, 13–14, 15; in More xiv, 4,
121; Plato on xixn., 28, 37; in
Utopia xxvi, 48–53, 63–4, 71, 73,
97–8; *see also* idleness
Adam of St Victor 26n.
Adams, Robert P. xxviin., 28n.,
85n.
Alaopolitans 85–6
Aldus Manutius 76n.
Allen, D. C. 66n.
Allen, John W. 32n.
Amaurot 5, 43, 44–7, 109
Ames, Russell 105n.
Anacharsis 127
ancillary materials xxxi, 110n.
Anemolian ambassadors 61–3
Anemolius 117
Anghiera, Pietro Martire d' 61n.
Anyder 5, 45, 109
Aquinas, St Thomas 66n.
Aratus 115
Aristophanes 76
Aristotle 75, 127. Works: *Nicomachean
Ethics* 36n., 65n., 69n., 73n., 107n.;

Politics xviii, xxiv, xxv–xxvi, xxviii,
32n., 39n., 41n., 49n., 55n., 56n.,
65n., 99n., 107n.
Augustine, St xxviii, 105n.
Aulus Gellius 5n.

Baker-Smith, Dominic xxn., 42n.
Beatus Rhenanus 126
Bible, books of: Acts 93n., 114n.;
Ephesians 55n.; Exodus 22n.; II
Kings 26n.; Luke 26, 36n.; Matthew
36n., 101n.; Proverbs 27; Psalms 26,
27n.; II Thessalonians 59n.
Budé, Guillaume 111, 126, 127
Busleyden, Jérôme de 120, 122
Buthrescas 97–8

capital punishment 15–16, 21–2, 23–4,
25, 81, 92
Carlyle, R. W. and A. J. 114n.
Charles, Prince of Castile 8, 29, 120n.,
127
children: *see* Utopia: children in
Cicero xviii, xxiiin., 10. Works: *Letters
to His Friends* 85n.; *On Invention*
xxiin.; *On Moral Obligation* xixn.,
xxiiin., 13n., 21n., 28n., 32n., 34n.,
35n., 85n.; *On Old Age* 73n.; *On the*

[1] 'Chronology' and 'Suggestions for further reading' are not indexed. Utopian ideas, attitudes, customs and institutions are indexed under 'Utopia (the country)'.

Orator 34n; *On the Supreme Good and Evil* 21n., 65n., 66n., 67n., 113n.; *Orator* 34n., 35n.; *Tusculan Disputations* 10n.
Clement, John 4–5
Colet, John xiv, 85n.
Colie, Rosalie L. xxin.
communism xxiii–xxiv, xxviii, 37–9, 93–4, 103–4, 106–7, 114–15, 124
confession (religious) 101
counsel xviii–xix, 13–14, 27–37

declamation xv
decorum 34n.
Desmarez, Jean 127
dialogue of friar and fool 25–7
dignity of labour 42n.
Diogenes Laertius 10n., 37n., 67nn., 68n., 73n., 100n.
Dioscorides 76
Du Ruel, Jean 117

education: *see* Utopia: education in
enclosure 18–20
England and Utopia 41n., 43n., 45, 47nn., 50n.
Epicureanism: *see* Utopia: hedonism in
Epicurus xxviii, 46n., 65–6n., 66n., 66–7n., 68n., 73n.
Erasmus xiv, xxn., 116; and ancillary materials, glosses to *Utopia* xxxi, 110n., 121n., 127n.; on More and *Utopia* 53n., 110–11. Works: *Adages* 30n., 38n.; *Colloquies* 50n.; *Complaint of Peace* 17n., 85n.; *Correspondence* 35n.; *The Education of a Christian Prince* 23n., 89n., 100n.; Letter to Dorp 6n.; Letter to Hutten 53n.; *The Praise of Folly* xxi, 6n., 64n., 65n., 70nn., 71n., 100n.
Euripides 76, 127n.
Europe and Utopia xxi–xxii, 39–40, 49–50, 51–3, 83–4, 101n., 103–7
euthanasia 78–9

fiscal policy 31–4
France, foreign policy of 28–30
Francis I of France 28n., 30n.
freedom xii, xxvii
Froben, Johann 88n., 110–11

Galen 76, 111–12
gambling 20, 50, 70
Gaza, Theodorus 76
Geldenhouwer, Gerard 125
Giles, Peter xvi, 9, 13, 39, 108–10, 116, 120, 127–8; and ancillary materials, glosses to *Utopia* xxxi, 119n., 121; on More and *Utopia* 120–2
Goodey, Brian R. 41n., 46n.
Grocyn, William xiv
Guy, J. A. xvn., xixn.

Harrison, William 43n.
health 72–3
hedonic calculus xxviii, 66, 69, 74
Henry VII of England 31nn., 34n.
Henry VIII of England 8
Herodian 76
Herodotus 76
Hesychius 76
Hexter, J. H. xvi–xvii, xix, 12n.
Hippocrates 76
Holbein, Ambrosius 118n.
Holinshed, Raphael 15n.
Holt, John xiv
Homer 10n., 12n., 76
honestas and *utilitas* xxii–xxiii
Horace xxi, 26
humanism xiii–xiv
hunting 70–1
Hythloday, Raphael: described 9–10; etymology of names of 3n., 5n.; learning of 3, 10; and More xx; travels of 10–12; whereabouts of 110, 121

idleness 16–17, 18, 20, 49, 51–2, 59, 104; *see also* action vs. contemplation
immortality 66, 95–6

justice, true and false xix, 15, 20–4,
31–2, 37–8, 82–3, 84, 104–5,
112–15, 123–4
Justinian 113n., 126

kingship 32–4
Kinney, Daniel 64n.
Kristeller, Paul Oskar xivn., xvn., 66n.

Lachner, Wolfgang 111n.
Lascaris, Constantinus 76
law 37, 54, 82–3, 105, 112–15; *see also* justice
Le Sauvage, Jean 128
Lily, William 111n.
Linacre, Thomas 111–12, 117
Livy 21n.
Logan, George M. 66n.
Lucan 10n., 124n.
Lucian xv, xx–xxi, 52n., 63nn., 76
Lupset, Thomas 112
Lupton, J. H. 100n.
Luther, Martin xvi

Macarians 34
Machiavelli, Niccolò xxiii, 83–4n.,
84n.
Manuel, Frank and Fritzie 42n.
Manutius, Aldus 76n.
Marc'hadour, Germain xivn.
marginal glosses xxxi, 121
Marius, Richard xiiin.
Martial 76n.
Menander xxivn.
mercenaries xxvii, 17, 29, 60, 88–9, 92
Miller, Clarence H. 3n.
monasticism 42n., 93–4, 97–8
money 37, 51, 70, 105–6
More, Cresacre xivn.
More, Thomas: biography of xiii–xvi,
8–9, 53n.; estimates of 110–11, 112,
116, 120–2, 122–3, 126, 127–8; and
Hythloday xx; and religious
persecution 95n.; and *serio ludere*
xxi; on *Utopia* 108–10, 110n.
Works: *The Answer to a Poisoned*

Book 73n.; *The Confutation of
Tyndale's Answer* 99n.; *A Dialogue
Concerning Heresies* 66n., 78n., 89n.,
95n., 97n.; *A Dialogue of Comfort
against Tribulation* 60n., 70n., 78n.;
Epigrams 30n., 33n., 71n., 111;
Exercises 111; *The History of King
Richard III* xv, 15n., 25n.; *The Last
Things* 70n., 78n.; letters 6n., 10n.,
34n., 53n., 64n., 101n., 110n.,
111n., 120n.; *A Treatise upon the
Passion of Christ* 60n., 63n., 70n.
Morton, John, Cardinal xiii, 15, 27
Mythra 93, 101

natural law 54, 113
Nephelogetes 85–6
nobility and gentility 16, 51, 62,
69–70, 106–7

Padover, Saul K. 29n.
Patenson, Henry 81n.
Peter of Spain 64n.
Phillips, Rowland 5n.
philosophy xxv–xxvi, 10, 28, 34–7,
64–74, 75
Pico della Mirandola xxn., 10n.
Pietro Martire d'Anghiera 61n.
Pirckheimer, Willibald 126
Plato xviii, xx, xxv–xxvi, 10, 28, 37,
75, 117, 120, 123. Works: Epistle
VII xixn., 28nn., 38n.; *Gorgias* 73n.;
Laws xviii, xx, 23n., 49nn., 54n.,
65n., 71n., 78n., 79n., 123n.;
Philebus 69n., 73nn.; *Republic* xv,
xviii, xixn., xxv–xxvi, 16n., 28, 35,
37, 38nn., 46n., 49n., 56n., 82n.,
99n., 117, 120, 124n.; *Statesman* xx,
38n.
Plautus 35
pleasure, true and false xxvi, 63,
65–74
Pliny the Elder 44n.
Plutarch 76. Works: *Moral Essays*
xixn., 33n.; *Lives* 28n., 38n., 51n.,
56n., 59n., 82n.

Index

Polylerites 22–4
popes 83–4
poverty xix–xx, 16–20, 33, 38, 104–6
pretenders, royal 29, 87–8
pride xix, 55, 106, 115
private property 37–9, 112–15, 124
Pythagoras 96n., 114

Quintilian xxiin., xxivn., 35n., 127n.

Rabelais, François 28n.
reason 66, 67, 74
republicanism 47n.
rhetorical theory xxii–xxiii, xxiv, 3nn.
Rhenanus, Beatus 126
Roper, William xiv
Ruel, Jean Du 117

Sallust 6n., 17
sanctuary 25
Sauvage, Jean Le 128
Saxo Grammaticus 127
Schoeck, R. J. 46–7n.
scholasticism 34, 64
Schrijver, Cornelius de 125
Seneca xixn., 10, 35
Skinner, Quentin xviii–xix,
  28n., 47n.
slavery: see Utopia: slavery in
Sophocles 76
Stapleton, Thomas 4n., 58n.
Stoicism 10n., 21, 65nn., 67
suicide 78–9
Surtz, Edward L. 29n., 54n., 65–6n.,
  66n., 94n., 102n.

Tacitus 61nn., 80n.
Terence 36, 82n., 109
theft 15–25
Theodorus Gaza 76
Theophrastus 75
Thompson, James W. 29n.
Thucydides 76, 89n.
toleration 94–5
treaties 28–9, 83–5
Tunstall, Cuthbert 8

Ulysses 10
Utopia (the book): ancillary materials
  in xxxi, 110n.; assessments by
  (1) Beatus Rhenanus 126; (2) Budé
  111–12, 114–17; (3) Busleyden
  122–5; (4) Desmarez 127–9; (5)
  Erasmus 110; (6) Geldenhouwer
  125; (7) Giles 120–2; (8) More
  108–9; (9) de Schrijver 125;
  composition of xvi–xvii, 3–4, 12n.,
  29n.; and the condition of England
  xix; and counsel xviii–xix; early
  editions of xxx; and humanism
  xvii–xxi; marginal glosses to xxxi,
  121; relation of Books I and II of
  xvii, xxi–xxiv; and rhetorical theory
  xxii–xxiii, xxiv, 3nn.; style of
  xxx–xxxi, 3, 28n., 31n., 121
Utopia (the country): age of 39, 46;
  attitude toward celibacy in 98;
  attitudes toward death in 78–9,
  96–7, 103; burial practices in 96;
  character of the citizens of 75, 90;
  children in 48–9, 54, 55, 57, 61, 63,
  101–2; and Christianity xxivn.,
  xxvi–xxvii, 93–4, 114–16; churches
  in 100; cities of 43, 44–7, 54, 55–6;
  and the city-state 43n.; and classical
  societies 39–40, 43n., 46n., 46–7n.,
  75, 100n., 119n., 123; climate of 74;
  clothing in 49, 53; colonies of 54–5;
  and communism xxiii–xxiv, xxviii,
  35–6, 37–9, 93–4, 103–4, 106–7,
  124; criminal justice in 61, 77–8,
  80–1; economy of 51–3, 59–60, 92,
  106–7; education in 50, 63–4, 90,
  99; the elderly in 54, 57–8; and
  England 41n., 43n., 45, 47nn., 50n.;
  and Epicureanism 46n., 65n.,
  65–6n., 66n., 66–7n.; and Europe
  xxi–xxii, 39–40, 49–50, 83–4, 101n.,
  103–7; excommunication in 98;
  farming in 43–4, 48–9, 58, 74–5;
  fools in 81; foreign policy of
  xxvii–xxviii, 54, 59–60, 83–5, 92;
  foreigners in 39, 56, 61–3, 77; and

Index

Utopia (*cont.*)
 freedom xii, xxvii; gardens in 46;
 gems in 61, 70; geography of 41–3;
 gold and silver in 60–1, 63, 87; and
 the Greek ideal commonwealth
 xviii, xxv–xxvii, 35–6, 37–8, 41n.,
 49nn., 51n., 54n., 56n., 59n., 65n.,
 71n., 78n., 79n., 117, 120, 123–4;
 hedonism in xxvi, 58, 65–74;
 holidays in 100; language of 64, 75,
 119, 121; laws in 37, 82–3; lawyers
 barred from 82; learning in 63–5,
 75–7; leisure activities in 50, 103;
 location 5, 115–16, 121; map of 118;
 marriage and divorce in 79–81;
 meals in 56–8; medicine in 56, 76,
 78–9; and mercenaries xxvii, 60,
 88–9, 92; military training in 85,
 103; miracles in 97; and
 monasticism 42n., 93–4, 97–8;
 music in 58, 102–3; and natural law
 54; occupations in 49; officials in,
 including (1) ambassadors 52; (2)
 governor 47–8, 52, 58, 81, 82; (3)
 priests 52, 80–1, 98–100, 102–3; (4)
 scholars 52, 63; (5) syphogrant or
 phylarch 43, 47–8, 52, 58; (6)
 tranibor or head phylarch 47–8, 52,
 58; officials in, respect for 82;
 philosophy in xxvi, 64, 65–74; and
 Plato's *Republic* xxv–xxvi, 35, 37,
 46n., 49n., 56n., 117, 120, 124n.;
 political organisation of 43, 47–8;
 population of 54; praise of 35–6, 37,
 39–40, 59, 74, 103–7, 114–16, 117,
 119, 120–1, 122–5, 128–9; and
 primitive societies 61nn., 66n.,
 80n., 102n.; printing in 76–7;
 religion in 66–8, 93–103, 106;

religious toleration in 94–5; and
 republicanism 47n.; senate of,
 national 43, 48, 61; sexual customs
 in 79–81; slavery in xxvii, 55, 56,
 61, 77–8, 80, 81, 92; social
 relations in 53–8; suicide and
 euthanasia in 78–9; trade of 59–60,
 77, 86; travel in 58–9; treaties
 contemned in 83–5; warfare of
 54, 60, 85–92, 99–100, 106; women
 in, in respect of (1) education 50,
 64; (2) marriage and divorce 54,
 79–81, 81–2; (3) occupations
 and domestic duties 49, 51n.,
 56–7, 99; (4) subordination to
 husband 55, 101; (5) warfare 85,
 90; work in 49–50, 52–3; worship
 in 100–3
utopia (the genre) xviiin.
utopia (the word) xi, 109
Utopus 42, 46, 94–5, 119

Valla, Lorenzo 65n.
Vespucci, Amerigo 10, 61n., 66n.,
 102n., 120
Virgil 10n., 12n., 46
virtue: attributed to individuals 8, 9,
 15; in Utopia xxvi–xxvii, 37;
 and Utopian education 78, 99;
 and Utopian religion 93, 95, 102;
 Utopian views on xxvi, 65,
 67–8, 73, 74, 82, 96, 99

war xxvii, 14, 16–18, 28–31, 42, 54,
 85–92, 99–100, 124
Wind, Edgar xxin., 66n.
women: *see* Utopia: women in

Zapoletes xxvii, 88–9

134

CAMBRIDGE TEXTS IN THE HISTORY OF POLITICAL THOUGHT

Titles published in the series thus far

Aristotle *The Politics* and *The Constitution of Athens* (edited by Stephen Everson)
0 521 48400 6 paperback

Arnold *Culture and Anarchy and other writings* (edited by Stefan Collini)
0 521 37796 X paperback

Astell *Political Writings* (edited by Patricia Springborg)
0 521 42845 9 paperback

Augustine *The City of God against the Pagans* (edited by R. W. Dyson)
0 521 46843 4 paperback

Augustine *Political Writings* (edited by E. M. Atkins and R. J. Dodaro)
0 521 44697 X paperback

Austin *The Province of Jurisprudence Determined* (edited by Wilfrid E. Rumble)
0 521 44756 9 paperback

Bacon *The History of the Reign of King Henry VII* (edited by Brian Vickers)
0 521 58663 1 paperback

Bagehot *The English Constitution* (edited by Paul Smith)
0 521 46942 2 paperback

Bakunin *Statism and Anarchy* (edited by Marshall Shatz)
0 521 36973 8 paperback

Baxter *Holy Commonwealth* (edited by William Lamont)
0 521 40580 7 paperback

Bayle *Political Writings* (edited by Sally L. Jenkinson)
0 521 47677 1 paperback

Beccaria *On Crimes and Punishments and other writings* (edited by Richard Bellamy)
0 521 47982 7 paperback

Bentham *Fragment on Government* (introduction by Ross Harrison)
0 521 35929 5 paperback

Bernstein *The Preconditions of Socialism* (edited by Henry Tudor)
0 521 39808 8 paperback

Bodin *On Sovereignty* (edited by Julian H. Franklin)
0 521 34992 3 paperback

Bolingbroke *Political Writings* (edited by David Armitage)
0 521 58697 6 paperback

Bossuet *Politics Drawn from the Very Words of Holy Scripture* (edited by Patrick Riley)
0 521 36807 3 paperback

The British Idealists (edited by David Boucher)
0 521 45951 6 paperback

Burke *Pre-Revolutionary Writings* (edited by Ian Harris)
0 521 36800 6 paperback

Christine De Pizan *The Book of the Body Politic* (edited by Kate Langdon Forhan)
0 521 42259 0 paperback

Cicero *On Duties* (edited by M. T. Griffin and E. M. Atkins)
0 521 34835 8 paperback

Cicero *On the Commonwealth* and *On the Laws* (edited by James E. G. Zetzel)
0 521 45959 1 paperback

Comte *Early Political Writings* (edited by H. S. Jones)
0 521 46923 6 paperback

Conciliarism and Papalism (edited by J. H. Burns and Thomas M. Izbicki)
0 521 47674 7 paperback

Constant *Political Writings* (edited by Biancamaria Fontana)
0 521 31632 4 paperback

Dante *Monarchy* (edited by Prue Shaw)
0 521 56781 5 paperback

Diderot *Political Writings* (edited by John Hope Mason and Robert Wokler)
0 521 36911 8 paperback

The Dutch Revolt (edited by Martin van Gelderen)
0 521 39809 6 paperback

Early Greek Political Thought from Homer to the Sophists (edited by Michael Gagarin and Paul Woodruff)
0 521 43768 7 paperback

The Early Political Writings of the German Romantics (edited by Frederick C. Beiser)
0 521 44951 0 paperback

The English Levellers (edited by Andrew Sharp)
0 521 62511 4 paperback

Erasmus *The Education of a Christian Prince* (edited by Lisa Jardine)
0 521 58811 1 paperback

Fenelon *Telemachus* (edited by Patrick Riley)
0 521 45662 2 paperback

Ferguson *An Essay on the History of Civil Society* (edited by Fania Oz-Salzberger)
0 521 44736 4 paperback

Filmer *Patriarcha and Other Writings* (edited by Johann P. Sommerville)
0 521 39903 3 paperback

Fletcher *Political Works* (edited by John Robertson)
0 521 43994 9 paperback

Sir John Fortescue *On the Laws and Governance of England* (edited by Shelley Lockwood)
0 521 58996 7 paperback

Fourier *The Theory of the Four Movements* (edited by Gareth Stedman Jones and Ian Patterson)
0 521 35693 8 paperback

Gramsci *Pre-Prison Writings* (edited by Richard Bellamy)
0 521 42307 4 paperback

Guicciardini *Dialogue on the Government of Florence* (edited by Alison Brown)
0 521 45623 1 paperback

Harrington *A Commonwealth of Oceana* and *A System of Politics*
(edited by J. G. A. Pocock)
0 521 42329 5 paperback

Hegel *Elements of the Philosophy of Right* (edited by Allen W. Wood and H. B. Nisbet)
0 521 34888 9 paperback

Hegel *Political Writings* (edited by Laurence Dickey and H. B. Nisbet)
0 521 45979 3 paperback

Hobbes *On the Citizen* (edited by Michael Silverthorne and Richard Tuck)
0 521 43780 6 paperback

Hobbes *Leviathan* (edited by Richard Tuck)
0 521 56797 1 paperback

Hobhouse *Liberalism and Other Writings* (edited by James Meadowcroft)
0 521 43726 1 paperback

Hooker *Of the Laws of Ecclesiastical Polity* (edited by A. S. McGrade)
0 521 37908 3 paperback

Hume *Political Essays* (edited by Knud Haakonssen)
0 521 46639 3 paperback

King James VI and I *Political Writings* (edited by Johann P. Sommerville)
0 521 44729 1 paperback

Jefferson *Political Writings* (edited by Joyce Appleby and Terence Ball)
0 521 64841 6 paperback

John of Salisbury *Policraticus* (edited by Cary Nederman)
0 521 36701 8 paperback

Kant *Political Writings* (edited by H. S. Reiss and H. B. Nisbet)
0 521 39837 1 paperback

Knox *On Rebellion* (edited by Roger A. Mason)
0 521 39988 2 paperback

Kropotkin *The Conquest of Bread and other writings* (edited by Marshall Shatz)
0 521 45990 7 paperback

Lawson *Politica sacra et civilis* (edited by Conal Condren)
0 521 39248 9 paperback

Leibniz *Political Writings* (edited by Patrick Riley)
0 521 35899 X paperback

The Levellers (edited by Andrew Sharp)
0 521 62511 4 paperback

Locke *Political Essays* (edited by Mark Goldie)
0 521 47861 8 paperback

Locke *Two Treatises of Government* (edited by Peter Laslett)
0 521 35730 6 paperback

Loyseau *A Treatise of Orders and Plain Dignities* (edited by Howell A. Lloyd)
0 521 45624 X paperback

Luther and Calvin on Secular Authority (edited by Harro Höpfl)
0 521 34986 9 paperback

Machiavelli *The Prince* (edited by Quentin Skinner and Russell Price)
0 521 34993 1 paperback

de Maistre *Considerations on France* (edited by Isaiah Berlin and Richard Lebrun)
0 521 46628 8 paperback

Malthus *An Essay on the Principle of Population* (edited by Donald Winch)
0 521 42972 2 paperback

Marsiglio of Padua *Defensor minor* and *De translatione Imperii*
(edited by Cary Nederman)
0 521 40846 6 paperback

Marx *Early Political Writings* (edited by Joseph O'Malley)
0 521 34994 X paperback

Marx *Later Political Writings* (edited by Terrell Carver)
0 521 36739 5 paperback

James Mill *Political Writings* (edited by Terence Ball)
0 521 38748 5 paperback

J. S. Mill *On Liberty*, with *The Subjection of Women* and *Chapters on Socialism* (edited by Stefan Collini)
0 521 37917 2 paperback

Milton *Political Writings* (edited by Martin Dzelzainis)
0 521 34866 8 paperback

Montesquieu *The Spirit of the Laws* (edited by Anne M. Cohler, Basia Carolyn Miller and Harold Samuel Stone)
0 521 36974 6 paperback

More *Utopia* (edited by George M. Logan and Robert M. Adams)
0 521 52540 3 paperback

Morris *News from Nowhere* (edited by Krishan Kumar)
0 521 42233 7 paperback

Nicholas of Cusa *The Catholic Concordance* (edited by Paul E. Sigmund)
0 521 56773 4 paperback

Nietzsche *On the Genealogy of Morality* (edited by Keith Ansell-Pearson)
0 521 40610 2 paperback

Paine *Political Writings* (edited by Bruce Kuklick)
0 521 66799 2 paperback

Plato *The Republic* (edited by G. R. F. Ferrari and Tom Griffith)
0 521 48443 X paperback

Plato *Statesman* (edited by Julia Annas and Robin Waterfield)
0 521 44778 X paperback

Price *Political Writings* (edited by D. O. Thomas)
0 521 40969 1 paperback

Priestley *Political Writings* (edited by Peter Miller)
0 521 42561 1 paperback

Proudhon *What is Property?* (edited by Donald R. Kelley and Bonnie G. Smith)
0 521 40556 4 paperback

Pufendorf *On the Duty of Man and Citizen according to Natural Law* (edited by James Tully)
0 521 35980 5 paperback

The Radical Reformation (edited by Michael G. Baylor)
0 521 37948 2 paperback

Rousseau *The Discourses and other early political writings* (edited by Victor Gourevitch)
0 521 42445 3 paperback

Rousseau *The Social Contract and other later political writings* (edited by Victor Gourevitch)
0 521 42446 1 paperback

Seneca *Moral and Political Essays* (edited by John Cooper and John Procope)
0 521 34818 8 paperback

Sidney *Court Maxims* (edited by Hans W. Blom, Eco Haitsma Mulier and Ronald Janse)
0 521 46736 5 paperback

Sorel *Reflections on Violence* (edited by Jeremy Jennings)
0 521 55910 3 paperback

Spencer *The Man versus the State* and *The Proper Sphere of Government* (edited by John Offer)
0 521 43740 7 paperback

Stirner *The Ego and Its Own* (edited by David Leopold)
0 521 45647 9 paperback

Thoreau *Political Writings* (edited by Nancy Rosenblum)
0 521 47675 5 paperback

Tonnies *Community and Civil Society* (edited by Jose Harris and Margaret Hollis)
0 521 56119 1 paperback

Utopias of the British Enlightenment (edited by Gregory Claeys)
0 521 45590 1 paperback

Vico *The First New Science* (edited by Leon Pompa)
0 521 38726 4 paperback

Vitoria *Political Writings* (edited by Anthony Pagden and Jeremy Lawrance)
0 521 36714 X paperback

Voltaire *Political Writings* (edited by David Williams)
0 521 43727 X paperback

Weber *Political Writings* (edited by Peter Lassman and Ronald Speirs)
0 521 39719 7 paperback

William of Ockham *A Short Discourse on Tyrannical Government* (edited by A. S. McGrade and John Kilcullen)
0 521 35803 5 paperback

William of Ockham *A Letter to the Friars Minor and other writings*
(edited by A. S. McGrade and John Kilcullen)
0 521 35804 3 paperback

Wollstonecraft *A Vindication of the Rights of Men* and *A Vindication of the Rights of Woman* (edited by Sylvana Tomaselli)
0 521 43633 8 paperback